MADRAS DISTRICT GAZETTEERS

DISTRICT GAZETTEER
CUDDAPAH

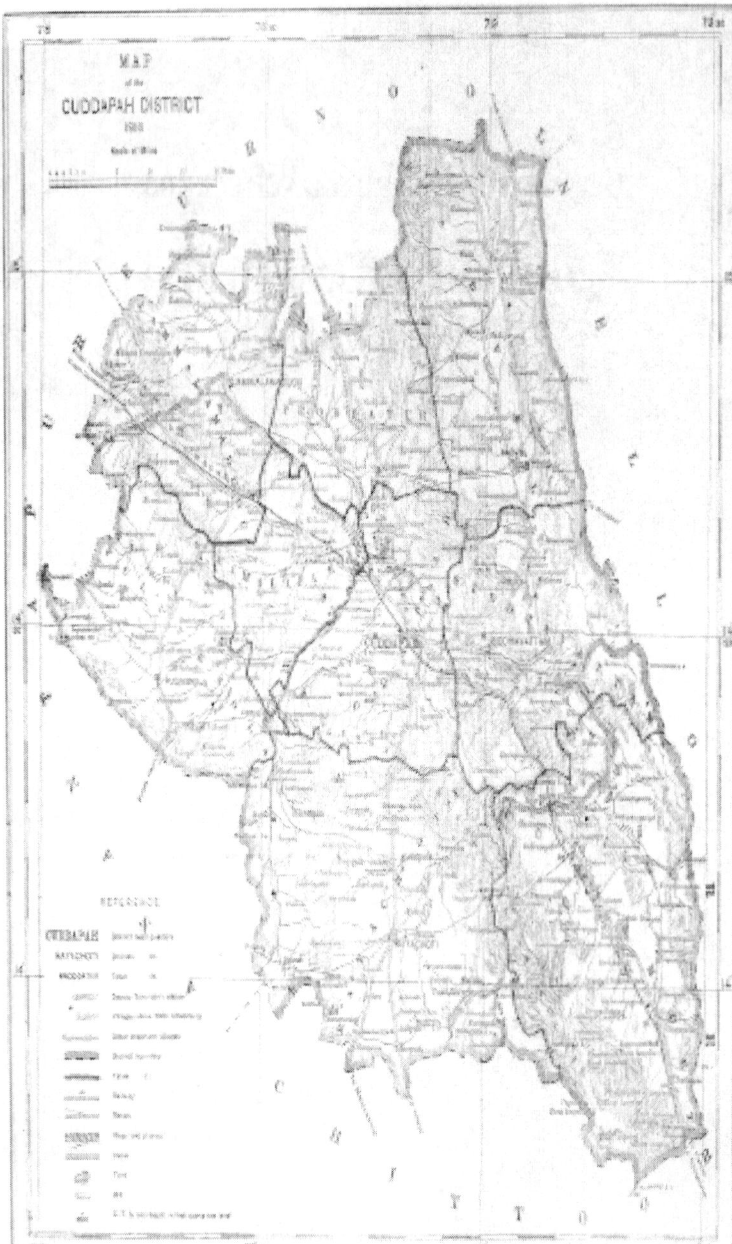
MAP
of the
CUDDAPAH DISTRICT
REFERENCE
CUDDAPAH

MADRAS DISTRICT GAZETTEERS

DISTRICT GAZETTEER
CUDDAPAH

C. F. BRACKENBURY

GYAN

Published by

Gyan Publishing House
5, Ansari Road
Daryaganj, New Delhi-110002
Phone: 011-47034999, 9811692060
E-mail: books@gyanbooks.com

Distribution Network
gyanbooks.com
India, USA, Canada, UK, Australia, France

ISBN : 978-81-212-3281-4 (PB)
First Published, Madras 1915

2nd Impression 2020

Printed at: Gyan Press, Delhi.

District Gazetteer Cuddapah
Author: C. F. Brackenbury

MADRAS DISTRICT GAZETTEERS

CUDDAPAH

BY

C. F. BRACKENBURY

INDIAN CIVIL SERVICE

MADRAS

PRINTED BY THE SUPERINTENDENT, GOVERNMENT PRESS

1915

NOTE.

The villages of Idupulapaya, Chilakampalle and Marellamadaka mentioned on pages 163, 214 and 217 of this volume were transferred from the Pulivendla to the Rāyachōti taluk under Notification No. 329, dated 13th May 1914, published on page 931 of Part I of the *Fort St. George Gazette*, dated 23rd June 1914.

PREFACE.

A "Manual" of the Cuddapah district, as then constituted, was compiled by the late Mr. J. D. B. Gribble, I.C.S., in 1875. The present gazetteer is prepared on different lines, and exigencies of form and matter have necessitated the omission of much that is still of interest in the old manual, which has thus not been revised so much as partially replaced. Statistics are under the present system relegated as far as possible to a separate volume of Appendices, which it is proposed to revise decennially, after every census.

Where so many have assisted me in the collection of material for this book it would be invidious to name a few. My thanks are due to them all, officials and others, for their prompt replies to my demands for information of all kinds, without which I could never have completed the work while engaged in the resettlement of another district.

SETTLEMENT OFFICE,
CHITTOOR,
October 1, 1914.

C. F. BRACKENBURY.

PLAN OF CONTENTS.

CHAPTER		PAGE
I.	PHYSICAL DESCRIPTION	1—23
II.	POLITICAL HISTORY	24—51
III.	THE PEOPLE	52—71
IV.	AGRICULTURE AND IRRIGATION	72—91
V.	FORESTS	92—107
VI.	OCCUPATION AND TRADE	108—117
VII.	MEANS OF COMMUNICATION	118—124
VIII.	RAINFALL AND SEASONS	125—138
IX.	PUBLIC HEALTH	139—142
X.	EDUCATION	143—145
XI.	LAND REVENUE ADMINISTRATION	146—160
XII.	SALT, ABKĀRI AND MISCELLANEOUS REVENUE	161—165
XIII.	ADMINISTRATION OF JUSTICE	166—173
XIV.	LOCAL SELF-GOVERNMENT	174—176
XV.	GAZETTEER—	177—247
	Cuddapah taluk	177
	Jammalamadugu taluk	187
	Proddatūr taluk	196
	Kamalāpuram taluk	204
	Pulivendla taluk	208
	Rāyachōti taluk	217
	Badvēl taluk	225
	Sidhout taluk	234
	Pullampet taluk	240
INDEX		249

SYNOPSIS.

CHAPTER I.

PHYSICAL DESCRIPTION.

PAGE

GENERAL—Natural divisions—Rivers—The western division—The southern division—The eastern division SOILS. CLIMATE—Rainfall—Temperature—Humidity—Winds. GEOLOGY—Two distinct rock areas—Of crystalline rocks—Of stratified rocks—Concealed by recent deposits—Upland rugged with scattered hill masses—Low country of hill-divided plains—Granitoid gneiss—Granite veins—Trap dykes—Brecciated quartz reefs—Sub-metamorphic series of Cuddapah and Kurnool—Cuddapah formation—In south-east taluks—Cheyyēr group—Cheyyērs in the Pulivendla taluk, volcanic—Pāpaghni group, oldest—Faulting near Cuddapah—Warm springs—Nallamalai group—Metalliferous—Cuddapah town on rocks of the Kurnool formation—Kundēr series of limestones—Narji beds—Banganapalle group of quartzites—Alluvium, soils, etc.—Implement gravels—Blown sands of Pennēr—Industrial products—Diamonds—Iron ore—Lead ore—Copper—Building materials—Limestones—Lime—Slates—Sandstones, etc.—Gneiss, etc. FLORA, FAUNA—Cattle—Buffaloes, Sheep and Goats—Game—Quadrumana 1–23

CHAPTER II.

POLITICAL HISTORY.

Introductory—Prehistoric remains—The Deccan politically isolated in earliest historical times—Earliest known dynasties—The Bānas—The Rāshtrakūtas—The Vaidumbas—Rise of the Chōlas—The eastern division of the district—The Telugu Chōdas—The Kākatīyas of Warangal—First Muhammadan invasion—The Vijayanagar Empire—Rise of the Poligārs—The Matla princes—The Nawabs of Cuddapah—Haidar Ali of Mysore—Transfer of Cuddapah to the British—The work of Munro—The Poligārs and their reduction—Conclusion 24–51

CHAPTER III.

THE PEOPLE.

PAGE

THE CENSUS—Density and growth of the population—Deficiency of females—Language—Education—Occupations—Religions. THE CHRISTIANS—The Roman Catholic Mission—The London Mission—The S.P.G. Mission—The Lutheran Mission. THE MUSALMĀNS—Their relations with Hindus. THE HINDUS—Villages—Houses—Dress—Food—Amusements. RELIGIOUS LIFE—The Village Deities—Peculiar religious practices and superstitions. SOCIAL LIFE—The more numerous castes—Tribes—Beggars ... 52–71

CHAPTER IV.

AGRICULTURE AND IRRIGATION.

INTRODUCTORY. WET CULTIVATION—Paddy—Ragi—Sugarcane—Garden crops. DRY CULTIVATION—The guntaka or scuffle—The gorru or drill—Weeding—Practices peculiar to the "black cotton" country—The pedda madaka or big plough—Harvesting—Cattle food—Modern changes. IRRIGATION—General—River channels—Tanks—Wells. IRRIGATION WORKS—The Kurnool-Cuddapah Canal—The Chāpād and Maidukūru Projects—The Sagilēr Project. ECONOMIC CONDITION OF AGRICULTURISTS—Indebtedness of the ryot 72–91

CHAPTER V.

FORESTS.

FORESTS—Their situation and area—Administration. CHARACTER OF THE FORESTS—The Redsanders tree—Its uses—Summary. CONSERVANCY—Prior to the Madras Forest Act of 1882—Subsequent operations. RECENT WORKING PLANS—Fuel—Timber. WORK IN PROGRESS—Fuel operations—Timber operations—Sandal sowing—Minor forest produce—Grazing and goat browsing—Forest offences—Fire Protection—Stream bunding—Cart tracks and bridle paths—Demarcation—Planting and sowing 92–107

CHAPTER VI.

OCCUPATION AND TRADE.

AGRICULTURE. ARTS AND INDUSTRIES—Textile—Condition of weavers—Cotton-weaving—Silk-weaving—Blankets and rugs—Cotton-printing and dyeing—Shoe-making—Wood—

PAGE

Metal—Stone—Other occupations. FACTORIES. TRADE—Exports—Imports. WEIGHTS AND MEASURES—Table of weight—Grain measures—Liquid measures—Lineal measures—Measures of time 108–117

CHAPTER VII.

MEANS OF COMMUNICATION.

ROADS—In 1854—Extension during famines—Present administration—Avenues—Travellers' bungalows and choultries. THE CANAL. RAILWAYS—Projected lines—Accidents ... 118–124

CHAPTER VIII.

RAINFALL AND SEASONS.

RAINFALL—Liability to famine. EARLY SCARCITIES. THE GREAT FAMINE OF 1876—78—Series of bad seasons—Beginnings of distress in July 1876—Relief works opened in September—Prices suddenly rise in October--December 1876; serious famine—Deputation of Sir Richard Temple—His views in regard to Cuddapah—Distress increases in 1877—June to August 1877—Rainfalls in September—The cost of the famine. SCARCITIES SUBSEQUENT TO THE GREAT FAMINE. The famine of 1891–92—The famine of 1896–97. FLOODS—In the first quarter of the 19th century—Great Storm of 1851—Excessive rains in 1874—The floods in 1903 125–138

CHAPTER IX.

PUBLIC HEALTH.

GENERAL HEALTH—Plague—Cholera—Small-pox—Malaria—Infirmities—Vaccination. MEDICAL INSTITUTIONS—Public —Private 139–142

CHAPTER X.

EDUCATION.

CENSUS STATISTICS— Progress since 1901—Education according to religions. EDUCATIONAL INSTITUTIONS—High schools—Lower Secondary schools—Education by the missions ... 143–145

GAZETTEER

OF THE

CUDDAPAH DISTRICT

CHAPTER I.

PHYSICAL DESCRIPTION.

GENERAL—Natural divisions—Rivers—The western division—The southern division—The eastern division. SOILS. CLIMATE—Rainfall—Temperature—Humidity—Winds. GEOLOGY—Two distinct rock areas—Of crystalline rocks—Of stratified rocks—Concealed by recent deposits—Upland rugged with scattered hill masses—Low country of hill-divided plains—Granitoid gneiss—Granite veins—Trap dykes—Brecciated quartz reefs—Sub-metamorphic series of Cuddapah and Kurnool—Cuddapah formation—In south-east taluks—Cheyyēr group—Cheyyērs in the Pulivendla taluk, volcanic—Pāpaghni group, oldest—Faulting near Cuddapah—Warm springs—Nallamalai group—Metalliferous—Cuddapah town on rocks of the Kurnool formation—Kundēr series of limestones—Narji beds—Banganapalle group of quartzites—Alluvium, soils, etc.—Implement gravels—Blown sands of Pennēr—Industrial products—Diamonds—Iron ore—Lead ore—Copper—Building materials—Limestones—Lime—Slates—Sandstones, etc.—Gneiss, etc, FLORA, FAUNA—Cattle—Buffaloes, Sheep and Goats—Game—Quadrumana.

CHAP. I.
GENERAL.

THE district of Cuddapah till recently ranked second in point of size among the Collectorates of the Madras Presidency. By the recent redistribution of districts, which chiefly affected the tract comprising the old districts of Cuddapah and North Arcot, the former lost three taluks representing an extent of 2,839 square miles, nearly 33 per cent. of its total area. Of these taluks Kadiri, the largest, was on

CHAP. I. GENERAL.

October 1, 1910, incorporated with the adjoining district of Anantapur on the west, while Madanapalle and Vāyalpād were absorbed by the new district of Chittoor, which came into being on April 1, 1911. With this change, so largely conducive to administrative convenience, Cuddapah loses much of its diversity, though the taluk of Rāyachōti still serves to point the distinction which marked off the "sub-division" from the "main division" of the old district. As now constituted the district lies between 13° 43′ and 15° 14′ N., and 77° 51′ and 79° 29′ E., with an area of 5,884 square miles. Each of its sides is bordered by a single district: Kurnool on the north, Chittoor on the south, Nellore on the east and Anantapur on the west.

Natural divisions.

It contains nine taluks which may be said to form themselves roughly into three natural divisions, the first of which, consisting of Jammalamadugu, Proddatūr, Kamalāpuram, Cuddapah and Pulivendla taluks, adjoins the Kurnool and Anantapur districts and contains large areas of black cotton soil; the second comprises Rāyachōti taluk on the plateau, facing the districts of Anantapur on the west and Chittoor on the south; and the third is made up of the three taluks of Badvēl, Sidhout and Pullampet, which constitute a fairly well defined valley separated from Nellore district by the Veligonda hills, and from the rest of Cuddapah on the west by a somewhat similar but more broken range extending from the spurs of the Nallamalais from Kurnool in the north to the Pālkonda and Sēshāchalam range which terminates in the south at the famous hill of Tirupati.

Rivers.

The whole of the district drains into one river, the Pennēr. This runs from west to east and passes into Nellore district by the gap in the Eastern Ghāts at Sōmasila. Its chief tributaries from the north are the Kundēr and Sagilēr, which flow respectively through Proddatūr and the taluks of Badvēl and Sidhout, while from the plateau it receives three important streams, the Chitrāvati furthest west, and the Pāpaghni and Cheyyēr, both of which pass through the taluk of Rāyachōti. All these streams have their original sources outside the district. The Chitrāvati rises near Nandidrug in the Mysore State, and for most of its course runs through Anantapur district. It joins the Pennēr in the north-west corner of Cuddapah district in the Jammalamadugu taluk. The Pāpaghni also has its source in Mysore and enters Rāyachōti taluk at a point not far from the trijunction of the three districts of Cuddapah, Chittoor and Anantapur. Piercing the Pālkondas near Vēmpalle it joins the Pennēr about two miles north-east of Kamalāpuram. The Kundēr rises in Kurnool, and drains the great cotton soil plains which stretch between Nandyal in that district and Proddatūr in Cuddapah. The Sagilēr springs from the higher peaks of the Nallamalai hills not far from Cumbum in Kurnool district and in Cuddapah flows in a deep channel along a narrow valley. The Cheyyēr rises within the Chittoor district under the name of the Bāhudānadi, and after being fed by several smaller streams, the principal of which is the Pinchanadi, flows through the Sēshāchalam hills and the rich valley which once formed the petty chiefship of Chitvēl, and falls into the Pennēr not far from the eastern limit of the district. None of these streams is in any sense perennial. They are filled from the drainage of bare, rocky country devoid of heavy forests and consequently become torrents for a few days and then as suddenly dwindle to thin trickles of water flowing through wide sandy beds.

The western division.

The five taluks of Jammalamadugu, Proddatūr, Kamalāpuram, Cuddapah and Pulivendla form perhaps the least picturesque part of the district. The monotonous contour of their hills, of insignificant proportions, lends but little distinction to the dead level of the intervening plains of black cotton soil, while the intractable nature of the rocks and the incessant depredations of mankind have thwarted the efforts of nature to cover their nakedness. A few trees growing round village sites, a fringe of stunted babools round some tank-bed, and here and there a tope of mango or tamarind trees afford the only relief to the eye. To the dull uniformity of the scenery there are however some striking exceptions. At Gandikōta, six miles west of Jammalamadugu, is the great gorge where the Pennēr has cut its way through sheer rugged cliffs of bedded sandstone 200 or 300 feet high crowned on the southern bank by a picturesque old fortress where Hindu and Musalmān held successive sway. It is not easy of access, but the interesting and extensive remains of the old fort and its enclosures and the magnificent view to be had from its battlements or from the roof of the old State granary sufficiently repay a visit. Scarcely less famous is the passage of the Pāpaghni through the Pālkonda range near Vēmpalle. Here the hills attain a height of nearly two thousand feet, and the river takes a winding course between towering cliffs till it emerges in the plain that stretches towards Cuddapah. The legend runs that when the news of Rāma's victory over Rāvana was brought, a triumphal wreath of gold was hung across the gorge, and it is said that its semblance, which is only seen

CHAP. I. GENERAL.

at the approach of death by those whom the gods love, appeared to Sir Thomas Munro on his last journey to Cuddapah.

The southern division.

Separated by the Pālkonda range of hills from the northern part of the district, at an altitude of from 1,000 to 1,500 feet above the plain, is the taluk of Rāyachōti, the sole remnant of the old "sub-division" of which it has been said that it differs so materially in general aspect and character from the "main division," that for climate, cultivation and condition, they might be in different degrees of latitude. From the foot of the Pālkondas this taluk forms a gentle upward slope towards the south till it culminates in the Mysore plateau, undulating so continuously throughout its extent that it would be difficult to find in the whole a perfectly level mile of ground. Isolated hills and masses of rock stud the country, some of which, though they present a rugged and inclement appearance, are not devoid of a certain grandeur. The soil is mostly red and of a poor quality, having but little depth, and the country presents an aspect of dryness and want of vegetation, which is but seldom relieved by an adequate and timely rainfall.

The eastern division.

The eastern division of the Cuddapah district, consisting of the three taluks of Badvēl, Sidhout and Pullampet, form a rough parallelogram of about 140 miles from north to south with a maximum breadth of 33 miles. In one respect the division is unique in that it has natural and well defined frontiers throughout except on the north where an irregular and artificial line divides it from the Cumbum taluk of Kurnool. About fifteen miles north of Rēnigunta a narrow gap in the Tirupati hills near Bālapalle leads the railway line into the Pullampet taluk. From this point the hills divide. On the right the Veligonda range runs in an unbroken line into the Kurnool district with a general north-north-west direction and separates the division from Nellore. On the left the great range of the Sēshāchalams, a much denser mass of hills of which the highest point rises 3,739 feet above sea level, divides the Pullampet and Sidhout taluks from the upland. Forcing its way through these hills by a narrow pass famous for the beauty of its scenery the Cheyyēr enters the low country and after crossing the railway just south of Nandalūr continues eastwards as far as Tangatūr where it takes a sharp turn and proceeds northwards to join the Pennēr in Sidhout taluk near the village of Mādhavaram. West of the confluence lies the Vontimitta valley formed by confused spurs thrown off by the Pālkonda range, which soon afterwards turns definitely westwards to form the northern boundary of Rāyachōti taluk, thus leaving a clear approach to Cuddapah but one of no great breadth, for the march of the hills continues northwards till they rise abruptly in an imposing and solid mass north of the Pennēr river where they are known as the Lankāmalais. Some twenty miles north of the river this great range suddenly dips nearly to the level of the plain, the road from Proddatūr to Badvēl passing over a low ghāt at their base. To the north of this two low ridges encircle the Jangamrāzupalle valley but gradually coalesce and swell into the great north and south system of elevations and depressions known as the Nallamalais which stretch beyond this district through Kurnool to the Kistna. In rough outline therefore these taluks form a depression between two hill ranges. This is, however, itself broken by minor undulations, some of which have been so denuded that mere humps of disintegrated rock now remain, while others rise as abrupt hogbacked ridges. Most noticeable is the long ridge running from Kalasapād to the Pennēr parallel to the eastern ghāts and enclosing a narrow valley wherein lie the great tanks of Pōrumāmilla and Badvēl. In Sidhout taluk this valley is named after its most important village, Ōbulām. Still further south a less elevated and more irregular group of hills marks off the historic valley of Chitvēl from the rest of the Pullampet taluk.

SOILS.

The soils of the whole district have been regarded by the Settlement Department as falling into the two main series of regar and red ferruginous. The presence of a large area of black cotton soil has already been mentioned as a predominant characteristic of the four taluks that abut on the districts of Anantapur and Kurnool. As we go eastwards through the taluks of Pulivendla, Kamalāpuram and Cuddapah, the black cotton soil disappears and we find the regar element less and less conspicuous till in the eastern division of the district it represents scarcely a fifth of the assessed area, while in the upland taluk of Rāyachōti over 90 per cent. of the soil is red ferruginous. There are three distinct regions in which the black cotton soil is found. It attains its finest development to the north of Jammalamadugu and Proddatūr, where it can sometimes be seen to reach a depth of twenty feet, though its maximum depth is probably much greater. Towards the Kōilkuntla frontier it is also of excellent quality but thinner as the underlying rocks keep cropping up to the surface. Next comes the wide plain round Yerraguntla extending south-west across the Pulivendla frontier. Much of the soil here, though of less depth, is scarcely inferior to that north of the Pennēr. Lastly comes the south-western

CHAP. I.
SOILS.

portion of the Jammalamadugu taluk where it abuts on the Tādpatri plain. Here the cotton soils show a fair general average of fertility rather than any marked superiority. The qualities of this soil are well known. It is very retentive of moisture and when wet exceedingly miry and tenacious. In the hot weather it crumbles into a fine dust on the top and cracks into adamantine blocks beneath, the fissures often being of great depth. Theories as to its origin differ, but the curious way in which in places it laps round the rocks when exposed, penetrating even to little nooks and crevices certainly goes to support the view that it is largely an aqueous deposit of lacustrine origin. Next in importance are the alluvial soils, which vary in texture and colour as the regar soil is more or less impregnated with other elements brought down by the rivers. As to the origin of other black soils it is unnecessary here to particularise. Loams largely predominate throughout the tract especially in Cuddapah and Pulivendla, where such land when commanded by wells is often very valuable. Turning to the red soils, in Jammalamadugu taluk they are almost entirely confined to the villages on and about the Gandikōta range of hills, from the quartzites of which they are derived. They are mostly shallow soils and of a poor quality. In Proddatūr and more especially in the Cuddapah taluk the red soils are more important as they often stretch for a considerable distance from the foot of the hills into the plains where they are not unfrequently beneficially affected by the alluvial deposits of the Pennēr. In the eastern division of the district where red soils predominate, the best and worst sorts are found. The stretches of good soil are nowhere very extensive, but mention may be made of the light red clay lands in the neighbourhood of Kottakōta in the north of Badvēl taluk, and there is also a tract of excellent red loam in the villages of Vontimitta and Mantapampalle under the Pālkonda hills. Smaller patches of fair quality are also to be found in parts of the Pullampet taluk, notably in the Chitvēl valley. In Rāyachōti taluk, where more than two-thirds of the dry area is assessed at 8 annas an acre and less, the vast, uneven expanses of coarse red soil often present a harsh and monotonous appearance.

CLIMATE.

An observatory, under the control of the Madras Meteorological Department, was instituted at Cuddapah in March 1884. The station is 433 feet above sea level. The duty of the officer in charge of the observatory is simply to observe and report his observations, all reductions of which are made at the Madras Meteorological office.

CHAP. I. CLIMATE.

Rainfall.

The rainfall of the district is referred to in some detail in a later chapter. The annual average for the district as now constituted is rather more than 27 inches. The least favoured taluks are Jammalamadugu and Pulivendla, where the fall is only 21 inches. The district does not lie definitely within either of the monsoon areas, but depends on a somewhat precarious supply from either or both quarters, so that the period of the main rainfall in any year is largely conjectural, and the precipitation is occasionally untimely.

Temperature.

The fact that Cuddapah is generally regarded as an unpleasantly hot place is probably due to the early setting in of high temperatures. It is almost always the first station in the Presidency to record a maximum shade temperature exceeding 100° Fahrenheit, and this is generally before the end of February. The average maximum temperatures of April and May are 105·2° and 106·3° respectively. A temperature exceeding 114° is occasionally recorded in the period from about May 16th to May 28th. The average minimum temperatures for these two months are 80·8° and 83·5°. From the second week in June the thermometer drops rapidly as the south-west monsoon declares itself, so that the maximum and minimum for this month average respectively six and three degrees lower than those of May. But though Cuddapah is thus unpleasantly hot for about four months, the climate is quite tolerable for the rest of the year. The coolest days and nights are from the middle of November to the middle of January, during the latter half of which period night temperatures not unfrequently drop below 59°. The maximum temperature reaches its lowest monthly average in December, while the lowest average minimum is recorded in January. The figures are 86·8° and 64·4° respectively. It should be mentioned that Rāyachōti taluk, most of which lies at an altitude of about 1,000 feet higher than Cuddapah, enjoys a temperature some five degrees cooler than that of the low country.

Humidity.

The annual average percentage of humidity at Cuddapah is 67·5. The average figures for May and December, which are respectively the driest and most humid months of the year, are 52·6 and 77·5. The most rapid transitions are from February to March when the air becomes very dry as the hot weather sets in, and from May to June when moisture is again brought up by the south-west monsoon.

Winds.

It is during the south-west monsoon that winds attain their highest velocity. They blow from the south-west in July, but in August and September when the rainfall is most frequent, the general direction of the wind is from the north-west. It veers to north-east during October, when the second monsoon is established and lasts for about two months. The average wind direction in December is south-east and it remains in this quarter till the latter part of the hot weather, when it again blows from the west or north-west.

GEOLOGY.

Two distinct rock areas.

[1] If Cuddapah district were denuded of the superficial deposits which so largely form the surfaces of its great plains and basins, it would be seen to be divisible into two well-marked areas of very different kinds of rocks. All that part of the country lying to the south and west of the Guvvalacheruvu and Yerraguntlakōta hill ranges with their extensions northwards to Pārnapalle and southwards to the Tirupati hills is made up of rocks of the *gneissic series* or as it is otherwise termed the *metamorphic* or *crystalline series.* The remainder of the district, viz., that lying to the eastward of, and including, the hill ranges just mentioned, consists of a succession of *slates, quartzites* (altered sandstones, etc.), *limestones and volcanic rocks* with their accompaniments, all of which have been classified into two series called the *Cuddapah and Kurnool formations.*

Of crystalline rocks.

Of stratified rocks.

Concealed by recent deposits.

At various places all over the district, but mainly in the taluks of Pullampet, Sidhout, Cuddapah, Pulivendla, Proddatūr, and parts of Badvēl, the rock series above given are concealed by *recent deposits,* such as cotton soil, river alluviums, blown sands, and stone implement gravels.

Upland rugged with scattered hill masses.

The upland, of which the taluk of Rāyachōti forms part, is characteristic of a country of the peculiar varieties of *gneiss* of which it is composed, being a rugged region broken by numerous great rounded hill masses with occasional steep faces, or by smaller hillocks and bosses, whose smooth-curved slopes and humpy form bear some resemblance to the *roches moutonnés* of the old ice-worn regions of Europe. Indeed, this ice-worn look of the country often derives apparent confirmation from the further occurrence of rounded blocks and odd-shaped "*tots*" which are left standing here and there over the country as though they had been dropped from icebergs, or rolled about and smoothed by ice action. There are also long wall-like ridges, with white serrated crests, which are peculiarly conspicuous, as well as others not so sharply serrated, which by their dark colour are easily distinguishable from the latter, and which occur mostly in the eastern part of

[1] The section of this chapter dealing with Geology is reproduced from the Cuddapah District Manual (1875) with certain modifications approved by the Director of the Geological Survey of India.

this country. The indented line of fine scarps and headlands on the eastern and northern edge of the Rāyachōti and Guvvalacheruvu country forms a well-marked hill barrier between this upland and the plains.

Low country of hill-divided plains.

Beyond, or to the northward of, this barrier stretches the wide plain of Cuddapah itself with its extension into the Kundēr valley, and the open country of Pulivendla and Chintakunta, the latter confined on either side by the Jammalamadugu and Pulivendla hills, while that of the Kundēr is shut in on the east by the much larger and more lofty range of the Nallamalais. At its southern and eastern sides the Cuddapah basin is completely closed in by hills, but the low saddle of Kanamalōpalle leads to a succession of flat valleys of Vontimitta, the Cheyyēr and Pullampet south-eastwards in the direction of Madras, which are confined on their eastern and western sides by lessening groups of hills and ridges. In addition to the great Cuddapah plain and these minor basins, there is a further series of long but narrow valleys lying to the eastward of the Nallamalais and their extension southwards in the Badvēl and eastern Cheyyēr country, which in its turn is closed into the east by the long range of the Veligondas, a portion of the true eastern ghats, and the boundary between this and the Nellore district or *coast* low-country.

The physical features of the country having already been described, the rocks may be classified as follows :—

(1) Superficial deposits (alluvium, gravels, soils, etc.), recent pleistocene.
(2) Kurnools (limestones, quartzites, shales) } pre-Cambrian.
(3) Cuddapahs (slates, quartzites, etc.) } pre-Cambrian.
(4) Crystallines (gneiss, granites, traps, etc.) } pre-Cambrian.

Granitoid gneiss.

Crystalline series.—The *gneiss* is very granitoid, scarcely any foliation or stratification being visible even over wide extents of country. This rock might in hand specimens be considered a fine-grained *granite*, for it has the composition of that rock; but there is no evidence of its being intrusive, or of its having altered other rocks in its vicinity. The general character is that of a more or less close-grained grey or pale-red compound of *quartz* and *felspar*, or a quartzo-felspathic gneiss. Locally it may be met within bands containing *hornblende* and *mica*, thus giving the greyer and foliated varieties; and a very pretty pink rock may be met with having pale-green *pistacite* distributed through it in grains, or running in irregular strings.

Granite veins.

Of the intrusive rocks associated with the *gneiss*, the granite occurs mostly in two forms. The larger veins are of

CHAP. I. GEOLOGY. — very coarse texture, often largely crystallised, and generally consisting of a white binary *granite* of *quartz* and *orthoclase*, through often containing mica and sometimes *pistacite*. This coarser granite is easily weathered or decomposed, as compared with the other rocks; and it is in great part owing to this that the harder *gneiss* traversed by it is often left standing out over the country in isolated masses. Besides the larger and more marked veins, there are numerous other smaller ones often of great length, but generally only a few inches in thickness and running in straight lines, of very close-grained white and pale flesh-coloured granite.

Trap dykes.

Next in importance to the *gneiss* itself is the enormous number and extent of the *trap* dykes. These are of a very compact, nearly black or dark-green *green-stone* or *diorite*, which is occasionally porphyritic with large crystals of white or very pale-green felspar distributed through the *hornblende* paste. Their direction is generally nearly E.—W., but some of them run N.—S. or nearly so; while their inclination is very nearly vertical, or at very high angles to east or west. They are often traceable for many miles, one to the eastward of Rāyachōti being 28 or 29 miles long. The east and west dykes are not traceable so continuously, but they in a few cases run for 20 miles.

This wonderful network of igneous outburst is most intense in the Gurramkonda, Rāyachōti and Pīlēr country; it decreases in the number of dykes, though not in their length towards Vellore and Arcot. The intrusion did not, however, take place all at once, but at long intervals. The E.—W. dykes appear to have been first formed; they were then broken and displaced to some extent by side-shifting during the filling in of the dykes of the N.—S. system.

Brecciated quartz reefs.

The remaining rocks of any physical importance in the upland are the brecciated *quartz rocks*. These generally consist of an amorphous quartz much seamed with oxide of iron, as also with strings of more compact silicious matter and they are mostly of dirty white colour. The rock looks as though it had been crushed and broken up and then re-cemented by silicious infiltration; in other words, it is an "infiltration breccia" filling up very long fissures of dislocation which are striking across the western part of the upland for long distances in NW.—SE. lines, forming the backbones as it were of many lofty and long hill ridges. These "runs" or reefs of quartz breccia are both older and newer than the dykes of trap or green-stone, though they are mostly crossed by the latter. Indeed, in some cases, they are possibly newer than the *Cuddapah formation*, for towards Kurnool they run in fractures which have affected rocks of that formation, and they are possibly contemporaneous with a series of great *faults* which was superinduced on the rocks of the Guvvala-cheruvu range to the south-west of Cuddapah.

Sub-metamorphic series of Cuddapah and Kurnool.

Cuddapah and Kurnool formations.—The rocks of the Cuddapah low-country are true sedimentary rocks with one exception, and show all the ordinary characters of such in a very clear manner; but they have been altered or metamorphosed to some extent in such a way that the original sandstones and *conglomerates* are now hardened and vitrified as *quartzites.* The *shales* and *clays* have been turned into *clay slates*, and in some cases porcellanised, and the *limestones* have been rendered more or less crystalline. This is the general character of the rocks; but it is often found that they are all weathered back again into their originally more sedimentary appearance. The ordinarily compact, flinty, homogeneous quartzites turn out after weathering to be the coarsest *sandstones* or the roughest conglomerates and shingle beds. The limestones become earthy and clayey, and the porcellanous beds are again ordinary soft pipeclay-looking shales.

The single exception to the usually aqueous character of the rocks is the occurrence of great flows of *trap* associated with *ash-beds* and other volcanic ejecta.

Cuddapah formation.

Cuddapah series.—Enclosing the Cuddapah plain and its continuation northwards is the hilly ground with the other valleys and basins of the low-country division of the district, and all this is made up of either quartzites, slates, limestones, or trap rocks. These constitute the much older series called the *Cuddapah formation*, which is divisible into many different groups, only some of which occur in the area under description.

In south-east taluks.

Commencing at the southern end of the district near the Bālapalle bank and cutting of the Madras Railway there are very hard splintery, compact, pale-grey, and nearly white quartzite beds which belong to the oldest group but one in this series called the *Cheyyēr group.* It is a series of great thickness consisting of two divisions, the lowest being conglomerates and sandstones which are very well represented in the famous Tirupati hills and on the summit of Nagari Nose in North Arcot.[1] On these quartzites lies the great *slate* series so well represented to the south of Vontimitta, and out of

Cheyyēr group.

[1] The wonderfully picturesque amphitheatre of cliffs and the narrow rift in these, called the Pedda Gandhi to the south of Cuddapah, have been cut out in the nearly horizontal quartzite beds of the lower division of this group.

CHAP. I. GEOLOGY.

which tolerable slates may eventually be got by deeper quarrying. There are also many bands of limestone (principally silicious) among these slates, the best and easiest worked being in the neighbourhood of Vontimitta.

Cheyyērs in the Pulivendla taluk, volcanic.

The *Cheyyēr group* is continued westward along the southern edge of the Cuddapah basin in a very narrow band bordering the Guvvalacheruvu hills into the Pulivendla taluk, but the character of the series is totally changed, or at any rate much modified by the occurrence of great flows of *trap (diorite)* and *ash-beds* of great thickness, while the bands of limestone are less numerous and thinner than in the Cheyyēr valley. Fine displays of these *ash-beds, traps, limestones, etc.*, may be seen in the Chintakunta and Kondāpuram hills lying to the westward of the line of railway.

Pāpaghni group, oldest.

The thin band of the Cheyyēr quartzites to the south of Cuddapah overlies the strata of the Guvvalacheruvu hills, which are here all quartzites, and form the lowest group or the *Pāpaghni beds*. These extend westward for some miles, and thence northwards all the way to Kurnool, forming the cliffy scraps overlooking the Bellary district, and often running up into peaks of considerable height.

Faulting near Cuddapah.

The Guvvalacheruvu hills[1] between the Cuddapah-Guvvalacheruvu road and the Pāpaghni are rather curiously cut up and broken by a series of stepped *faults* running in a nearly E.—W. direction, by which a long patch of the crystalline rocks of the upland has been left inside the area of quartzites.

Warm springs.

The warm springs of the Buggavanka to the south of Cuddapah, and those of Putalēshwar a few miles further west, are probably connected with this system of faults.

Nallamalai group.

Metalliferous.

A further and higher set of quartzites overlies the Cheyyēr beds of the Pulivendla valley, viz., those of the Jammalamadugu hills, through which the grand gorge of the Pennēr at Gandikōta has been cut. These belong to, and are the lowest beds of, the *Nallamalai group*, but their continuity with the greater mass in the Nallamalai mountains is hidden by strata of the *Kurnool* series in the Kundēr valley. This, like the rest, is made up of quartzites and slates, but in more numerous and varied bands than in the two groups already enumerated. It is also the group which is richest in resources, for it has given and still shows signs of treasures of lead, copper and iron ores; and there are fair indications of various building materials. The lie of the Cuddapah rocks until they get close to the Nallamalais is tolerably easy, that

[1] A portion of the Pālkonda range.

is, they are dipping gently to the north-east as the edging beds of a great bay or gulf; but in this range of hills and southward all along the eastern side of the Cheyyēr valley considerable crushing, folding, and breaking of the strata have been superinduced and have in great measure helped to elevate the varied strata in the great mountain mass, with its flanking valleys and ridges carved out by the great denuding forces which were afterwards brought to bear upon this part of the surface of the Indian Peninsula.

Cuddapah town on rocks of the Kurnool formation.

Kurnool series.—The town of Cuddapah stands on a wide plain underneath the soil of which, and visible in most of the wells, are reddish-purple and chocolate-coloured (with greenish seams) calcareous *shales* and *slaty* shales lying nearly horizontal or undulating slightly, but having a general basonal position; these have been called *Nandyal shales.*

Kundēr series of limestones.

They show all up the middle of the Kundēr valley and repose on, but graduate quickly down into, pale-grey and dark limestone flags and thicker beds of limestone called the Koilkuntla limestones. The latter dip or rise up gently from under the purple shales to the south of Cuddapah and Chintakommadinne, and to the west of the town in a narrow belt by Kamalāpuram, Proddatūr and so into the Kōilkuntla taluk of the Kurnool district, whence they are named.

Underneath the Kōilkuntla limestone are sandstones or quartzites, locally intercalated in the limestones and known as the Paniam series, after the town of that name. These outcrop between the open Kundēr valley and the western ranges or Erramalais, forming some low flat hills such as the plateaux of Uppalapād and Undutla. The greatest thickness of the quartzites is only 100 feet, and the series disappears altogether to the north and south, nor has any sign of it been observed on the eastern edge of the basin. An upper portion formed of firm white sandstone has been distinguished as the "pinnacled quartzites" from its mode of weathering; the lower beds, or "plateau quartzites" are coarser, more earthy and ferruginous, of various rusty tints. Again, still further underneath is a thin band of white, pale-yellow and buff non-calcareous shales, traces of which show near the line of railway about eight miles north-west of Cuddapah. These are underlaid by a set of beds in the Cuddapah district, called the *Narji limestones*, which have become an industrial resource of Cuddapah.

Narji beds.

The Narji beds are typically very compact, sub-crystalline, and extremely fine-grained—so fine-grained that it is from this series of beds that the so-called lithographic limestone of

CHAP. I. GEOLOGY.

the Madras Presidency has in some cases been obtained. They are generally of a grey colour with a blue shade, sometimes nearly black, and occasionally of pale-buff and fawn colours. These strata crop up on either side of the Cuddapah basin and its extension northwards.

Bangana palle group of quartzites.

In the Kurnool district, the whole group of buff shales and limestones is underlaid by a thin series of *quartzites*, which are peculiarly interesting in that they contain diamonds. There is unfortunately no good evidence that the lower group is represented in the Cuddapah district, unless the quartzites capping the Chintakunta hills towards the Chitrāvati are their representatives. There is no case of the rocks on these hills having ever been worked for diamonds, and it is almost certain that the natives would have known of them long ago were they to be found.

Alluvium, soils, etc.

Recent deposits.—The special superficial deposits worthy of notice, leaving out the usual sandy soils of red or brown colours which are mainly derived from the disintegration of the adjacent rocks by atmospheric agency, are the gravels and alluvial deposits of the proper plains of the district, the cotton soil, and to a small extent the blown sands. The alluvial deposits are mainly of two kinds—a hard calcareous clayey drift with bands of heavy conglomerate and shingle, and a set of softer, somewhat sandy loams. The latter appear to be strictly fluviatile and lacustrine in their origin, while the coarser deposits are possibly estuarine, and may even be partly marine. Stone implements chipped out of quartzite have been dug from seams of gravel in the lower clays (though not as yet in the Cuddapah basin) of the western side of the Kundēr valley in a nullah five miles north of Mutyālapād in the Kurnool district, and at other places; and hence those older clays are sometimes called "implement gravels." Other stone implements have been found lying among the much more recent sandy soils a short distance to the east of Rāyachōti. The upper alluvial deposits occupy a large part of the middle of the Kundēr valley and nearly the whole of the Cuddapah plain, but they are every now and then covered up by extensive patches of cotton soil, particularly in the direction of Nossam and Kōilkuntla (Kurnool district) and the wide valley west and north of Pulivendla. The heavier clays and gravels only show on the east side of the Kundēr valley. The diamond mines of Chennūr were worked in some gravel banks of these deposits.

Implement gravels.

Blown sands of Pennēr.

Blown sands are only exceptionally accumulated in the district, and mainly along the banks of the Pennēr. The sands from this river are blown from the bed in the dry seasons by the high winds as they rush through the different gorges, particularly the long one of the Gandikōta. At both ends of the Gandikōta gorge there are heavy accumulations piled up by the westerly and easterly winds which blow during the two monsoons. The larger drift is at the eastern end towards Jammalamadugu, which village is often largely invaded by the sand during the westerly winds. From Jammalamadugu, there is a belt of low sand hills bordering the left bank of the river as far down as and beyond the confluence of the Pāpaghni and Kundēr.

Industrial products.

The geological resources of this district are diamonds, iron, lead and copper, to which may be added building stones, road materials and cements.

Diamonds.

Diamonds have been worked for and found only in one part of the district, at or in the neighbourhood of Chennūr on the right bank of the Pennēr, about seven or eight miles north of Cuddapah. The diamonds were obtained from a hard gravelly deposit, or rough conglomerate underneath the rather thick covering of soils and clays at Chennūr, which is made up of fragments of rocks and smaller *débris* from the proper diamond-bearing strata of the adjacent Kurnool district, the whole making up a bank or banks of rearranged materials among the recent deposits lying around a spur of the Nallamalais which here drops down into this part of the Cuddapah basin. The extent of these gravels is of course not known, except in so far as their area is indicated by the pits dug down to them; but, from all inquiry made on the subject, it would appear that further lateral extension of the search was not considered worthy of trial, or that the landholders opposed it. There is no reason, however, against the supposition that the conglomerate does extend much further, and that it may even be found in other parts of the valley. The deposit lies about six feet below the surface. The mines are generally of a square form, and from 4 to 12 feet deep. The pebbles most commonly met with are ferruginous, gritty and schistose sandstones, sandstone-conglomerates, including rolled pebbles of quartz, chert and jasper, claystone porphyry, with crystals of felspar; blue jasper, veined with oxide of iron; coarse, red jasper and quartz crystals. Some of these pebbles have evidently been transported from the adjacent hills, but the porphyritic and felspathic pebbles must have travelled a much greater distance. Near the base of the hills the cotton soil is covered with red gritty earth, arising from the disintegration of the sandstone rock. The process of mining consists merely in digging out the rolled pebbles and gravel, and washing them carefully in small square reservoirs raised on mounds having their bottoms paved with stones. At the foot of the mound is a clear space surrounded by heaps of refuse, where the washed gravel is again carefully spread out and examined in presence of the diamond contractors; the diamonds are easily recognized in the moist state by their peculiar lustre. These mines were formerly let out by the Government to native contractors. In 1834 the mines proved profitable, but in the following year the miners lost a considerable sum. The sum paid to Government by them for the privilege of mining a piece of ground, 100 yards long by 50 broad, for four months was Rs. 200. In 1840, the contract rose to about Rs. 250. When a diamond of more than a gold pagoda in weight (52·56 grains at Madras) was found, it was sold by public auction, and one-third of the proceeds went to Government, the remainder to the mining contractor. Dry weather was selected to carry on operations to avoid the inconvenience and expense of draining. Previous to British rule all the diamonds produced were carried for sale to Vijayanagar and Golconda. In those days very large diamonds were found. Dr. Heyne and Captain Newbold, when describing their visits to these mines, mentioned that the natives objected to their approaching them on horseback, as it would, they said, irritate Ammavāru or Lakshmi, the goddess of riches, who was the patroness of the mines. Newbold stated that he witnessed sacrifices made to propitiate her. The different pebbles considered indicative of the presence of diamonds bear the following names in Telugu:—Tella bendu, decomposed hornstone; Binga bendu, transparent quartz; Pacchai bendu, epidote; Gāju bendu, pebbles with an ochreous encrustation; Baggira, jasper of various colours; Karla, basalt; Yerra bendu, sandstone; Kanna, small globular ironstone; Korund or Corundum, which is considered to be the best sign. Besides these there are many other pebbles, chiefly varieties of sandstones.

The mines were leased collectively for a time by Mr. Richardson, of Madras, who applied to the Collector of Cuddapah, for permission to work them in 1869, at the favourable rent of Rs. 100 per annum. This attempt was not attended with success, but there are accounts of two diamonds having formerly come out of the field which were eventually sold, respectively, for Rs. 50,000 and Rs. 30,000.

In the *Kurnool formation* there is a group of quartzites which is actually mined at Banganapalle for diamonds; but, though other members of this series are found in the Cuddapah

CHAP. I. GEOLOGY.

area, this particular group, to which the name Banganapalle has been given, does not occur in the district. The nearest point of occurrence of this group is some miles to the west of Tādpatri.

Iron ore.

Iron ore is scattered pretty generally over the country, but only in any quantity at two or three localities, in the neighbourhood of which it used to be smelted according to the demand, the latter being always very small. Usually the ore is some variety of the *peroxide of iron*, mostly a grey micaceous ore. Some old iron-smelting villages lie along the eastern side of the Kundēr valley from Nandyālampet northwards. The form of ore here worked was a massive shaly ferruginous sandstone mainly made up of *hæmatite*. Several furnaces were worked at Yerraguntlakōta in the Chitvēl country, the ore being brought from the eastern slopes of the hills west of the village. In the Rāyachōti taluk, near Madicheruvu, this manufacture was also carried on, though not to any great extent, the ore being quarried and brought from the hills to the westward. The industry ceased to be remunerative about forty years ago, owing to cheaper foreign imports.

Lead ore.

Lead, in the form of *galena* or *sulphide of lead,* is found in the Nallamalais in the neighbourhood of the old mines at Jangamrāzupalle. The workings are now, and have long been, deserted, and much of the lead has probably been worked out; but there are still good indications of this mineral. The locality is wild, much overgrown with jungle, and feverish.

Jangamrāzupalle is on the pass of that name across the Nallamalais, some five miles north of the road from Cuddapah to Badvēl. The lead-workings were at the south end and east side of a low ridge north-north-east of the village. The galleries were excavated between beds of dark-grey silicious limestone traversed by strings of white and dull-blue quartz. Granular sulphide of lead is disseminated in very small quantities through the blue quartz, and it was doubtless in strings like these in the excavated beds of the same rock that the extracted lead occurred. These strings of quartz are in north-north-east—south-south-west fissures having a dip of 60° westward, the beds of silicious rock dipping at 50° east by north. Further south and west of the village there are again numerous old galleries excavated in the same series of beds; and the adjacent strata still show traces of the ore. There are also other old workings to the westward on the flanks of the Nallamalais opposite Vanipenta but no traces of lead were seen.

CHAP. I. GEOLOGY.

The lead found in this region is very rich galena, containing silver; and, though only poor specimens were found *in situ* at the time of the visit of the Geological Survey of India, many of the quarried fragments or *débris* from the mines were very rich in ore; and fine and massive specimens have been found since then by subordinates of the Public Works Department. There seems on the whole every probability of this being a good mining region as far as the traces of ore can show; and Mr. Wall, the then Mining Engineer of the Madras Government, at the time of his inspection reported very favourably on it. It is now within more easy reach of Madras, owing to the proximity of the railway, than it was in Mr. Wall's time. There is not a good supply of water for working machinery, etc., but this might be met by damming up some of the streams which are full enough during the rains; and indeed the other obstacles in the way of opening out the mines, such as the unhealthiness of the place, the poorness of junglegrowth to meet the requirements in the way of fuel, and the scarcity of labour might all be met to some extent by care and good management.

Copper.

Copper shows only in traces associated with the lead ore in this same Jangamrāzupalle region. These were only cupreous stains,—impressions of crystals of *copper pyrites* and faint traces of *native copper.* They occur in the strings of quartz already detailed as traversing the beds of silicious limestone.

Building materials. Limestones.

Good building stone is common all over the district, but some of it is of special adaptation, one variety having become worthy of exportation into other districts. Among these are the various limestones, commencing first with the fine *narji stone.* The best description of this was, and possibly is, yet procurable from the original quarries at the village of Narji, about 24 miles west-north-west of Cuddapah. It is a regular-bedded, compact, dark-grey, semi-splintery rock; and, being well jointed at right angles to the bedding, is easily obtainable in blocks and thin slabs. The colour is so dark at times as to give almost a black marble when the stone is polished. As the group in which this limestone occurs underlies the great Cuddapah plain and crops up to the surface on either side of it, it follows that good varieties are quarried, or can be obtained anywhere along the base of the Nallamalais, as also to the westward of a sinuous line drawn from Chintakommadinne (south of Cuddapah) through Kamalāpuram, Proddatūr, Peddapasupula and Pattūr.

Other almost equally good limestones occur in the Nallamalai side of the valley, though these belong to the upper group of the Kurnool formation. It is from this upper series that the coarser and more clayey limestone flags, so largely used in Cuddapah and the villages up the middle of the Kundēr valley, are obtained.

Besides these easily procurable and extensively distributed limestones, there are frequent bands of other but often harder—as being very silicious and splintery—calcareous beds especially around Vontimitta, and so down through the Pullampet taluk. A very thick series crops up along the course of the Pāpaghni just before it enters the Cuddapah basin, and thence continues westward below the main Pulivendla ridge. There are some thin bands of limestone running for miles in long north-west—south-east outcrops across the plains north of Pulivendla, the highest and thickest bands crossing the Chitrāvati (not seen in river) a few miles above the railway bridge.

Lime.

Of all these limestones perhaps that from the Narji quarries, or from the corresponding beds on either side of the Kundēr valley, is best adapted for lime burning, though in many cases good lime may be produced from nearly all the varieties if care in selection and a judicious mode of burning be adopted. The country is, however, so generally productive of the peculiar nodular and concretionary fresh-water and subærial deposit called *kankar*, both in the upland taluks and in the low-country that, except for large works, the proper limestone is seldom brought into extensive use as a source of *lime.*

Slates.

The next most frequently-occurring stone in the district, which at first sight might seem of great value, is the *clay-slate.* These slates are never seen to come near the true slates of commerce either in hardness, fineness of texture, or intensity of cleavage. It may be said of these rocks that they are simply *clay-slates,* describing them as to their composition as evident to the eye and touch, the true roofing material being distinctly a *slate.* However, there are regions in the district where some of these clay-slates are much more suitable for roof-covering or for flags than the generality of the rock; and it is not improbable as the country is opened up and quarries cut into the rock, that even better materials may be found.

The best slates, or such as seem capable of being split into slabs of any moderate size and tenuity, are near the upper Ahōbilaṃ temple in the Nallamalais. Again, large slabby slates are quarried to some little extent on the eastern flanks of these mountains at about the parallel of Badvēl.

Sandstones, etc.

The remaining rocks in the low-country are the numerous *quartzites,* or altered sandstones. These are all hard, difficult

CHAP. I. GEOLOGY.

to be worked, and only suitable for local construction. Occasionally they are thin-bedded and jointed sufficiently to give small-sized slabs easily split up. The numerous railway works along the line of railway south of Vontimitta are mostly built of blocks from these thin beds of the quartzites; and the cutting at Bālapalle may be pointed out as a piece of work excavated in about the most intractable rock in the country.

Gneiss, etc.

In the upland region the prevalent rock is a variety of the gneissic series, or what is usually wrongly designated as granite; and it is hardly necessary to refer here to the building material obtainable therefrom as it is so well known, and so frequently used in large structures all over Southern India.

FLORA.

From what has already been said of the situation of the district and its scanty rainfall the nature of its flora may be readily inferred. The whole district falls within what has been called the dry zone of the Presidency, depending for its moisture on the fringes of both monsoons. A few weeks after hot weather conditions are established, everything begins to wear a withered appearance. Herbaceous vegetation is burned up, many trees are leafless, and the aspect of the country is dreary in the extreme. The main characteristic of the stretches that intervene between cultivated areas is a rather sparse scrub jungle, variegated by more or less isolated rocky hills of no great elevation which are as often as not devoid of any growth except thin grass and scattered Euphorbia or Cactus bushes. I omit here all reference to the reserved forests which cover the slopes of the main hill ranges of the district, as they are treated in some detail in another chapter. Among the characteristic shrubs of the district may be mentioned Carissa carandas, Calotropis gigantea, Opuntia dillenii, Cassia auriculata, Euphorbia antiquorum, Euphorbia neriifolia, Euphorbia tirucalli and Ixora parviflora. Of these the Cassia auriculata—the yellow-flowered *tangēdu*—though found throughout the district is perhaps commonest in Rāyachōti taluk and often thrives over rocky and gravelly wastes where seemingly nothing else can grow. Tamarind topes abound throughout the district and there are but few camping grounds where other trees such as mangoes afford an adequate shade. Of scattered trees other than the tamarind, the babul and margosa are perhaps the commonest, though in Rāyachōti taluk no tree seems to occur so frequently as the kānuga (Pongamia glabra) which thrives better on the plateau, while its growth is encouraged for the manurial value of its leaves. Of fig trees, the ragi (Ficus religiosa) and juvvi (Ficus tsiela) are most frequently met with, especially the

FLORA.

former. It is said that at the top of the Pālkonda hills a hamlet of Tāllapalle-Yelamavāripalle of Pulivendla taluk contains an immense banyan tree capable of sheltering about three thousand people. The place is very difficult of access and I have never had an opportunity of visiting it to verify the truth of this statement.

FAUNA. Cattle.

Live-stock has increased with the spread of cultivation; but the indigenous cattle of the district, which are of the small black and white and red breed common in the Ceded Districts and southern portions of the Presidency, are generally of poor quality, being undersized, ill-fed and ill-cared for. The universal system of common pasturing, in which cattle of all ages wander in promiscuous herds over the open arable lands and village wastes, ensures immature, mongrel breeding and the spread of disease; and since, in general, there is no system of fodder growing, only the scanty wild pasture of the unoccupied lands, and the grazing and stubble on the arable lands and leaves from trees are available for ordinary cattle. Of the better cattle there are two kinds, both imported or from imported strains. Around Cuddapah and on the black cotton plains the cattle are almost all of the Nellore breed, tall, bulky, clumsy and flat sided animals, which however possess great strength, and when cared for are very useful beasts. They are imported from the breeding districts of Nellore, being brought over annually by drovers who seldom obtain full payment at the time of sale, the purchase money being spread over several years. The best animals weigh up to 1,500 lb. and are excellent milkers. Brought over when just ready for use, their life under the plough is said to last for about eight years. The other imported strain is the Mysore breed, which is nowhere found pure in the district and is practically confined to the upland taluk, where good results have been obtained by intermixing this breed with the common indigenous kind. Cattle disease which is prevalent in various forms often causes immense loss to the ryots, who are nevertheless slow to abandon time-honoured and ineffectual remedies in favour of more enlightened methods of combating the evil.

Buffaloes, Sheep and Goats.

Buffaloes are of the usual variety. They are occasionally used for heavy ploughing, and frequently in Rāyachōti taluk for slow heavy draught such as carting slabs from granite quarries on the most primitive vehicles imaginable, formed of two or three heavy planks on solid wooden wheels. But probably most of the buffaloes are sacrificed at shrines, one of which, at the small village of Anantapuram in Rāyachōti taluk, is responsible for the slaughter of hundreds every year.

CHAP. I. FAUNA.

Of sheep the three principal breeds found in the Presidency are all represented in the district. The small woolly kind is found in the upland taluk, all the wool which is of a hairy quality being consumed locally in the manufacture of coarse blankets. The other small variety which is red in colour and covered only with short coarse hair is found all over the district as is also the third species, a long-legged goat-like animal, characterized by two tassels dependent from its neck, of larger size than the two first named, but producing coarse mutton and no wool. The goats are of the ordinary breed. Together with sheep they are largely used as manuring agents, wandering over the village by day and penned at night on the fields of those who have hired their services. In folding the sheep on the land hurdles are very seldom used in this district, the flock being simply herded on a particular field and guarded by the shepherd assisted by two or three savage dogs according to his need. No fixed lambing season is known, owing to the universal practice of letting the rams and ewes run together; but the shepherds acknowledge that the best season for the lambs being dropped is February.

Game.

The most important species of game are to be found in the reserved forests along the slopes of the main hill ranges. Tigers are not very common but are well known to haunt the south end of the Sēshāchālam range where the Pullampet taluk adjoins the well-known Chāmala valley in Chittoor district. This valley is so well stocked with game and so carefully preserved that the forests in its neighbourhood have become the tiger's permanent habitat. Leopards are very common, especially in the rocky hills of Rāyachōti taluk, and do Considerable damage by killing cattle. The hunting cheetah, Cynælurus jubatus, is no doubt occasionally seen. One was recently heard of at the southern end of the Nallamalais in Proddatūr taluk, but as the people do not clearly distinguish this species it is difficult to record its appearances with exactitude. Other smaller species of the wild cat tribe are said to be found in all parts of the district. Bears are to be found, as also wolves. The latter are less common, but have been seen in recent years near Agudūr in Pulivendla taluk and in the neighbourhood of Veligallu in the extreme west of Rāyachōti taluk. The Indian wild dog, Cyon dukhunensis, occurs wherever deer and sambhar are found. The latter haunt the larger forests, while spotted deer are common at the foot of all the big hill ranges. The same may be said of jungle sheep (Cervulus muntjac) and wild pig. Outside the forests chinkara (the Indian Gazelle) and the Indian Antelope or blackbuck, especially the latter, are often seen. Some three years ago black buck was very plentiful in the north of the Pullampet taluk, west of the road from Pottapi to Mādhavaram. In addition to these, no doubt the mousedeer, Tragulus memimna, also occurs, as it is known to frequent all hilly jungle tracts south of the Gōdāvari, though I have no record of its having been actually seen in Cuddapah district.

Of game birds, partridges and quails are the commonest, and sandgrouse also occur in all parts of the district. In and near the forests peafowl are fairly plentiful, and one of the localities specially favoured by them appears to be a stretch of jungle and forest a few miles east of Sidhout, where they are often to be seen from the road leading to Badvēl. Junglefowl and spurfowl are also common in all the forests of the district. The Indian Bustard (Eupodotis Edwardsi) though generally scarce, is said to be fairly common over a small area in the north-west of Jammalamadugu taluk beyond Talamanchipatnam towards the Kurnool frontier. The Lesser Florican (Sypheotis aurita) is also occasionally seen and I learn that two specimens have been shot in recent years within a few miles of Cuddapah town. Besides the usual species of plovers which occur in all parts of South India, it is interesting to note that a portion of Cuddapah district, corresponding roughly to the Badvel taluk, is included in the very limited area to which is confined the rarer species of double-banded plover (Rhinoptilus ditorquatus), which is said to be scarcely ever found outside scrub-jungle and is not known to exist except in parts of Nellore, Cuddapah and Kurnool districts. Of water-loving birds, snipe are less common than on the east of the Veligonda hills, but in some years they are very plentiful, especially in parts of Cuddapah taluk. Several kinds of teal and duck are found throughout the district and are seen in good years on nearly all the larger tanks after the cessation of the north-east monsoon. Barheaded geese, which visit the country in the cold season, are also occasionally met with.

Quadrumana.

Finally, the quadrumana of the district may be briefly noticed, as they comprise, besides the common Bonnet Monkey (Macacus sinicus) of South India, two rarer species, namely, the Madras *Langur* (Semnopithecus priamus), which is the large grey monkey found in the Sēshāchalams, and the curious little slender *Loris* (Loris gracilis) which, owing to its nocturnal disposition, is seldom seen unless searched for.

CHAPTER II.

POLITICAL HISTORY.

INTRODUCTORY—Pre-historic remains—The Deccan politically isolated in earliest historical times—Earliest known dynasties—The Bānas—The Rāshtrakūtas—The Vaidumbas—Rise of the Chōlas—The eastern division of the district—The Telugu Chōdas—The Kākatīyas of Oarangal—First Muhammadan invasion—The Vijayanagar Empire—Rise of the Poligārs—The Matla Princes—The Nawabs of Cuddapah—Haidar Ali of Mysore—Transfer of Cuddapah to the British—The work of Munro—The Poligārs and their reduction—Conclusion.

CHAP. II. INTRODUCTORY.

IT has been truly said that in any account which may be given of the literature proper to South India, one capital defect must be obvious, that history finds in it no place. The Muhammadan historians have confined themselves to their own period, and the records of Golconda and Bijāpur do not touch that part of the Deccan which includes the present district of Cuddapah. It is only in the last quarter of a century that means have been found through antiquarian research of supplementing the deficiency caused by the absence of materials constructed or collected by usual historic methods. That epigraphy has thrown and continues to throw a flood of light on what has hitherto been obscure or conjectural is proved by results. The neglect of history as a branch of the literature of the country is in marked contrast to the care which has been taken from very early times to as recent a period as the 18th century of our era to record matters of local interest on stone and copperplates. It is fortunate that the exigencies of the climate and the voracity of white ants, which perhaps alone precluded the use of a more perishable substance for the purpose of making what were intended to be permanent records, have preserved to us the means of reconstructing the history of the past. Old copperplate records are commoner than might be supposed, and are very carefully preserved, being handed down as heir-looms from generation to generation. Their possessors value them highly and, though often ignorant of their contents, are glad to show them to enquirers. Lithic inscriptions are mostly found in temples but were also not infrequently set up near the entrance to a village or at the

KISTVAENS.

KISTVAENS.

spot referred to in the inscription. They most commonly record grants to temples, remission of taxes, gifts of land in consideration of the performance of services to the community, settlement of land disputes and the like. Their historical value is to be found not so much in the details they relate as in the fact that they nearly always give the date of the event recorded, with the name of the reigning king, and his dynasty. If the event recorded is a public work redounding to the merit of the king, such as the construction of a tank or irrigation channel, the titles of the king, indicating the principal military achievements of his reign, are often recited, and his genealogy is sometimes given. Such inscriptions are fortunately very numerous, and several may be found relating to the same period, so that a little understood allusion in one may often be elucidated and explained by another. They constitute practically the only material for an authentic history of Cuddapah district up to the fall of the Vijayanagar Empire.

Prehistoric remains.

That parts of the district, notably the river valleys in the low country, were inhabited ages before the earliest of these records which have come down to us, is proved by the existence of kistvaens or cell-tombs. They are locally known to the present day as *Pāndavagullu*. There are two types found in the district, one being constructed of irregular unfashioned stones, examples of which are to be seen near Yerraguntla, and the other bearing signs of more or less rough workmanship. They are always found in groups and not scattered about singly. Good examples of the latter type have been found at Amilēpalle.[1] They have not yet been surveyed by the Archæological Department, but it is conjectured that they contain cinerary urns filled with fine red earth and bone ash, with perhaps the remains of a few corroded iron implements. The curiously shaped stones planted alongside some of the tombs are peculiar and hitherto unexplained, but they appear in some way to serve the purpose of memorial stones. The constructions of unhewn stone near Yerraguntla are of course to be referred to a still earlier civilization, but as they too have never yet been scientifically examined it can only be recorded that they are the oldest surviving monuments of human activity in the district.

The Deccan politically isolated in earliest historical times.

The earliest historical notices of the south of India lack all reference to this part of the Deccan, and the key to the obscurity of its history is probably to be found in its geographical position. The Eastern Ghāts cut it off from the sea-coast country while on the south and part of the west the

1 In Vāyalpād taluk, now included in Chittoor district.

CHAP. II.

intervention of the Mysore plateau constituted a natural barrier to intercourse with regions for which easier access to the sea secured an earlier development. While we know from the Greek geographer Megasthenes (302 B.C.) and the inscriptions of Asōka (250 B.C.) of three Dravidian kingdoms in the south-east, the extreme south, and the south-west of the Peninsula, there is no evidence of any kingdom having been in existence in the Deccan at this early period. Further, to judge from the configuration of the country and the present aspect of its wilder parts, it appears certain that at that time and long afterwards what is now Cuddapah district was a mere tract of impenetrable forest, barren rocks and stony wastes. With its later development it offered means of expansion to the kingdoms surrounding it, and its history for many centuries affords but an index to the varying fortunes of neighbouring dynasties.

Earliest known dynasties.

The three Dravidian kingdoms above referred to are the Chōla, Pāndya and Kērala or Chēra. With the Pāndyas and Kēralas, about the latter of which little appears to be known, we are not concerned. The Chōlas who appear from earliest times to have been firmly established in Tanjore and South Arcot found in the early centuries of our era a check to their expansion to the north in the growing power of the Pallavas who had become firmly settled at Conjeeveram by the middle of the 4th century A.D. From here the Pallava kings controlled an extensive territory to the north, which included the present Nellore district and probably all the Telugu country on the east coast as far as the Kistna. From Nellore they penetrated for a time into the north of Cuddapah district, presumably following the course of the Pennēr up stream, for it is in the neighbourhood of this river in the taluks of Jammalamadugu and Proddatūr, that the earliest historical evidence, in the shape of lithic monuments, has been collected. From this and similar evidence elsewhere it appears tolerably certain that the growing power of the Pallavas was checked almost simultaneously in the north and the south in the latter part of the 5th century, when the Chōla dynasty under its famous, and hitherto mythical, king Karikāla attained unprecedented ascendency and captured Conjeeveram from Trilōchana-Pallava, while on the north the same Pallava king suffered defeat at the hands of the Chālukyan adventurer Vijayāditya, who claimed to come from Ayōdhya (Oudh). This battle probably took place in Cuddapah district, as the village of Mudivēmu where the queen of the victor Vijayāditya who lost his life took refuge after the battle, is no other than Peddamudiyam in Jammalamadugu taluk. Yet this district never came under the sway of the Chālukyans, whose power developed much later, for the dominions of their two branches, the Eastern and Western Chālukyans, scarcely touched the middle country. On the other hand, with the capture of the Pallava capital, it seems that the Chōlas overran the Pallava territory as far north as Nellore, for a branch of them undoubtedly penetrated inland and established themselves for a century or two in the black cotton country on the banks of the Pennēr in this district. The recent discovery of some copper plates at Malēpād and stone inscriptions at Peddamudiyam and Muddanūr conclusively prove that at least four generations of the earlier Chōla kings ruled this country. That this dynasty succeeded the Pallavas, politically, in at least a portion of their extensive territory is also rendered probable by the fact that they adopted titles and names current among the Pallava kings of the Simhavishnu line. The full extent of this Chōla kingdom has not yet been discovered, but the fact of its existence throws an interesting light on the account of a "Choolya" State described by the Chinese traveller Hiuen Tsiang who visited India about 640 A.D. and compiled a geographical treatise of the south of the Peninsula. From the boundaries given by him of the various divisions of the country and the order in which he mentions the Choolya State it used to be thought that it might correspond to part of the Kurnool district, though others considered that the names of Choolya and Dravida had been transposed and that the Choolya State really referred to the Chōla kingdom of Tanjore. The doubt has now been cleared up. The Choolya State referred to by Hiuen Tsiang was the Telugu Chōla kingdom occupying most of the black cotton country of this district and perhaps parts of Kurnool and Anantapur. The same authority says it is a small State, about 400 miles in circumference. In inscriptions we find the name of this Chōla country to be Rēnandu (the 7000) and a division of it is called Rēnādu (the 70). The rule of the Telugu Chōlas appears to have lasted till the latter part of the 8th century, when they were probably dispersed by the Rāshtrakūtas of Warangal in the north Deccan, whose king Gōvinda III (A.D. 783-84 to 814-15) is recorded to have taken Conjeeveram from the Pallavas. At this early date, however, the Rāshtrakūtas do not appear to have obtained any permanent foothold in the district of Cuddapah, and the next dynasty which established its authority, for a time at least, in these parts appears to be that of the Bānas. This presumption is

CHAP. II. supported by the discovery of an inscription at Pottipād in Jammalamadugu taluk, the date of which corresponds to A.D. 884. It records a grant made by a Bāna king or chief named Dhavalēyarasa, which shows that by the end of the 9th century an outpost of the Bānas had at any rate penetrated to the heart of the kingdom formerly held by the Telugu Chōlas. As a last word in regard to these Chōlas it may be mentioned that they seem to have retreated northwards, as a record of the 11th century from the Bastar State in the Central Provinces states that a chief named Chandrāditya, a feudatory of the king of those parts, "was a descendant of Karikāla Chōla of the solar race," etc., giving practically the same family titles to this chief as were borne by the Chōla kings of Cuddapah.

The Bānas. The Bāna kingdom, records of which in Canarese are chiefly to be found in the eastern fringe of Mysore and in Punganūr, was established early in the 8th century in a tract of country of which the north and south boundaries roughly corresponded to those of the present district of Chittoor, while it extended from Kolar on the west to Kālahasti on the east. Later in the century this kingdom evidently increased rapidly in power and absorbed large territories to the north. Bāna inscriptions of this period boast of possessing "the country west of the Āndhra dominions," or all the country west of the "road to the Telugu country," by which must be meant the east coast road from Conjeeveram to Nellore. That all this country was effectively ruled by the Bāna is not probable, but as already stated his authority was undoubtedly acknowledged in the north of Cuddapah district in the last quarter of the 9th century. In this connection it is interesting to note that with the coming of the Bāna we get apparently the first historical evidence of the opening of a route to Cuddapah from the due south or south-west. It seems natural to suppose that the Bānas entered the north portion of the present Cuddapah district through the Vēmpalle gorge, following the course of the Pāpaghni from its sources which lay within the Bāna territory. But at the very time of this sudden accession of power to the Bānas, another dynasty of Chōlas was being founded in the south by Vijayālaya, before which the Bāna kings failed even to conserve their old territories, for they became feudatories of Vijayālaya's grandson the Chōla king Parāntaka I (A.D. 907 to 940), with whose family they effected an alliance by marriage.

The Rāshtrakūtas. With the retreat of the Bānas the fertile plains of north-west Cuddapah came beneath the sway of a dynasty of kings

CHAP. II.

from the north and west. These were the Rāshtrakūtas who, though they attained pre-eminence in their own country prior to the 9th century, only adopted a policy of expansion and conquest in the reign of Indra III (fl.c. A.D. 915). Canarese verses in praise of this king's general are found recorded at the village of Dānavulapād on the north bank of the Pennēr five miles south of Jammalamadugu. We know more about a later king of this line, Krishna III, who reigned from A.D. 940 to 956. In his reign the power of the Rāshtrakūtas reached its zenith. He must have held the whole of Cuddapah district except the eastern portion beyond the Sēshāchalams, for he penetrated as far south as Mēlpādi in Chittoor district. He is said in an inscription near Pōlūr in the North Arcot district to have "taken Kachchi and Tanjai." That he took Conjeeveram is possible, as a large number of his inscriptions are found in the districts of Chingleput and South Arcot, but that he held it for any length of time is most improbable as he must have come into violent collision with the now rapidly-growing power of the new dynasty of Chōlas. The boast that he took Tanjore is no doubt a mere exaggeration. In his expedition to the south it is not to be supposed that Krishna III effectively conquered the south country of Cuddapah district through which he passed. We have evidence, however, that he exacted allegiance from the local chiefs, among whom may be mentioned the Vaidumbas who became his feudatories.

The Vaidumbas.

As to these Vaidumbas they seem to have ruled independently a tract comprising part of Mysore and the south of Anantapur district from very early times, and to have extended their power into Rāyachōti taluk as early as the 8th century to which period is ascribed an inscription at Nerusupalle in the Surabhu valley, which refers to a Vaidumba king. They were evidently on friendly terms with the Bānas, on whose side they fought at the battle of Sōremati possibly Sōmapalle of Madanapalle taluk, in A.D. 900, of which we learn from a lithic record set up near Pedda Tippasamudram.

With the death of Krishna III the power of the Rāshtrakūta dynasty declined, and we find the Vaidumbas acknowledged, apparently as the sovereign authority, as far north as the village of Animela in Kamalāpuram taluk in the year A.D. 975-976.

Rise of the Chōlās.

About this time the Chōlas began to establish their authority in these parts, for in the reign of the Chōla king Rājarāja I, who ascended the throne in A.D. 982, a Vaidumba chief was his feudatory and ruled over the "Ingallur-nâdu"

CHAP. II. in the Cuddapah district. The Ingallur-nâdu must correspond to a tract in Pulivendla taluk, with the present village of Inagalūr as its headquarters. From an inscription, the date of which corresponds to A.D. 1056-57, we learn that a Vaidumba king or chief named Bhīma Mahārāja restored a temple at Pālagiri in Kamalāpuram taluk, and the same record refers to a previous grant made to the same temple by the Rāshtrakūta king Krishna III (died A.D. 956). The Vaidumbas were still feudatories of the Chōla kings in A.D. 1102, as we learn from an inscription discovered at Rāyachōti. This date falls in the reign of the Chōla king Kulōttunga I of whom we know from another source that his dominions extended even to Kurnool. They must have included the whole of Cuddapah district, for the taluks of Sidhout and Pullampet were at this time held by the Telugu Chōdas who were also feudatories of the Chōlas and originally belonged to the same family.

The eastern division of the district

By the incursion of the ancient Chōlas into the Pallava country at the end of the 5th century A.D., of which one, if not the only, lasting result had been the establishment of a small Chōla State in the north-west of Cuddapah district, the power of the Pallavas suffered only a temporary eclipse. During the next four centuries, with Conjeeveram as their capital, they ruled all the eastern country, including the present eastern taluks of Cuddapah district, and their authority as far north as the Kistna was undisputed. Their power in the south was however permanently crippled by the severe defeat inflicted on them by the Chōla king Āditya I under whom the new dynasty of the Chōlas first assumed importance. This was at the end of the 9th century. The Pallavas, though they still retained their hold on the north of their dominions, gradually retreated, till at the beginning of the 11th century we find the Telugu Chōdas governing the country corresponding to the modern district of Nellore, and the taluks of Pullampet, Sidhout and possibly Badvēl.

The Telugu Chōdas.

The Telugu Chōdas claim the same ancestry and possess the same family titles as the Chōlas. That the word Chōda is really only a variant of Chōla now admits of no doubt. They became established in the Telugu country in the century following the recrudescence of the Chōla kingdom already referred to. It is recorded that one Dasavarman, the grandfather of a Chōda chieftain, conquered the Pâka-Rāshtra and ruled at Pottapi. This must have been about A.D. 1000 Pottapi has been identified with absolute certainty with the village of that name situated on the bank of the river Cheyyēr in Pullampet taluk. Later Chōda chieftains who ruled this part of the country generally assumed the title Madurāntakan-Pottapi-Chōla. They were thus feudatories of the Chōla kings. What Madurāntakan means is not clear. It is curious to note that the name of the Chōla king who immediately preceded Rājarāja I and ruled from A.D. 970 to 984 was Madurāntaka Uttama Chōla, and it is suggested that a younger branch descended from this sovereign held this part of the country as viceroys. On the other hand the name Madurāntaka may be merely a title. But from the fact that several inscriptions of Madurāntakan-Pottapi-Chōlas have been found in the Chingleput district as far south as Māmandūr, it is not impossible that Madurāntakan-Pottapi-Chōla was the official designation of the officer or viceroy of the Chōlas administering for the time being the province extending from Madurāntakam (a town some ten miles south of Māmandūr) on the south to Pottapi on the north. The portion of this Chōla province corresponding to the district of Nellore and the eastern division of Cuddapah district was known as the Pâka-nâdu, and the Cuddapah portion, of which Pottapi was the headquarters, was the Mêrpâka-nâdu, or the west Pâka country. The coast part of the province was presumably Kīl-pâka, of which perhaps the name of the Kīlpauk division of Madras city is a reminiscence. A rich harvest of information has been obtained from lithic records discovered in or near several villages on the banks of the Cheyyēr river in Pullampet taluk, such as Nandalūr, Lēbāka, and Tangatūr. The great Chōla king Kulōttunga I (A.D. 1070 to 1118) is mentioned in an inscription at Nandalūr. He must have passed through this province on his expedition against the Kalinga country (Vizagapatam district). His successor's name Vikrama Chōla is also found in two inscriptions of the same place, to which are assigned dates corresponding to A.D. 1121 and 1126 respectively. In the same place again there is a record of Kulōttunga III (A.D. 1178 to 1216), of whom we know from another source that his territory included Nellore. The name of his successor Rājarājadēva III is also found on an inscription at Nandalūr. During this and the following century the province was actually administered by the Telugu Chōdas and from their inscriptions which contain genealogical accounts it is clear that the office of governor became hereditary. It happened at times, through the weakening of the central authority, that these Madurāntaka-Pottapi-Chōlas exercised practically sovereign powers. Such a period occurred towards the end of the 12th century when another feudatory or viceroy of the Chōlas, who was in

CHAP. II. charge of a province of which the headquarters were at Vallūr, near Cuddapah, boasts to have "levied tribute from Kanchi." This appears to refer to a general insurrection of the northern provinces of the Chōla kingdom in the early years of the reign of Kulōttunga III, the rebels being probably set on or encouraged by the Eastern Chālukyas or Pallavas. Their success, however, was shortlived, for in A.D. 1196 Kulōttunga III regained Conjeeveram and "made the kings of the north prostrate themselves to the ground." This sovereign entirely re-established the Chōla power in the Pâka-nâdu. During the reign of his successor Rājarājadēva III (A.D. 1216 to 1243) the power of the Chōlas suffered a temporary eclipse, chiefly owing to the aggression of the Pāndyas in the south. That the Chōlas survived this set-back is chiefly due to the prowess and loyalty of the Madurāntaka-Pottapi-Chōla Tikka who was then administering the Pâka-nâdu. We find him actually at Conjeeveram during the reign of Rājarājadēva III helping that weak monarch to repel the attacks of the Pāndyas, one of whose allies was the Hoysala king from the west, whose name was Vīra-Sōmēswara (A.D. 1234 to 1253). Not only did Tikka, who was also known as Gandagōpāla, establish the Chōla king on his throne, but he defeated the Hoysala king and "played ball with the head of Prithviswara" who apparently threatened the Pâka-nâdu from the north. It is interesting to note that after the defeat of Vīra-Sōmēswara the ambitions of the Hoysala kings found an outlet further north, for his successor Narasimha III, who reigned from A.D. 1254 to 1291, is referred to in an inscription found at Dēvagudipalle of Rāyachōti taluk, which shows that by that time at any rate the Vaidumbas, who formerly held that part of the country, had been dispersed. Both Tikka and his son and successor Manumasiddhi ruled the Pâka-nâdu from Nellore, though both of them held the title Madurāntaka-Pottapi-Chōla. Till their time Pottapi had been the headquarters of the Madurāntaka-Pottapi-Chōlas who governed the Mêr-pâka-nâdu, the rest of the Pâka-nâdu being administered from Kandukūr by another branch of the same family of Telugu Chōdas whose distinguishing name or title seems to have been Gandagōpāla. Manumasiddhi, who ruled at Nellore and owed allegiance to the Chōla king Rājēndra-Chōla III (A.D. 1246 to 1268), was the patron of the Telugu poet Tikkana-Sōmayāji who translated a portion of the Sanskrit Mahābhārata into Telugu and from whose writings we learn something of Manumasiddhi's genealogy. It happens that there has been preserved to us the story of a land dispute in the Pottapi division, which was enquired into and settled by Manumasiddhi. The account of it is as follows. Certain Brahmans of Perungandura got into trouble with the Vellālas and sought the intervention of the Madurāntaka-Pottapi-Chōla to set matters right. The Brahmans represented to him that a grant of land had been made to them in fifty-two shares "very long ago" by a certain Pallava king named Mukkanti-Kāduvetti, and that they had been enjoying the same from the time of their forefathers. But recently the villagers of Sākali-Kōdūr being obliged to emigrate owing to a disturbance in their country had arrived and settled near the village tank. The cultivators of Inumbrōlu or Inumpudōli, had also put up some huts in the fields of Perungandura as they could not stop in their own village on account of plague. But they agreed to pay compensation amounting to the total produce of the fields occupied by them. Subsequently the Brahmans temporarily left Perungandura owing to a famine in those parts. When they returned they found that the settlers from Sākali-Kōdūr had named their new settlement Kōdūr. The Inumbrōlu cultivators also refused to pay the stipulated compensation for their occupation of the fields of Perungandura. Moreover the original grant made to the Brahmans by the Pallava king was ignored, and the lands had become escheat to the reigning king. On the complaint of the Brahmans an enquiry was held by Manumasiddhi, and both parties were invited to adduce proof by ordeal. In the result, the ancient grant was confirmed to the Brahmans and the village of Kōdūr restored to them by Manumasiddhi in order to secure religious merit for his father Tikka. It is noticeable that the inscription makes no mention of the Chōla king, which leads us to presume that Manumasiddhi practically ruled independently of Rājēndra Chōla III though nominally his viceroy: a presumption which is strengthened by the fact that we know from other sources that the power of the Chōlas was at this time declining. As to the identity of the places mentioned in the inscription my authority conjectures that the Kōdūr referred to may be Kōdūr in the south of Pullampet taluk, and states he is unable to identify Perungandura. Its identification does not, however, present much difficulty. It must be Penagalūr, on the east bank of the Cheyyēr river in that taluk. Very near Penagalūr are two villages Kondūr and Indlūr, of which the former must have been the settlement from Sākali-Kōdūr, while Indlūru is none other than Inumbrōlu or Inumpudōli of the inscription. As to Sākali-Kōdūr, Sākaḷi is the name of a division of the district, as we learn from a Kākatīya record of the end of the 13th century, and that it practically corresponded to the present Badvēl taluk is conclusively proved by a later inscription discovered at Pōrumāmilla, to which reference will be made below. Sākali-Kōdūr is therefore the village of that name in Badvēl taluk. It is possible that Sagilēr, which is the name of the only river of importance in Badvēl taluk, merely connotes 'the river of the Sākali country.' The rule of Manumasiddhi in the Pâka-nâdu was not uneventful. In the earlier years of his reign he was dispossessed by a cousin, Vijaya Gandagōpāla, of the branch that up to the time of Tikka ruled the east portion of the province from Kandukūr or Nellore. Manumasiddhi being ousted sought the assistance of the Kākatīya king Ganapati of Warangal and obtained it by himself fighting on the side of that king in a battle on the banks of the Godavari. It also appears that the poet Sōmayāji used his influence with the Kākatīya king on behalf of his patron. In the result Manumasiddhi was restored. He formally acknowledged the suzerainty of the Chōla king Rājēndra Chōla III till the latter's death in A.D. 1268, when the Chōlas seem to disappear from history altogether owing to their conquest by the Pāndyas.

The Kākatīyas of Warangal.

From this date the Pottapi country, as was already the case with all the tract corresponding to the taluks of Jammalamadugu, Proddatūr, Cuddapah, Kamalāpuram and probably Pulivendla, fell into the hands of Ambadēva who had temporarily usurped the Kākatīya crown. He ruled this part of his territory from Vallūr, some ten miles west of Cuddapah, and the administrative divisions were the Gandikōta-sīma, the Muliki-nādu, Rēnādu and, in the east of the district, the Sākali, Yēruva and Pottapi divisions. During the time of Ambadēva a land survey of Pottapi-nādu was carried out under the direction of his subordinate Peddināyaka, and a river channel was constructed at Lēbāka. A flood bank was also thrown up to prevent the waters of the Cheyyēr from inundating a temple in the village of Athirala. Pratāparudra was the Kākatīya king who succeeded to the throne at Warangal after the death or downfall of the usurper Ambadēva. The Pottapi country continued to form part of the Kākatīya dominions, and with the death of Manumasiddhi we hear no more of the Telugu Chōdas who ruled the Pâka-nâdu as feudatories of the Chōlas of the south.

First Muhammadan invasion.

With the opening of the 14th century we thus find the whole of Cuddapah district, except Rāyachōti taluk, under the sway of the great northern kingdom whose capital was

Warangal while Rāyachōti taluk was, as we know, in the latter part of the 13th century, included in the territories of the Hoysalas. In A.D. 1309 came the invasion of the Deccan by the Muhammadans during the reign of the Khilji Emperor Allah-ud-din. Warangal fell and with it the Kākatīya dynasty. The whole of the Carnatic and the Coromandel was overrun by the invaders, who penetrated to the extreme south of the Peninsula. The subjection of the country was completed about A.D. 1325 when Warangal was captured and king Pratāparudra carried a prisoner to Delhi. But in A.D. 1336 the Vijayanagar kingdom was founded by Harihara and Bukka, two Hindu refugees from Warangal, and in A.D. 1344 a Hindu confederation, consisting of the son of Pratāparudra of Warangal, Krishna Nāyakkar of Vijayanagar, and the Hoysala king from Mysore, with an immense force drove the Muhammadans out of Warangal and rolled back the tide of their advance. The outcome of this was the establishment of the Vijayanagar Empire. During the two centuries of its ascendency it included the whole of the present Cuddapah district.

The Vijayanagar Empire.

No general account is necessary here of the rule of the Vijayanagar Emperors, but the political condition of Cuddapah district from the 14th to the middle of the 17th century, on which some interesting light has been recently thrown by the discovery of inscriptions may be briefly summarised. Within a very few years of the founding of the empire we find the whole of Cuddapah district and probably most of Nellore included in the province of Udayagiri (in Nellore district). This province was ruled over by a son of the Emperor Kampa I as early as A.D. 1356, and this fact illustrates what was apparently the fixed policy of the Vijayanagar dynasty, namely, that of appointing close relatives of the reigning emperor as viceroys of outlying provinces. The great importance of this province is shown by the fact that in the next reign also a son of the emperor was viceroy. This was in the reign of Bukka I (A.D. 1352 to 1376), when we learn that his son Bāskara when viceroy of the Udayagiri province constructed the great irrigation tank at Pōrumāmilla in the Badvēl taluk in the year A.D. 1369. From the inscription which records this event and from others we find that the whole of the Cuddapah district fell within the Udayagiri province, which was bounded on the south by the Chandragiri province, and on the west by the Penukonda province. It contained two main districts in the country that now includes the Cuddapah district. These were the Siddhavattam-sīma and the Gandikōta-sīma. The former comprised among others the Sākali and Pottapi sub-divisions

CHAP. II. corresponding respectively to the Badvēl and Pullampet taluks, so that the Siddhavattam-sīma must have represented roughly the three eastern taluks of the present district. All the rest of the Cuddapah district except Rāyachōti taluk fell in the Gandikōta district, one sub-division of which was the Muliki-nādu. This latter was extensive, for it included Chennūr, Potladurti and Pulivendla, all of which appear to have been the headquarters of still smaller administrative units. Rāyachōti taluk was also included in the Udayagiri province but apparently in a different district. From an inscription at Chilamakūr which records a transfer of land in A.D. 1382-83 we again find that the Udayagiri province is ruled by a son of the reigning emperor Harihara II. This was Prince Dēvarāya Odaiyār. The latter name, sometimes spelled Odeya, was, as is made clear from other records, merely a title of the viceroys of the Vijayanagar provinces. This prince subsequently became Emperor and ruled from A.D. 1406 till at least 1417. The history of Cuddapah during the 15th century A.D. is marked, as far as we know, by no event of importance. The rule of the Vijayanagar emperors was now acknowledged through all the region south of the capital, and the country enjoyed peace and comparative prosperity. The military forces of the empire were, however, continually engaged in resisting the Muhammadans on its northern frontier, while on the east, north of Udayagiri province, its borders were from time to time harassed by the Gajapati king of Orissa and his southern feudatories, of whom probably the most important were the Reddis of Kondavīdu. At the end of this or the beginning of the following century Udayagiri must have been temporarily lost to the empire through the aggression of its enemies in the north-east, for it is recorded that about A.D. 1514 Krishnarāya, the greatest of the Vijayanagar emperors, captured Udayagiri and defeated and pursued the Gajapati king Pratāparudra as far as Kondavīdu, who subsequently sued for peace and acknowledged Krishnarāya as his overlord. An inscription found at Katteragandla in Badvēl taluk, from which we learn that one Yellamarasayya was administering the Sākali district as agent of the Governor of the Udayagiri province, shows that the Emperor Krishnarāya was ruling as late as A.D. 1530. From the year A.D. 1544 several inscriptions have been found in the district in which mention is made of the Emperor Sadāsiva. During his reign and that of his predecessor Achyuta the decline of the empire began. The empire was actually governed, while Sadāsiva still occupied the throne, by his brother-in-law Rāmarāja, the

CHAP. II.

great Hemrāj of Muhammadan historians, and his brother Tirumala, the founders of the Karnāta dynasty of Vijayanagar rulers. In A.D. 1557-58 an inscription at Munelli in Badvēl taluk shows that Tirumala was then administering the empire on behalf of the puppet Sadāsiva, while Rāmarāja as we know from other sources was engaged in incessant warfare on the northern frontier. Rāmarāja was the only ruler of the empire who ever made any headway against the Muhammadans. We are told that he wrested several districts from Bijāpur, overran Golconda, laid seige to the capital and exacted large concessions from its king. But his unprecedented success had the effect of impelling the Muhammadan kingdoms to suspend their mutual jealousies and unite to crush the Hindu sovereignty of the Deccan once for all. Thus it came about that at the famous battle of Tâlikōta in January 1565, the Hindus and Muhammadans, with forces of almost fabulous strength, contested for the supremacy of the Deccan. In the result the Rāja was totally defeated and slain, and his capital taken and looted by the Muhammadans. The Hindu power in the south was irretrievably broken, but dissensions among the victors enabled Tirumala, the brother and successor of Rāmarāja, to conserve a part of his territory, which we may note still included the whole of Cuddapah district, and to carry on the government from Penukonda. He was succeeded in 1573-4 by his son Ranga who shortly afterwards transferred his capital to Chandragiri in the Chittoor district on the capture of Penukonda by the Muhammadans in 1576-7. Ranga was followed in 1586 by his brother Venkatapati. A record from Varikunta in Badvēl taluk mentions this king as ruling from Chandragiri in 1602. He died in 1614. For thirty years afterwards his successors continued to rule the remnants of their territory with Chandragiri as their capital; but in 1646 this stronghold as well as Chingleput, a royal retreat still further south, fell into the hands of the king of Golconda. But long before this time they had ceased to exercise any real authority, as first one, then another of their viceroys threw off their allegiance. It appears, however, from numerous inscriptions that up to the death of Venkatapati the Vijayanagar suzerainty was nominally acknowledged throughout most of the Cuddapah district. This was due not only to the prestige of the dynasty and its former magnificence, but to the fact that, unlike the rest of the Ceded Districts, this part of the country was not immediately affected by the Muhammadan irruption which followed the track of the retreating emperors. In pursuing Sadāsiva and Tirumala to

CHAP. II. Penukonda after the battle of Talikōta the king of Golconda left Cuddapah district on the east, and after dislodging the emperor from Penukonda and establishing Muhammadan influence throughout Bellary and Anantapur, the trend of the Muhammadan invasion turned east and south leaving Cuddapah district untouched on the north. It was not till the beginning of the 17th century that the Golconda kings turned their attention to the present Cuddapah district and surveyed the country for revenue purposes. The survey took four years to complete and the amount of revenue they hoped to realise is known in revenue history as the kamil assessment. This was a singularly ineffective undertaking, for all traces of the survey were soon obliterated and it does not appear that a tithe of the assessment was ever collected, nor is this a matter for surprise as the country had never been conquered; yet the kamil assessment was utilized by later governments down to the British occupation as a sort of standard by which to measure the tax-paying capacity of the district. Till the reduction of the Golconda kings in 1687 by Aurangzebe the only representatives of the central authority in the Cudappah district appear to have been the Nawabs of Gandikōta and Cuddapah, but as they had not the means of reducing the local chiefs who had rendered military service during the Vijayanagar period their political importance was almost negligible. Subsequently Aurangzebe was continually engaged in withstanding the aggressions of the Mahrattas, so that with the opening of the 18th century the condition of this part of the Deccan fell little short of anarchy.

Rise of the Poligars.

It is accordingly from the date of the battle of Talikōta and the failure of the Golconda kings to establish a political ascendancy in any way comparable to that of the Vijayanagar dynasty that we trace the rise of local chiefs and poligārs, fostered by the absence of any effective central authority. These petty chieftains who in fact exercised sovereign rights within their jurisdiction were moreover never adequately dealt with by the Nawabs of Cuddapah whose authority subsequently received nominal recognition throughout the district, with the result that after two hundred years of practical independence, their reduction was only accomplished by British troops and their allegiance won by the unflinching determination and never-failing tact of Sir Thomas Munro.

The Matla princes.

Some of the local chiefs of Cuddapah district deserve more than a passing allusion. By far the most important was the Matla or Matli family of chieftains. They were more than poligārs, for their territory amounted to a principality, and from the beginning of the 17th century at least they assume the title of Rāja. As early as A.D. 1524 we find a chief of this family exercising some political authority in the Pottapi subdivision of the Siddhavattam-sīma, and a member of his family constructed an anicut near the village of Kondūr. In the reign of the Vijayanagar king Sadāsiva the Matla family became allied to that dynasty by marriage and acquired considerable local importance. In A.D. 1570 Matla Timmalarāja who was ruling the Pottapi-nādu granted the revenue of some lands in the village of Pondalūr to a temple of that place. At the beginning of the 17th century they seem to have extended their authority, now practically uncontrolled, over the three taluks of Badvēl, Sidhout and Pullampet. This was in the time of the best known ruler of the line, whose name was Anantarāju or Anantarāmarāju. He is credited with having constructed the Badvēl tank, and one of the villages it irrigates is called Anantarājupuram. There is also a tradition that Chennampalle some four miles from Badvēl is named after his wife Chennamma. In A.D. 1604 he repaired the walls of the temples at Sidhout and created the nucleus of the fort which was afterwards completed by a Nawab of Cuddapah. He appears to be the nephew of another Matla Ananta, who was the author of the Telugu poem Kākusthavijayamu and one of the brothers of Timmalarāja referred to above. The Matla princes spent a good deal of money on irrigation works. In addition to the construction of the Badvēl tank and the anicut at Kondūr already alluded to a later prince named Perumallarāja built a sluice in the big tank at Lēbāka in the year A.D. 1718 while it is recorded that yet another ruler of this family dug an irrigation channel from the Cheyyēr in Pottapi village. It is interesting to note that they took the title of Dēvachōdamahārāja and claimed descent from the Chōla kings, thus establishing their political continuity with the Telugu Chōdas who ruled the Madurāntaka Pottapi country as feudatories of the Chōlas in the 13th century. Towards the end of the 17th century in the time of Venkatarāmarāja we find the old Pottapi-nādu split up into two divisions known as the Pulugunati-sīma and the Pottapi-sīma. On the whole the administrative changes that took place seem to be as follows. Under the Vijayanagar kings the Matla family ruled the Pottapi division from Pottapi. There is a tradition that Pottapi was abandoned as headquarters on account of its inferior strategical position. The Matlas therefore moved their headquarters to Yerraguntlakōta, but this too was finally relegated to the sub-divisional officer in charge of the

CHAP. II. Pulugunāti sub-division, while the old sub-division of Pottapi was administered from Tangatūr, and the headquarters of the Raja became Chitvēl. This last change must have occurred about the time that Abdul Nābi Khan became Nawab of Cuddapah, for in 1801 Munro writes of the Matla family, "They obtained Chitvēl about ninety years ago to support a body of peons, and pay an annual peshcash which, at the time of the conquest of Cuddapah by Haidar, was paid to the Nawabs of that province and amounted to above a lakh of rupees." It was either the son or the father of Venkatarāmarāja, named Tiruvēngalanātha rāja, who built the magnificent gōpura of Gōvindarāja at lower Tirupati. The second Tiruvēngalanātha was ruling in A.D. 1705. An interesting old document of the beginning of the 19th century gives us the genealogy of the Matla rajas from A.D. 1721-22 to the year A.D. 1801-02 when came the "Kumphani Government," in connection with which is mentioned Colonel Mantolu Sahib (Munro). This record tells us that about A.D. 1780 the Raja governed under the Sultan for six years, and for three years subsequent thereto "the Sultan ruled." Thereafter the Rāja seems to have come to his own again until the time of Company. "The Sultan" here referred to is Haidar Ali, who died in 1782 and his son Tipu Sultan. Under Haidar Ali, the old sub-division of Cuddapah district which includes the present taluk of Rāyachōti was administered by Mir Sahib, the Governor of Gurramkonda. Haidar Ali himself, assisted by Mir Sahib, finally reduced the Cuddapah Nawab and carried him and his family prisoners to Seringapatam in A.D. 1780. The effect of this event was not only felt by the Matla princes but by the poligārs throughout the district. As Munro points out in his letter dated 20th March 1802 to the Board of Revenue concerning the poligārs " Haidar Ali was the only Indian sovereign we know of who ever subdued all his petty feudatories and was really master of his country." Unfortunately for the peace of the country Tipu was obliged to cede all his Cuddapah possessions to the Nizam in A.D. 1792 with the result that the local chieftains all returned and resumed their independence confident in the weakness of the central authority. Munro's reports are eloquent of the effect on the country caused by a period of eight years' anarchy immediately preceding the transfer of the Ceded Districts to the British in A.D. 1800. But before giving a more general account of the poligārs of the district and Munro's administration we must revert to a closer consideration of the history of the country under the Nizam, when the whole of the present district was, at least nominally, governed by the Nawab of Cuddapah.

The Nawabs of Cuddapah.

As already stated, a pretty long period elapsed between the battle of Talikōta and the establishment of Muhammadan rule in Cuddapah district, for the reason that the Muhammadan kings of the Deccan, besides continually quarrelling with each other, were occupied during the next century in the final annihilation of the Vijayanagar Empire and in continual wars with the Mahrattas. It is not until the Nizam of Hyderabad began to rule the Deccan as a practically independent monarch in the early part of the 18th century that the Nawabs of Cuddapah attain to any political importance. For a whole century their authority must have been very restricted, for we find that as late as A.D. 1694 a governor of the Siddhavattam-sīma was appointed by the Nawab of Arcot and given by him a jagir of three villages. The first Nawab of Cuddapah to assert his control of the district was Abdul Nābi Khan whose governorship began in the year A.D. 1714. He was a man of considerable energy and ability, for he extended his province as far south as Punganūr and even levied tribute in the Bārāmahāl. He established garrisons at Gandikōta in the north and Gurramkonda in the south, but made no real attempt to reduce the country to order. The local poligārs in the Gurramkonda country were allowed to continue undisturbed as long as they shared their ill-gotten gains with the Muhammadan governors. In 1732 the name of the ruling Nawab was Mahazid Khan, the son of Abdul Nābi Khan. But in the year 1740 a Nawab of the latter name is mentioned in connection with a raid by the Mahrattas. This Nawab was probably a grandson of the first Abdul Nābi Khan. In military prowess he was certainly far inferior to the earlier Nawab. In May A.D. 1740 the Mahrattas invaded the country, defeated the Nawab of Kandanūr (Kurnool) and marched against Cuddapah with a force of cavalry said to have been 40,000 or 50,000 strong. A day's fighting then ensued between the Mahrattas and the Nawab. Abdul Nābi Khan was defeated and sent away his family for safety to the fort of Gandikōta, himself retreating southwards. He was again engaged by the Mahrattas "in the defile," which seems to indicate the Guvvalacheruvu ghāt. Here he was once more defeated but made his peace with the marauders by giving them a lakh and a half of rupees and other presents. The Mahrattas then proceeded southwards, defeated and killed the Nawab of Arcot, Dost Ali Khan, in a cavalry engagement at "the pass" which must have been the descent from the

CHAP. II. plateau from Pīlēr to Dāmalcheruvu, and overran all the south country. After subsisting for several months on the proceeds of raids and robbery they finally invested Trichinopoly which was surrendered to them by Chanda Sahib, its Governor, on March 30th, 1741. They then returned to their own country. Early in 1743 the Nizam himself with a huge following visited the south country and made a friendly arrangement with the Mahrattas by ceding to them Penukonda in exchange for their restoration of Trichinopoly. In this expedition the sons of Abdul Nābi Khan followed in the Nizam's train. Their names are given as Fath Miah and Baday Miah. A crowd of poligārs also accompanied them. It may be mentioned here that the opinion sometimes held that the Mahratta and Muhammadan descents from the north into the south country were by way of Tirupati seems to be incorrect. The route taken from Cuddapah on both occasions was almost certainly through Rāyachōti, Kalakada, Pīlēr and Dāmalcheruvu, and so to Arcot. That the Nizam did not get to Arcot by way of Tirupati on this occasion is beyond doubt, for we are told that it was rumoured after his arrival at Arcot that he would visit Tirupati and from thence pass south through Conjeeveram. If he had already passed Tirupati on his way to Arcot, this statement would be incomprehensible. Besides, so far as the Muhammadans were concerned, the route from Rāyachōti to Pīlēr lay entirely within that part of the country controlled by their stronghold at Gurramkonda, whereas the eastern division beyond the Sēshāchalams was, as far as is known, ungarrisoned.[1] The presumption that they took the central and more direct route is also supported by the fact that at the present day Musalmāns are far more numerous in the towns and villages through which it passes than in the east of the district.

After concluding his treaty with Morāri Rao at Trichinopoly the Nizam left that place in October 1743, and returned northwards. But before he reached his capital his army was intercepted early in 1744 by another Mahratta force which broke through his lines and penetrated to the Carnatic. For many years subsequently the country stretching from Kurnool on the north to Arcot on the south was distracted by similar conflicts between the Muhammadans and the Mahrattas. The latter were almost always successful, though one exception is recorded, when in May 1746 Muhammad Ali Khan, son of the Nawab of Arcot, marched to Kurnool, and with the assistance of the Nawabs of Kurnool and Cuddapah defeated the Mahratta chief Bāpōji Nāyakkan, who retired with loss. In 1750 a

[1] Sidhout was fortified at a later date.

tragedy, which plays an important part in Indian history, took place, in which a Cuddapah chief took a prominent share. In this year Nasir Jung was besieging Ginjee and was attended by his vassals, the Nawabs of Cuddapah, Kurnool and Savanore. His title of succession as Nizam had been disputed by his nephew Muzaffar Jung, whose cause had been adopted by the French. Under the orders of M. Dupleix, M. Bussy, by a daring attack, captured the fort of Ginjee, hitherto deemed impregnable. Nasir Jung advanced to recapture it and Muzaffar Jung marched to relieve the garrison. Previous to the meeting, however, Dupleix deserted his ally, and Muzaffar Jung, thinking his cause hopeless, surrendered to his uncle Nasir Jung. The desertion of the French troops was only a part of a deep-laid conspiracy, to which the principal chiefs of Nasir Jung had been gained over. On the occasion of a sally from the Fort, Nasir Jung went forth to head his troops and passing by the elephant of the Nawab of Cuddapah he paused to salute his vassal. The salute was not returned; and, thinking that in the dim light of the morning it had not been perceived, Nasir Jung raised himself in his howdah to repeat it. He was, however, greeted with a salute from a loaded carbine and fell mortally wounded by two bullets. Muzaffar Jung was at once proclaimed Nizam and proceeded to Pondicherry, where he was formally installed by Dupleix with much solemnity and state. The opening scene of this tragedy took place in the present district of South Arcot, but the closing scene took place in the Cuddapah district, and in this the Nawab of Cuddapah plays an equally conspicuous and discreditable part. Whilst Muzaffar Jung was lingering in Pondicherry, bestowing lavish presents on the French, and discussing treaties for the joint government of Southern India, the Nawab of Cuddapah, disgusted that he had not gained as much as he had expected, had retired to his district. Indeed, the only persons who seem to have benefitea by this act of treachery were the French and Haidar Ali, whose clevei thieves, in the confusion resulting from Nasir Jung's death, had managed to decamp with two elephants loaded with treasure, which afterwards proved of much servict to Haidar when recruiting his army. When he arrived in his district, the Cuddapah Nawab formed a conspiracy with other Pathan Chiefs, and when Muzaffar Jung was marching northwards from Pondicherry to Hyderabad, to take possession of his new Government, the conspirators met him at the narrow pass of Lakkireddipalle in the Rāyachōti taluk of the Cuddapah district. In the conflict that ensued, Muzaffar Jung fell struck

CHAP. II. down by a javelin thrown by the Nawab of Kurnool (January 1751). The name of the dastardly conspirator who engineered this double treachery has not come down to us. It has been thought that he was merely the guardian of the minor Abdul-alam Khan. But that he was the *de facto* Nawab of Cuddapah admits of no doubt. He seems to have been mortally wounded at this very affray at Lakkireddipalle, and it is probable that Abdul-alam Khan, the minor, then assumed the governorship. This latter is the last of the Nawabs of Cuddapah. In his time (1757) the Cuddapah district was overrun by the Mahrattas under Balavanta Rao who gained a decisive battle over the Muhammadans near the town of Cuddapah. It was apparently on this occasion that the Mahrattas were bought off by the cession of Gurramkonda.

Haidar Ali of Mysore.

About this time the rise of Haidar Ali constitutes a new element in the political forces which shaped the destinies of Cuddapah. This daring adventurer had obtained complete control of the Mysore army by 1761 when he persuaded the feeble Rāja to resign the sceptre to him and to retire into private life on an annuity. Haidar Ali obtained possession of Gurramkonda in 1766, temporarily lost it to the Mahrattas in 1772, but regained it early in 1774 through his son Tipu. Until 1779 Haidar had no excuse for extending his raids into Cuddapah any further than Gurramkonda, but in that year the Nawab of Cuddapah, Abdul-alam Khan, having refused to supply the military contingent he had bound himself to furnish when Tipu re-conquered Gurramkonda from the Mahrattas, Haidar despatched a force under Mir Sahib, the Governor of Gurramkonda, to punish him for his disobedience. This force was too small to effect anything decisive, but in the following year Haidar himself took the field and, effecting a junction with Mir Sahib, gave battle to the forces of the Nawab near the small fortified town of Duvvūr on the banks of the Kundēr, about ten miles north-east of Proddatūr. The Nawab's cavalry were defeated in the open field and driven into the town, which they surrendered at discretion. The Nawab himself escaped to the fort of Sidhout, which was at once invested by Haidar and captured without much difficulty. The Nawab and his family were then sent prisoners to Seringapatam where he finally died in captivity. At the close of this conquest Haidar Ali left for Mysore, having first added Sidhout and Cuddapah to the jagir of Gurramkonda held by his brother-in-law, Mir Sahib, who was now left in charge of the whole district on the condition of maintaining the requisite garrisons and 3,000 horse. Mir Sahib, who died in 1781, and his son and successor Kamal-ud-din, were the first rulers of the district who seriously grappled with the problem of the poligārs, the importance of which was fully recognised by Haidar Ali. In the words of Munro "The Cuddapah Nawabs expelled some of them (poligārs), but neither they nor the Mahrattas were ever able to reduce the rest, or even enforce the regular payment of their peshkash. Haidar was engaged in such constant and extensive wars that he had not leisure to root out the poligārs so entirely as he would otherwise have done. He however took the surest means of disabling them from disturbing his Government. Those who fled were deterred from returning by a strong detachment stationed in their country and those who fell into his hands were ever after obliged to remain near him." As an example of this it may be mentioned that Haidar took away the Matla Raja of Chitvēl with him in 1780. Munro continues "Tipu in the early part of his reign pursued the same measures, but when his power was reduced by the campaigns of Lord Cornwallis, and when he afterwards weakened it still more himself by parcelling out his country into a vast number of minute amildaris in order to provide for a host of ignorant, corrupt and needy Musalmāns, the fugitive poligārs, though they did not think it prudent to risk their own persons in the country, contrived by means of their emissaries to obtain the consent of the Asophs to their collecting most of their ancient *rusums* and even the rents of their villages on condition of their giving them a part . . . so that several years previous to the death of the sultan the poligārs of Gurramkonda were without his knowledge drawing large annual contributions from their old possessions. When Kamal-ud-din Khan besides his jagir in Gurramkonda received from the Nizam the management of the remaining part of that province, he found himself too weak to drive out the poligārs who had recovered their hereditary districts during the war, and he therefore granted them terms which he meant to observe only while he found it convenient; but they broke them before him by withholding their kists, and a fruitless expedition, which he undertook for the purpose of enforcing payment, only ended in laying waste the country and in placing the recovery of the balances at a greater distance than ever. In that part of the Ceded countries which fell to the Nizam by the treaties of Mysore and Seringapatam," *i.e.* in 1792,—they included the whole of Cuddapah district—"his officers, from indolence or weakness, not only allowed the poligārs to return but sometimes invested them with the

CHAP. II. management of sircar villages in addition to their own . . . The Mysore system, which resumed all poligārships, expelled their turbulent chiefs and levied an additional body of troops to prevent their return, was in every respect, whether for maintaining the authority of Government, or the tranquillity of the country, infinitely preferable to that of the Nizam which, at a greater expense incurred by the necessity of frequent expeditions, suffered them to retain their power, to commit every kind of depredations, and on every favourable conjuncture to set the Government itself at defiance."

Transfer of Cuddapah to the British.

In the year 1800 the Hyderabad contingent was increased to eight battalions, and districts (including the whole of modern Cuddapah) yielding sixty-three lakhs a year were made over by the Nizam in perpetual sovereignty to the East India Company, under the stipulation that the British Government should guarantee all the remaining territories of the Nizam from every attack. In their order, dated October 24th, 1800, the Government of Madras acquainted Major Thomas Munro, as he then was, with the particulars of this treaty, and posted him as Principal Collector of "the whole of these extensive territories," with four Sub-Collectors under his immediate authority. For the purpose of establishing the British authority in the Ceded Provinces, Colonel Wellesley (afterwards the Duke of Wellington) was simultaneously ordered to move with all the troops under his command at Hubli to Ādōni, and to detach a small portion of the troops in Mysore in order to meet the Principal Collector's "unavoidable demand for military aid." Less than a month after taking charge, Major Munro reports as follows: "By every report which has reached me, it appears that almost every poligār, however insignificant, who had been expelled since the beginning of Haidar's usurpation, has been within these few years permitted to resume the management of his district."

The work of Munro.

At the opening of the 19th century we thus enter on the last phase of the history of the Cuddapah district, namely, the subjugation of the poligārs, the establishment of a well ordered government and the inauguration of the revenue system which obtains at the present day. All this was the work of the great Munro, who later became Sir Thomas Munro, Governor of Madras. Of so high an order were the energy, ability, foresight and determination which he brought to the task that he accomplished in the short period of seven years what might have taxed the powers of a whole generation of administrators endowed with less extraordinary talents. To these qualities was added also the incalculable factor of a magnetic personality, to which much of his success with the people of the country must be attributed. It made such an indelible impression on all who came in touch with him, that they remembered him all their lives and bequeathed to their children the story of his greatness, which so grew in the telling that by the middle of the century many traditions and legends of a semi-sacred character were associated with his name. These survive to the present day, and though what he did is now forgotten, the memory of the man is preserved in the hearts of the people for ever.

The Poligārs and their reduction.

In describing the state of the country when the Ceded Districts passed into the hands of the Company, Munro enumerates 80 different poligārs, of whom a large number were in the present Cuddapah district. Most of these were grouped round the more influential poligārs to whom they paid the same sort of allegiance as their nominal chiefs paid to the ruling sovereign power. A peculiarity of all these poligārs was that every one, however petty his territory, kept up a mimic court; nominal officers were appointed, holding the same titles as similar officers in the sovereign courts, and a small standing army was maintained of permanently appointed peons, aided by a militia of relatives of these peons, who were liable to be called out in times of disturbance. These small standing armies were but seldom paid, and the greater part of their earnings were gained by their depredations in time of war. During peace these bodies of peons continued their usual practices and earned their livelihood by pillaging border villages. The consequence was that every village exposed to their ravages (and the territories of each poligār were so small, that there were few that were not more or less affected by them) endeavoured to put itself in a state of defence sufficient to ward off these attacks. In most villages of the district are still to be seen a ruined watch-tower or the outline of a fort, and sometimes the vestiges of turrets and bastions. Where a village was wealthy or populous enough to be able to defend itself against the attacks of these border robbers, it advanced in the course of a few years from the defensive to the offensive. The principal inhabitant became the chief of the village, the servants employed by the villagers to defend their common property were under his orders, and so, after a few years (supposing that in the interim his village had not been sacked or burnt), the village chief emerged as a petty poligār. A few years more added somewhat to his pretensions, and in a short time he attempted to imitate the poligārs who were

CHAP. II.

so lately his aggressors, and established his mimic court, his standing army, and his raids of plunder. The consequence was that the Ceded Districts, and more especially that portion of them above the ghāts, were nothing more than a nest of robbers, and the ryots and country people were tormented by a continual state of violence and rapine. It is almost impossible to imagine a country from which it would be more difficult to raise a permanent revenue; for payment of any kind was exactly what every one from the highest to the lowest was the least accustomed to.

In order to deal more promptly with the prevalent disorder the Government of Madras had, when appointing Munro as Principal Collector of the Ceded Districts, directed that until his authority should have been established in the country his correspondence should be "immediate with his Lordship," but as soon as circumstances should appear to render it expedient he should subject himself to the authority of the Board of Revenue. Munro carried out his operations so quickly and effectually that in March 1801 he was able to settle the revenues of the Gurramkonda country and in April we find from his correspondence that the Board of Revenue had assumed control of the whole district. One of the difficulties confronting Munro at the outset was the presence of bodies of the Nizam's troops who refused to leave the country until their arrears of pay were settled. This Munro did at once, leaving the money to be recovered afterwards. At the same time the poligārs were kept in check by a proclamation declaring that every chieftain who garrisoned a fort, maintained an armed force, or levied contributions, would be treated as a rebel. This was not a mere threat, as in May 1801 Major-General Campbell marched against Vēmula in the Pulivendla taluk and reduced the poligār to obedience by demolishing his fort. From there the general proceeded to Pullampet taluk and forcibly dispossessed the Matla raja of Chitvēl. But Munro's summary manner of treating these petty chieftains did not meet with universal approval. The Governments of Madras and Calcutta gave it their sanction, but the Court of Directors condemned it in the strongest language as "not only disingenuous, but harsh and ill-considered," and called upon Munro for a complete explanation of his motives, threatening that, if this proved unsatisfactory, he would be removed from his appointment and never again employed on revenue work "for which the violent and mistaken principles of his conduct seemed to render him unfit." The Directors wished the poligārs to be upheld in their right and enjoyment of the soil, and trusted that a gradual course of good government would wean them from "their feudal habits and principles," and turn them into peaceful citizens. Munro's reply of 22nd February 1805 is an unassailable defence of his position. He shows that neither on the ground of their ancient rights nor of their later conduct were the poligārs entitled to "gentle measures" and that their "feudal habits and principles" consisted of crimes, oppressions and contumacies which if permitted to continue would have rendered good government impossible. The Directors said no more and Munro's policy gave the district the first taste of tranquillity which it had known for many years. He steadily followed each delinquent; and, though at times when the forces under his orders were employed on other duty he was compelled to remain quiet (for he made a point of never using force until he knew that he had sufficient troops to render resistance unavailing), he always carried his purpose in the end. For months perhaps the fugitive poligār would be going from one friendly chief to another, endeavouring to incite each into rebellion, and at the commencement of Munro's rule these men perhaps ridiculed the ineffectual manner in which the Company's Collector carried his orders into force; but Munro never moved from the line he had adopted. He had at first only a limited number of troops at his disposal. He employed them, as occasion demanded, in hunting out or reducing the forts of the absconding poligārs, but he never allowed them to be diverted from the object they had in view. Other poligārs might disobey his orders, might abscond or attempt to raise rebellion; but for the present Munro would be hunting down the Poligār of Nossam or some other particular recusant, and until this task was accomplished, others could wait. Frequently a passage like the following occurs in Munro's despatches: "I was not prepared at the time to enforce my demands, and I therefore took no notice of his conduct." But when the time came that Munro was able to enforce his demand, the rebel poligār was hunted from place to place. If he took refuge with a chief beyond Munro's jurisdiction, no force was used. Munro would quietly look on and remark to the Board that, since for each protection the poligār's friendly ally would squeeze as much money from the fugitive as he could, the poligār would, after a few more such visits, be left without any more resources, and as none of his friends would think of protecting him when he had no more money, he would then be compelled to surrender to the troops who, for days and weeks, had been following and waiting for

CHAP. II. him as patiently as a cat for a mouse. The whole of the first eighteen months of Munro's rule was taken up by these incidents. The history of one tells us of all; the beginning and the end are always the same. The poligār begins by refusing payment, he becomes refractory or absconds, and he ends by being captured, his estate is confiscated, and he is confined in the fort of Gooty. The following despatch of Munro's gives us a clear indication of the methods he adopted in dealing with refractory poligārs: "The poligār of Uppalūr, about 80 miles to the west of Cuddapah, disobeyed the summons I sent him in February last to meet me in order to settle his rents, and he also refused to relinquish two sircar villages which he had obtained on rent a few years ago from one of the Nizam's Amildārs. I was not prepared at the time to enforce my demands, so I took no notice of his conduct until the division under Major-General Campbell encamped in this neighbourhood in June, when I directed the Amildār (Tahsildar) to take possession of the sircar villages, which were given up without opposition. The poligār was permitted to keep his hereditary village of Uppalūr on the idea that he would in future show more obedience to the civil authority. On my arrival here on the 20th instant, I found that he would neither come to the cutchēry himself nor allow the karnam of his village to bring me his accounts. All the poligārs of Gurramkonda had come in with their accounts, and as I was sensible that their example being followed by those in other parts of the country would depend in a great measure on his treatment, I resolved to seize him without delay. As he had only 20 armed followers, the Amildār's peons would have been sufficient for the purpose, but as there was a chance of his escaping and collecting more followers, and committing depredations before he could be taken, I requested Colonel St. Leger, commanding at Kamalāpuram, to send a detachment against him. The Colonel in consequence marched himself last night with these troops, and surprised and made him prisoner without any loss. I shall keep him in confinement in Gooty, and allow him such a proportion of his revenues as the Right Honourable the Governor in Council may be pleased to direct." At the end of 1807 Munro resigned his post of Principal Collector and proceeded home on leave, having first received the following handsome acknowledgment of his services from the Madras Government :—

"From disunited hordes of lawless plunderers and free-booters they (the people) are now stated to be as far advanced in civilization, submission to the laws, and obedience to the Magistrates, as any of the subjects under this Government. The revenues are collected with facility ; every one seems satisfied with his situation, and the regret of the people is universal on the departure of the Principal Collector."

The following extract from a letter, dated 6th November 1805, is significant of the change which had taken place in the feelings of the Court of Directors:—"The reports of Colonel Munro now brought under our observation afford new proof of his knowledge of the people and the lands under his administration, and of his ability and skill as a Collector. We see reason to be surprised at the industry which had carried the Collector into a detail of no less than 206,819 individual settlements of this nature (ryotwar) averaging only pagodas 65 each of annual rent."

Conclusion.

With the departure of Munro and the assimilation of Cuddapah district to the more orderly parts of the Madras Presidency its history as a separate political unit comes to an end. No event of any political significance has since occurred within its limits, if we exclude the rising of Narasimha Reddi, a descendant of a dispossessed poligār, in 1846, the story of which would more properly find place in a history of Kurnool district, on the frontiers of which his former jagir lay. After two or three months' lawless marauding with a band of followers numbering, according to various estimates, from 400 to 5,000, he was captured and hanged at Kōilkuntla in that district.

An account of the revenue administration of the Cuddapah district, more particularly from the time of Munro to the present day, will be found in another chapter.

CHAPTER III.

THE PEOPLE.

THE CENSUS—Density and growth of the population—Deficiency of females—Language—Education—Occupations—Religions. THE CHRISTIANS—The Roman Catholic Mission—The London Mission—The S.P.G. Mission—The Lutheran Mission. THE MUSALMANS—Their relations with Hindus. THE HINDUS—Villages — Houses — Dress—Food—Amusements. RELIGIOUS LIFE—The Village Deities—Peculiar religious practices and superstitions. SOCIAL LIFE—The more numerous castes—Tribes—Beggars.

CHAP. III.

THE CENSUS.

FOR purposes of the decennial census Cuddapah district forms part of the Deccan division and in regard to its population exhibits in itself all the more striking peculiarities which are characteristic of the whole.

Density and growth of the population.

First in importance is the sparseness of its population.[1] Its mean density per square mile is only a little more than half that shown for the whole Presidency. Conditions of life in Cuddapah district are in fact such as to prevent anything but a scanty population and a slow rate of increase. Less than six per cent. of the cultivated area is grown with rice and the ryot, whether he lives on the cholam that he raises on his own land or buys his food with the price of his cotton, requires a greater acreage for his livelihood than the southern cultivator. The climate moreover is inclement to the idle or physically weak, and the position of the district in the heart of the famine zone occasionally entails violent set-backs to what may be regarded as the normal rate of increase in the population. Thus in the ten years ending with 1901 we find a positive decrease in the population by over two and a half thousand, largely attributable to the famines of 1892 and 1897. The statistics of the following decade, which affords no instances of similar acute distress, furnish a truer criterion of the normal movement of population in the district, which is represented during this period by an increase of 1·6 per cent.; though it is

[1] The census of 1911 gives the total population of the district as 893,998.

CHAP. III. THE CENSUS.

difficult to conjecture why the difference in variation in the two decades should be so marked in the taluks of Badvēl, Cuddapah and Sidhout. A cursory examination of the figures noted in the margin almost suggests that an appreciable proportion of the population of this tract finds it difficult to decide in which taluk ultimately to settle down. All the other taluks of the district show an increase in 1911 over the population of 1901, the variation being most marked, after Badvēl, in Kamalāpuram, and least in Rāyachōti. Emigration, except to adjoining districts, is rare, and is practically unknown in the *regada* taluks, where the ryot will scarcely ever be found to live elsewhere than in the village of his ancestors. On the other hand, there is naturally no appreciable immigration to an inland district possessing no important industrial centre, where agriculture is the largely predominant occupation. It is therefore only by an examination of vital statistics for a series of unexceptional years that we can arrive at any definite conclusion regarding the normal rate of increase in the population. For each of the ten years from 1901 to 1910 the birth-rate of Cuddapah district was lower than for the Presidency as a whole, while the death-rate for the whole period is slightly higher.

Percentage of variation.

	1891 to 1901.	1901 to 1911.
Badvēl taluk ...	− 4·1	+ 7·3
Cuddapah taluk ...	+ 2·2	− 1·4
Sidhout taluk ...	+ 1·9	− 5·5

Deficiency of fameles.

Another characteristic of the Deccan division and of each of its constituent districts is that the males outnumber the females. The fact that certain other districts in which this peculiarity was also found to occur at the last census are just those districts which are most susceptible to famine has given rise to the suggestion that, in the long run, the sufferings entailed by a famine wear out more women than men. But it is to be noted on the other hand that during the ten years ending with 1900, a period which saw two famines, there was a slight increase in the number of females per 1,000 males over the figures recorded in 1891, while though there has been no famine in the present century, the number of females per 1,000 males has rather markedly decreased; and it is in fact generally considered that women are less susceptible than men to the effects of famine. The two theories are not irreconcilable. It may be that though the mortality observed to be directly due to famine is smaller among women than men, yet the male survivors have greater powers of recuperation. The subject seems to deserve further investigation.

CHAP. III. THE CENSUS. — Language.

Ninety per cent. of the people speak Telugu, and nine per cent. representing practically the Musalmān population, speak Hindustani. Of other languages Tamil, Canarese and Marathi account for about six persons per thousand of the inhabitants of the district, in nearly equal proportions. The higher grade of railway employees throughout the district are nearly all Tamilians, as are many Government officials. It is curious to note that the author of the original Manual of this district, writing in 1875, states: "The number of the Tamil-speaking population is yearly increasing" and "it is quite possible that . . . this district may at the end of the century be a Tamil-speaking one." There is in fact no indication at all at the present day that Tamil is in any degree whatever displacing Telugu as the vernacular of the natural population.

Education

The education of the people is dealt with more particularly in a subsequent chapter. It is sufficient to note here that though Cuddapah district is included for statistical purposes in the backward Deccan division, it compares favourably in point of education with two districts that adjoin it outside this division, namely, Nellore and Chittoor, in each of which there are fewer literate persons per mille than in Cuddapah.

Occupations.

Nearly three-quarters of the entire population depend for their livelihood on agricultural and pastoral pursuits. The subject of occupation and trade is separately dealt with elsewhere.

Religions.

Rather more than six-sevenths of the inhabitants are Hindus. As in other districts of the Deccan the proportion of Musalmāns is high. They constitute in Cuddapah district more than 11 per cent. of the total population, but comparatively few of them obtain their livelihood by agriculture. It follows that they are chiefly settled in the larger villages and towns along the main lines of communication. The Musalmān element is most noticeable in the towns and villages situated on the Kurnool-Chittoor road which passes through the taluks of Proddatūr, Cuddapah and Rāyachōti.

THE CHRISTIANS.

The Christians of Cuddapah district number twenty-five in every thousand, a proportion which largely exceeds the average for the Deccan as a whole and is only surpassed in three other Telugu districts, namely, Guntur, Kurnool and Nellore. The vast majority belong to the London Mission which has mainly confined its operations in this district to the taluks of Jammalamadugu, Pulivendla, Kamalāpuram and Cuddapah. A branch of the S.P.G. Mission numbers more than three thousand converts, principally in the Badvēl taluk.

CHAP. III. THE CHRISTIANS.

The remainder, numerically unimportant, are Roman Catholics and Lutherans.

The Roman Catholic Mission.

Of these missions the first in point of seniority is the Roman Catholic. The origin of this mission in the district as now constituted dates from the middle of the 18th century. At that time, when the political influence of the French was in the ascendant, some French Jesuits from Pondicherry to whom the neighbouring mission of the Carnatic had been entrusted extended their activities to this part of the country. It is recorded in the diary of the late Bishop Bonnand who visited these missions about the year 1830 that by the middle of the 18th century there had been a Christian settlement at Sidhout with a resident missionary, a certain French Jesuit, who on account of his great skill in medicine had acquired much influence at the Court of the Nawab of Cuddapah. But with the suppression of the Jesuits in 1773 their society's missions came gradually to be abandoned, and their work was ultimately carried on by missionaries from the west of the peninsula.

It was the Rev. Joachim D'Souza, a native of Goa, called by the Telugu Christians Father Ādikanada, who succeeded in founding a more lasting settlement of Christians in the Cuddapah district. This was at Sathyapuram, a suburb of the present Proddatūr, and was established at the end of the 18th or the beginning of the 19th century. Father Ādikanada had before this founded churches at Bellary and Ādōni in the Bellary district and at Yālēru in the Anantapur district. Some five hundred caste Hindus (reddis, weavers and goldsmiths) were converted in Cuddapah district. They appear to have enjoyed certain privileges from the Government of the Nizam; but in 1800, when the country was ceded to the British, these privileges were withdrawn, and for this and other reasons the community broke up and dispersed into different localities. Many of them, particularly the goldsmiths, followed their spiritual father Ādikanada to Bangalore, where he had joined the Fathers of the Foreign Missions Society of Paris. He subsequently died there in 1829. Others, notably the weavers, went and settled in the Rāyachōti taluk, where their descendants live to this day in the village of Kātimāyakuntla. Again some others of the same caste settled in the Nellore and Guntur districts. The greater number of cultivators went from Sathyapuram northwards and eastwards into the Kurnool, Nellore and Guntur districts where they became the pioneers of later Christian communities.

The spiritual care of these scattered Christians remained with the missionaries of Pondicherry, who periodically

CHAP. III. THE CHRISTIANS.

visited them once a year or once in two years, until in 1843 the Telugu districts were handed over to the Vicar Apostolic of Madras. But owing to a scarcity of missionaries for the Telugu missions progress has hitherto been slow.

In the town of Cuddapah itself there are only a few Roman Catholics, most of them being servants of officials or railway employees. They have a substantial chapel. During the time that Cuddapah was a cantonment[1] (1821–68) the station was regularly visited from Bellary, and the late Rev. Father Patrick Doyle registered about 200 baptisms during his visits.

Fresh conversions have taken place here and there in the Jammalamadugu taluk, but the greatest number of new converts are found at Urutūr, a village in the newly formed taluk of Kamalāpuram. In this village through the heroic exertions of the late Monsignor J. Balanadar, himself a native of these parts, a great many families of the Reddi caste have become Christians and have built for themselves a handsome church.

According to the latest returns of the mission there are only between five and six hundred Roman Catholics in the Cuddapah district; but what the late Right Rev. Bishop Stephen Fennelly wrote concerning them in 1875 remains true: "They are for the most part Reddis or *Kāpuvāndlu*, who live by cultivation. They renounced paganism and caste as far as its observance is incompatible with the honest profession and practice of the Catholic religion, retaining those social observances of caste which have no religious significations. They have hitherto lived in friendly intercourse with their pagan neighbours and relations, who associate with them on terms of equality in all the relations of life, and not unfrequently give their daughters in marriage to our Christians, allowing the girls to be instructed and baptized previous to their marriage."

The London Mission.

The activity of the London Mission in this district dates from 1822 when the Rev. John Hands, whose headquarters was Bellary, began work in Cuddapah town. In 1824 he was joined by Rev. W. Howell who was the first missionary to be permanently located in Cuddapah. It was in his time, about the year 1840, that a large number of Mālas began to accept Christianity, since when, and notably in later years, remarkable progress has been made by the London Mission with this community. In the early fifties of the last century

[1] The number of Catholics among the sepoys is said to have been considerable.

when the mission was in charge of the able and energetic Rev. Edward Porter further considerable advances were made, and by the year 1875 there were 80 outstations, 31 teachers, some 1,400 converts and thrice as many 'adherents,' and 27 boys' schools with 419 pupils. But in the great famine of 1876-78 out of more than five thousand converts and adherents the mission lost no less than eleven hundred and fifty.

CHAP. III. THE CHRISTIANS.

Previous to 1890 very few caste people joined the mission, but in that year a large number became Christians, notably in Pulivendla taluk, where they continue to increase to the present day.

In 1891 a new station was opened in Kadiri, which now belongs to Anantapur district. The Rāyachōti taluk is in charge of the Kadiri missionary.

In 1893 the first lady missionaries came to Cuddapah and took charge of the Girls' Day and Boarding schools, which were transferred to Jammalamadugu in 1899. The mission hospital had also been built at Jammalamadugu, which thus became an important mission station.[1]

"From 1890 to 1900," says the Rev. G. H. Macfarlane, the present head of the Mission staff, "about ten thousand adherents were gathered into the mission. Since then the rate of progress has not been so rapid, but a great internal advance has been made by the organization of the Christian community into circle churches . . . A third station in the mission was opened in 1903, when a missionary was settled at Kamalāpuram . . . The mission now (1914) numbers a Christian community of 18,500 people."

The S.P.G. Mission.

The Society for the Propagation of the Gospel has a mission station at Kalasapād. The Superintending Missionary is at present the Rev. Canon Inman. The converts of this mission are distributed over some fifty villages of the Badvēl taluk. The mission was established in 1861. The church at Kalasapād was built in 1887 and dedicated by the Bishop of Madras at the end of the same year. About ten years ago another church was built at Palugurāllapalle and dedicated by the present Bishop in 1904.

The Lutheran Mission.

The headquarters of this mission in Cuddapah district is Kōdūr in the Pullampet taluk. The present missionary in charge is the Rev. J. N. Wittmann. About eight years ago this gentleman, who has studied medicine in Germany and London, established a Leper Asylum about a mile and a half

[1] For particulars of the medical and educational institutions of the Protestant missions, see Chapters IX and X.

CHAP. III. THE CHRISTIANS.

from Kōdūr, which is known as Krupapalle. It has between thirty and forty inmates. The converts attached to this mission number about three hundred. The mission has looked after their material welfare in a very practical way by constructing an anicut across the Gunjāna river for the benefit of some sixty acres of land belonging to them. It has also made experiments in the plantation of leguminous trees with the view of demonstrating to the ryots what are the best green manures.

THE MUSALMĀNS.

That Musalmāns should be relatively more numerous in the Ceded Districts than in other parts of the Presidency is only what the political history of the country would lead us to expect. This is particularly the case in Kurnool and Cuddapah. But with the overthrow of the Pathan Nawabs by Haidar Ali at the end of the 18th century, thousands of Musalmāns must have lost their employment. Many of them to the present day are in very needy circumstances and occupy a low place in the social scale. They are often weavers, but by far the majority are engaged in trade. Nearly 17 per cent. of them are Dūdēkulas, who follow indiscriminately both Musalmān and Hindu ways and customs. These speak Telugu far more often than Hindustani and dress like Hindus rather than Muhammadans. Though they attend mosques and submit to the authority of the kazi, they nevertheless consult Brahmans regarding auspicious days, tie *tālis* at their weddings, do occasional worship at Hindu shrines and follow the Hindu law of inhoritance. Their proper occupation is the cleaning of cotton, but this is chiefly done in factories nowadays, so that many of them have taken to weaving or agriculture. Of the other sects Sheikhs are the most numerous, constituting more than five-eighths of the whole Musalmān population of the district.

Their relations with Hindus.

Of the antagonism which must have existed between Hindus and Musalmāns in the century following the downfall of the Vijayanagar Empire, it is difficult to find any trace at the present day. For the most part they live on the most amicable terms. Musalmāns often dress like Hindus, and in many villages the same wells are used by both communities. There are several examples in the district of their mutually tolerant attitude in the matter of religion. It is of course a common practice for Hindus to assume *pulivēshams* and take an active part in the Muharram. What is more strange is that in parts of Badvēl, and in Yetūr village of Jammalamadugu taluk certain Musalmāns regard the Hindu god Narasimhaswāmi with peculiar reverence. They worship him at the festival of *sankarānthi*, especially, and also before the performance of a marriage as their family god. If they fail to do this, they apprehend that great misfortune will overtake them. These devotees of Narasimhaswāmi, except that they do not eat beef, follow all the customs of other Musalmāns, with whom they freely mix. Again, in the village of Kondūr in Cuddapah taluk Hindus hold in great respect the mosque of Masthān Sahib, which was constructed by the villagers within the last ten years in honor of a holy Musalmān whose tomb is said to be in Kottacheruvu of Penukonda taluk of Anantapur district. His sanctity is acknowledged in many villages of this district, and in Kondūr it is said that Hindus will, out of gratitude for offspring long delayed, take their children to the mosque and name them Masthān Reddi or Masthānamma, after the saint.

THE HINDUS.

The Hindus constitute so predominant a factor in the population of the district that any account of their characteristics is for all practical purposes an account of the people in general.

Villages.

Of the total number of towns and villages in Cuddapah district more than five-eighths consist of villages containing less than a thousand inhabitants, and in about 62 per cent. of these the population is below five hundred. Though the villages within each natural division of the district present practically identical features, there are noticeable differences between the village of the black cotton country and that of the upland taluk of Rāyachōti, while the villages of the east part of the district are in some respects again distinguishable from either. For example, in the north-west taluks the villages are almost always enclosed by ring walls which generally contain a gateway, and houses are not constructed outside this rude fortification. They are therefore very often inconveniently crowded, while their expansion is further rendered impossible by the fact that all the land up to the very walls has long ago been appropriated and brought under cultivation. In the south of this tract, in Pulivendla taluk, the village gradually conform more closely to the type which is common in Rāyachōti. This is pre-eminently the country of the old poligārs. Here the ring wall disappears and we find a ruined fort overlooking nearly every village, where the poligār used to dwell with his liliputian court. He in his stronghold was responsible for the protection of his villages, themselves unfortified, whereas in the northern taluks where poligārs were scarce it devolved on the community itself to make the villages secure. A feature common to both tracts is the *buruz* or stone-constructed tower

CHAP. III. THE HINDUS.

situated a short distance from the village site. These are of no great size, but very strongly built. They evidently served the purpose of watch-towers in more turbulent times, but are now all ruined. They are more frequently seen on the plateau, where it is said they were also utilized for storing grain. In the eastern taluks of the district, Badvēl, Sidhout and Pullampet, there are no fortified villages or watch-towers, while such forts as are found owe their existence to a period anterior to the poligārs. During the 18th century while the rest of the district was exposed to the alarm and danger of every Mahratta raid, not to mention the mutual hostilities of the local poligārs, the part of the country east of the Nallamalais and the Sēshā-chalams was generally undisturbed and acknowledged, through nearly allits length and breadth, the authority of the Matli rajas of Chitvēl, who ruled the country under the nominal overlordship of the Nawab of Cuddapah.

Houses.

In the construction of their houses the ryots of the black cotton country follow a type different from that adopted in the rest of the district. Where the well-known Cuddapah slabs are available these are used for building up the walls, which are otherwise constructed of stone and mud. Where the walls are built of stone a characteristic feature of the houses in this part of the district is the flat roof. Two wooden pillars in the middle of the house lend support to the rafters on which stems of the cotton plant and other twigs are thrown in two layers cross-wise. Upon this foundation is deposited about a foot of earth surmounted by a few inches of clay or *tsoudu* so as to render the roof watertight. This construction is called a *midde.* Ventilation is obtained by openings in the roof, generally square, which are covered by slabs in wet weather. When Cuddapah slabs are not used the *midde,* properly so called, will not be found unless some other stone of sufficient strength to bear the immense weight of this peculiar flat roof is available. Nearly al! houses are provided with verandahs throughout the district, but from the verandah one descends to the street and not, as is generally the case in the Tamil country, to an outer verandah or pial. There are no courtyards within the houses of this district, and in the black cotton country backyards are very exiguous. The *gadi,* or place where the cattle are kept in the house, is generally on the right hand side as one enters. Further within, on the same side as the cattle, are the masonry *geriselu* or huge basket *gādelu,* in which grain is stored. On the opposite side of the house will be the living rooms, the cooking place and the *dēvunimūla.* The better sort of house generally has a carved doorway, with the figure of a horse, or occasionally an elephant, at the top of each post. On auspicious occasions a festoon of mango leaves is hung from one to the other across the entrance. Verandah pillars are also sometimes carved. With these exceptions, the houses display no ornamentation.

Dress.

Of the well-to-do farmers of the district, the Kāpus of the north-west taluks have proved the most conservative in the matter of dress. Until comparatively recently, their costume comprised, besides the voluminous white turban which is characteristic of the black cotton tracts, a plain unbleached upper cloth and a pair of drawers, both of very coarse material. These coarse fabrics are woven principally by the Mālas, the yarn, which used often to be homespun, being supplied for the purpose. But there has been a noticeable change in the last fifteen years. The cotton drawers or *tsallādamulu* are now rarely worn except by Gollas, and the locally made upper cloth is not nearly so frequently seen as before. So far as the men are concerned Manchester goods are steadily gaining ground, and on special occasions shirts are worn. The change is much less marked in the women's dress. Their clothes are for the most part still made of the coarse country stuff, with a black or red border, and it is only by the women-folk of merchants or very well-to-do ryots that a superior 'cotton and silk' material is used. Very little yarn is homespun by the ryots nowadays, the Mālas being supplied with yarn from the bazaar as occasion arises. In other parts of the district, in regard to male attire, there is little worthy of remark. It may be noted that *tsallādamulu* are also occasionally worn by agriculturists in the north of Badvēl taluk. Women generally wear the cotton or 'silk and cotton' cloths which are woven in the district, but the Brahmans and the richer classes follow Madras fashions. The tight-fitting bodice or *ravika* is very generally worn with certain marked exceptions, for example, it is never worn by Oddes nor yet by some gotrams among the Pākanāti Kāpus, and except in the lower castes it is not used by a woman after she becomes a widow. Certain jewels are said to be less frequently seen than formerly; for example, the *bulāki* (nose ornament), *vadyānam* (waistbelt) and *sandibandi* (elbow ornament) are not in general use nowadays. In all matters of women's dress and jewellery the fashion is set by the Brahman ladies of Madras.

Food.

Cholam is the staple food-grain of the country people in the black cotton taluks of the district, where the principal meal of even wealthy Kāpus is cholam pudding garnished with chillies. Korra is in these parts much less favoured than

CHAP. III. THE HINDUS.

formerly, though it is still largely consumed in parts of Kamalāpuram and in Badvēl taluk, where the other principal food-grain is ragi. This latter constitutes the usual food of the ryots of Sidhout and Pullampet taluks, who also consume a large quantity of cumbu. Cumbu and ragi are also the principal food-grains of Rāyachōti taluk. Rice is only eaten on special occasions. The Kāpus of the north-west of the district call it *dēvuni boova (bhōjanam)*, which sufficiently indicates the rarity of its use. In towns and large villages where there is a non-agricultural population and rice is sold in the bazaars, it is eaten by most classes once a day, at the evening meal.

Amusements.

Some of the children's games and amusements bear a curious similarity to those prevalent in Europe. The game of marbles is a very common pastime with boys. They also spin tops and fly kites. Tipcat is a favourite amusement, but played somewhat differently to the English game. The absence of breakable windows permits a degree of wildness in street games which would not be tolerated in the west. The bigger boys play a sort of prisoners' base and also indulge in games of ball somewhat resembling rounders and cricket, the latter being played with a brick for a wicket. The girls enjoy games of a quieter sort. They play with dolls much like the children of the west; for example, dolls' weddings are not unfrequently celebrated. Dancing is the main feature of their more active amusements. Singing and dancing with clasped hands, jumping and skipping are favourite pastimes. The universally known *kōlāttam* is danced not only by children but also by grown-up youths who are sometimes most expert in its performance, going through the most complicated figures with the greatest grace and precision.

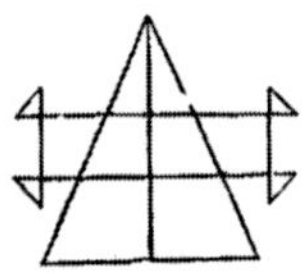

The chief recreations of adults seem to be card-playing and cock-fighting. They also play several varieties of draughts. One of the commonest is known as *pulijūdam*, which is played with stones on any surface marked out with a diagram like that shown in the margin.

It is a game for two players. One takes three large stones which are called *pululu* or tigers, and the other has about fifteen smaller stones called *mēkalu*, goats. The stones are moved from point to point on the figure, the objects of the game being for the tigers to eat up the goats and for the goats to hem in the tigers so that they cannot move. The tigers take the goats by hopping over them, as in draughts. The apex of the triangle is called *konda*, hill, and the tiger that is placed there never leaves his post. This brief description of the game shows that it corresponds in principle and part of the play to the English game of fox and geese. The principal card games appear to be *iruvai okati*, which is almost exactly the same as vingt-et-un, *munūta nālugu* (304), which is a kind of whist—the trump suit being declared by the highest bidder—and *minap* which corresponds roughly to poker. Gambling at *minap* is said to be generally very heavy, though it is of course made the feature of all adults' games. It is said to be exceptionally prevalent in Pulivendla taluk, to a certain village of which people from Anantapur and Kurnool districts resort for the purpose of high play. It is said that a certain Guntakal gentleman who visits the place never stakes less than a thousand rupees on a single throw, the corresponding amount on the other side being made up of the numerous petty stakes of less adventurous players.

The villagers occasionally amuse themselves with rude dramatic performances and side shows. *Bommalātam*, a marionette display, is very common. A cotton screen is erected, backed by lights, and dolls made of oiled paper are held up on sticks and moved about, while the action is explained or commented on by singers behind the screen. A favourite play in the black cotton country is *Chenchunātakam* which relates the amours of the god Ōbalapati, whose temple is in the Nallamalais, with a Chenchu girl. The story, which is unfit for publication, was introduced into these parts from Nellore district only some twenty years ago; but it has become so popular that, as I was informed, "any child can tell you what it is."

The wandering Dommaras also travel round and give gymnastic and acrobatic displays.

RELIGIOUS LIFE.

In Cuddapah district the followers of Vishnu far outnumber all other Hindu sects. The Lingāyats, who muster so strongly in Bellary district, have not extended their influence in these parts to any marked degree, though they are represented by the Linga-Balijas in some places, notably Rāyachōti, where there is an important temple of Vīrabhadraswāmi. Of specially sacred places within the district, Pushpagiri, some ten miles from Cuddapah town, alone deserves mention here. Some account of it will be found in a subsequent chapter. Tirupati is so easily accessible and offers religious opportunities to so predominant a proportion of the Hindu population, that the temples of the district have perhaps suffered by comparison. But in any case the real religion of the people throughout the district finds its expression not so much in

CHAP. III. RELIGIOUS LIFE.

devotion to the orthodox Hindu gods as in the worship of the tutelary deities of the village.

The village deities.

The tutelary deity of a village is always a goddess. Her name varies. Over the greater part of Cuddapah district she is known as Gangamma. Theoretically she is one of several sisters, of whom Pōlēramma and Ellamma are also known and worshipped in several villages. In Anantapuram village of Rāyachōti taluk Ellamma is worshipped as well as Gangamma at the great annual *jātra*. In the black cotton tracts the village goddess is almost invariably named Peddamma. In her resides pre-eminently the *bhū-sakti* which makes the earth bring forth her fruits in due season, just as Gangamma is the goddess to be propitiated to ensure an adequate supply of water in the tanks. But whatever be the goddess' name and peculiar attributes, these are lost sight of in the general worship accorded to her for all purposes, and one and all demand the same bloody sacrifices and the same barbaric rites as in other districts of the Presidency. The officiating priest at the annual Peddamma *jātra* is either a carpenter or a potter according as the image of the goddess is made of wood or clay, while the *pūjāri* in a Gangamma *jātra* generally belongs to the Golla (herdsman) caste. Particular care is taken at the time of sacrifice to the goddess that no one should pass beyond the village boundary, as it is held that if any of the sacrificial blood is carried outside the limits of the village, the sacrifice itself is rendered nugatory. It is said that, to prevent such a catastrophe, the villagers would not hesitate to take life.[1]

Peculiar religious practices and superstitions.

As every evil that besets mankind is thought to be the work of some malignant sprite it follows that, besides the little temple of the village goddess, other shrines are found in every village. These are of very rude construction. The commonest type consists of three stones set up on a low platform between two trees. The middle stone is a big one and has a little stone on each side of it. These stones are daubed with red and yellow spots. The trees are often a margosa and ragi tree which have been "married" with due ceremony. Shrines of this sort are generally found near the village site. Another is often seen on the tank-bunds, and generally consists of four stone slabs about a yard square in size. Three of these are set up on end like the walls of a room, and the fourth is laid on top as a roof. The "walls" are generally painted with

[1] The subject of village deities may be further pursued in Bishop Caldwell's "Demonolatry in Southern India;" "Census of India, 1891, Madras;" and in Bishop Whitehead's "Village Deities of Southern India."

CHAP. III.
RELIGIOUS
LIFE.

red and white stripes. The inmate of this little chamber is the usual decorated stone. In addition to these one often notices that some attention has been paid to natural peculiarities, such as a tree twisted into a weird shape or a rock of unusual appearance, it being supposed that the stranger the appearance of a natural object the more likely is it to harbour some demon who has to be propitiated. The earth will therefore be smoothed and levelled round the foot of such a tree and the trunk will be smeared with saffron and *kunkumam*. Somewhat different is the practice of doing puja to stones inscribed with *antrams* consisting of weird and unintelligible combinations of letters and figures. Such a stone is called *saktibanda*. They are generally shaped like large tombstones, and sometimes bear representations of snakes or of a female figure above the inscription. Some of them are very old, but it is interesting to note that this is not always the case. In the village of Utukūr, in Cuddapah taluk, such a stone has recently been erected as a prophylactic against cholera. Its surface is divided into sixteen squares in each of which is a character of the Telugu alphabet together with one or more unintelligible symbols. The virtue of these stones no doubt resides in the *antrams* which are considered as charms to keep off epidemics. The value of charms in general is of course universally recognized. In parts of Badvēl taluk it is customary to tie silver "arithmetical" charms of the sort shown in the margin round the necks of children, with the idea of keeping away sickness. In some villages of Proddatūr taluk it is usual, when an epidemic has made its appearance, to tie two cocoanuts and a small bottle of arrack or toddy to the roof of the house, to secure immunity for its occupants.

6	1	8
7	5	3
2	9	4

The practice of hookswinging,[1] in its modern form, is very common at village religious festivals in many parts of the district. It was in fulfilment of vows to the village goddess that human beings used to submit to the uncomfortable process of being suspended in mid air by iron hooks passed through the fleshy part of the back and swung round a maypole. When Government forbade this inhuman practice, live goats were substituted, the animals presumably being supplied for the purpose by the human devotees. The cruelty of swinging goats is however recognized, and though this is still being done it is more common to use a wooden dummy. It is said

[1] A description of this ceremony will be found in the *Madras Museum Bulletins*, Vol. V, No. 1.

CHAP. III. RELIGIOUS LIFE.

that at the great jātra at Anantapuram village human beings are actually swung to the present day, but that the hooks are attached to the waist cloth: which probably occasions the victim no more inconvenience than would a merry-go-round at an English fair.

Before leaving the subject of religion and religious observances brief reference may be made to the practice of canonization. The mosque of Masthān Sahib at Kondūr has already been mentioned. A similar case is to be seen at Lingāladinne in Proddatūr taluk, where there is a temple of "Brahaswāmi," a Brahman who died in the village about twenty-five years ago. He attained this unusual honour partly by his asceticism, but chiefly by his accurate prognostication of future events and his miraculous power of being in several places at the same time. Various extravagant things are said of him, one of which is that he gave birth to a son. Upon this son and his descendants devolve the duty and privilege of maintaining the temple. A Brahman pūjāri is employed for the daily worship of this strange saint.

SOCIAL LIFE.

There are no important social communities in Cuddapah district that are not also found in other parts of the Deccan. The vast majority of Telugu-speaking Hindus in the district are, according to the latest census, comprised in twenty-five castes.

The more numerous castes.

First in numerical importance are the Kāpus, who are the principal landowners of the Deccan. They constitute nearly one-fourth of the total population of the district, and consist of many sub-divisions. Of these the Peddakanti, Mōtāti, Kodide and Pākanāti[1] Kāpus are chiefly found in the taluks of Jammalamadugu, Proddatūr, Pulivendla, Cuddapah and Kamalāpuram; while the Velanādu and Yelama Kāpus, the latter of whom are vegetarians, seem to be the commonest sub-divisions in the three eastern taluks of the district. In Rāyachōti taluk the caste is not quite so common, many cultivators on the plateau being Balijas and Kammas. The Kāpus are good steady farmers, true sons of the soil, and very conservative. Having no interest in life beyond the welfare of their crops, their natural obstinacy and love of contention finds an outlet in forming factions and fomenting the bitterest quarrels. Though there are factions in every village of the district, and these are by no means confined to Kāpus, yet in the black cotton country where this caste largely predominates they are developed to a very high degree

[1] In some places called Pōkanāti. The two names seem to denote the same sub-division; but the matter is not free from doubt.

of animosity and are a fruitful source of crime, as they not infrequently result in regular blood feuds. The highest ambition of a wealthy Kāpu in Jammalamadugu taluk is to become the leader of a powerful faction. Such a man will not leave his village unaccompanied by a body of armed retainers, so that free fights occur with passable regularity. In this part of the district it is a curious custom of the Kāpus, and consequently also of the lower castes who all take their cue from them, to bend the head and take off the turban with both hands as a mark of respect when presenting a petition: which appears at first sight to be very similar to the western practice of taking off the hat. It has however been suggested that the action probably signifies the *sāshtāngamulu*, or prostration of eight members, in the performance of which the turban will not stay on the head and so is removed beforehand.

Next to the Kāpus, in point of number, come the Bōyas, but they are of little importance as a distinct social element and occupy but a low place in the social scale. In old days their proper occupation was that of palanquin bearers. It is also said that the poligārs' forces and Haidar Ali's famous troops were largely recruited from these people. This may account in part for the tradition, preserved in many stories, that they are blood-thirsty and cruel. They are good shikaris and at the foot of the great hill ranges they trade in forest produce and are said to be versed in forest lore. In the towns they live by cooly. Balijas, though somewhat fewer in number than the Bōyas, have a larger stake in the country. It has already been stated that in Rāyachōti taluk many of them are landowners. In the rest of the district they are mainly occupied in trade. Many of them are Lingāyats. Next come the Gollas who slightly outnumber both the Mālas and the Mādigas. The Gollas are herdsmen, and, perhaps from their being accustomed to handle cattle, the pujaris who perform animal sacrifices are generally of this caste. They are also largely employed as agricultural labourers. The Mālas and Mādigas are the lowest in the social scale, and, like the Paraiyans of the Tamil country, occupy separate hamlets apart from the rest of the village community. The Mālas' principal occupation is weaving. The Mādigas are the leather workers and coolies of the community. In the black cotton country there is a marked antagonism between these two classes, of which the longstanding bitterness is illustrated, if not sufficiently explained, by the currency of various mythological stories which present either Māla or Mādiga in a very discreditable light. For example, in one of

CHAP. III. SOCIAL LIFE.

these stories a Māla is represented as having fled from a Mādiga, leaving his sword and turban behind. Their enmity is kept alive at the present day by disputes regarding the division of the flesh of dead cattle. The rights of the Mālas and Mādigas in this respect are immemorial, the Mādigas taking the skin and one share of the flesh, and the Mālas taking two shares of the flesh. It appears that in some villages the owners of the dead beasts claim to sell the skin, and the Mādiga to make up for his loss tries to appropriate part of the Mālas' perquisites. Strife having once arisen, the spark is speedily fanned into a flame by taunting references to the old stories, and the great opportunity comes at the annual Peddamma festival, when the Mādigas perform the "*Chindhu* dance," wearing red turbans and carrying swords when feeling runs high, in reference to the discreditable story of the Māla alluded to above: which they also sing as they dance, so as to place their meaning beyond reasonable doubt. It is interesting to note that on occasions of "*Chindhu* dancing" the whole village joins in supporting one side or the other. The castes who encourage the Mādigas are, principally, Kamsalas, Kurubas and Bōyas, while on the other hand those who agree with the Mālas in objecting to the dance are the potters, barbers and washermen as well as Balijas and certain sub-divisions of the Kāpu caste. So, if the dance ends in a fight, as is not infrequently the case, it involves not only the parties immediately concerned but the whole village: and the *Chindhu* becomes a 'shindy' of the liveliest description.

Of other communities, the Kōmatis are the principal traders of the district. The trade of the big towns is chiefly in their hands. The weaving castes, excluding the Mālas who only weave coarse cotton stuffs, are represented by the Togatas, Sāles and Dēvāngas in the order of their numerical importance. Of the village artisans no special mention need be made. The only notable caste occupied in agriculture outside the Kāpus and Balijas, is that of the Kammas. The Oddes, or navvies, are fairly numerous. The toddy-drawers are Īdigas. The Upparas furnish an interesting example of a caste whose occupation is gone. They used to live by making earth-salt. When the manufacture of salt became a Government monopoly, the Upparas took to agriculture, and this is their usual occupation nowadays.

In the latest census report all the wandering tribes known to Cuddapah district are returned partly as Hindus and partly

CHAP. III. SOCIAL LIFE. — Tribes.

as Animists. The former predominate. The most important of these tribes, in point of numbers, are the Yānādis, Yerukulas, Lambādis and Chenchus. The Yānādis reside principally in Nellore district, and have overlapped into the east of Cuddapah. There are now less than two thousand in this district. At Srīharikōta on the east coast, which is their original settlement, they are said still to be very backward. But elsewhere they are becoming more civilized and some have given up their wandering habits and are found permanently domiciled in towns and villages.[1] The Chenchus are often regarded as a sub-division of the Yānādis, but they hold themselves distinct, and claim consanguinity with Narasimha of Ahōbilam in Kurnool district, who, so they say, married a Chenchu maid, and gave them the whole of the Nallamalais. They are probably as distinct from the Yānādis as, for example, are the Mālas from the Mādigas. Between the Chenchu and the Yānādi there is no love lost. They may be seen living close together on the Nallamalai hills, but they do not intermingle, and their social habits differ. To quote an instance, the degree of importance attached to the marriage tie differs very considerably in the two tribes, for while the Chenchu wife is renowned for her fidelity the Yānādi marriage is at best but a loose bond and readily dissolved.

The Yerukulas appear to be more addicted to a life of crime than either of the tribes already mentioned. They are more frequently met with on the plateau than in other parts of the district. They occasionally settle down, and there is a community of them at Mailavaram in Jammalamadugu taluk, where they are known by two names according to their occupations. Those who live by selling baskets, tatties and the like are known as *Dabbala* Yerukulas, and others, who make 'sizing-brushes' (*kunchulu*) for weavers are known as *Kunchugattu* Yerukulas, and generally travel round with monkeys. The women tell fortunes from house to house and take notice of their construction and other details with a view to informing their menfolk of likely 'cribs to crack.' When a woman of this tribe marries again, the relatives of her first husband have to be indemnified for the expenses of the previous marriage. No woman is allowed to marry more than seven times, though if she accomplishes this remarkable record she is regarded with considerable respect. Their tutelary deity is said to be named Yerukula Nāncharamma.

[1] An unusally full account of the Yānādi tribe will be found in the *Madras Museum Bulletins*, Vol. IV, No. 2.

CHAP. III. SOCIAL LIFE.

The Lambādis, who are generally known as Sugālis in the Telugu country, are commoner in Rāyachōti taluk than the rest of the district. They live chiefly by collecting firewood and other forest produce which they sell in towns and villages. Formerly, it appears, they did considerable business in the transport of merchandise by means of pack-bullocks. With the opening up of communications they naturally lost this trade, and some of them have taken to agriculture or live by cooly. There are several Sugāli hamlets to be found in Rāyachōti taluk. The women of this tribe, by their dress and appearance, are quite unmistakable. They wear patch-work petticoats and tight-fitting bodices of the same material, with several rows of bead necklaces, while their arms are covered with bracelets up to the elbow. In appearance they are not very dark, and this fact, together with the regularity of their features and the brightness of their costume, reminds one vividly of the Romany gypsies of Europe, with whom indeed they may be allied, if the prevalence of Indian words in the language of the Romanies is the key to their true origin.

A curious custom, which is nevertheless extremely widespread and is known to exist in countries so far apart as Greenland and Borneo, obtains among both the Yerukulas and the Sugālis. It is technically known as the *couvade* (hatching) and is thus described in Brett's 'Indian Tribes of Guiana.' "On the birth of a child, the ancient Indian etiquette requires the father to take to his hammock, where he remains some days as if he were sick, and receives the congratulations and condolences of his friends. An instance of this custom came under my own observation, where the man in robust health and excellent condition, without a single bodily ailment, was lying in his hammock in the most provoking manner, and carefully and respectfully tended by the women, while the mother of the new-born infant was cooking, none apparently regarding her." With the Yerukulas and Sugālis, similarly, the father of a new-born child will take to his bed for fifteen days and observe a very strict diet, being constantly attended by the women of the house as if he were sick. On the sixteenth day he undergoes a ceremony of purification and gives a feast to his relatives. During all this time the mother pursues her usual avocations, and no particular attention is paid to her.[1]

The district is not remarkable for the frequency of beggar castes, the only one of any numerical importance being that

[1] For a fuller acconnt of the convada custom the reader is referred to the *Madras Museum Bulletins*, Vol. IV, No. 2.

Beggars.

of the religious mendicants known as Dāsaris.[1] This community is recruited from several castes, such as the Kāpus, Balijas, Kurubas, Bōyas and Mālas, and members of it who belong to the two last of these, being low in the social scale, do not intermingle with the others. All Dāsaris are Vaishnavites and admission to the community is obtained by being branded by some Vaishnavite *guru*. Thenceforward the novice becomes a Dāsari and lives by begging from door to door. The profession is almost hereditary in some families. The five insignia of a Dāsari are the conch-shell which he blows to announce his arrival; the gong he strikes as he goes his rounds; the tall iron lamp he keeps lighted as he begs; the brass or copper vessel in which he places the alms received; and the small metal image of Hanuman which he hangs round his neck. Of these the iron lamp is at once the most conspicuous and the most indispensable. It is said to represent Vēnkatēsa, and it must be kept burning, as an unlighted lamp is held to be inauspicious. It is also an important function of the Dāsaris to officiate at certain ceremonies of the Mālas and other low caste communities.

Of other beggars mention may be made of the Bhatrāzus and Budubudukulas. The Bhatrāzus carry a little book but use no musical instrument of any kind. Their practice is to extol the virtues of the principal villagers in extempore verse, and the longer alms are withheld the more persistent and extravagant grow their praises, till the object of them in very shame is compelled to bestow upon them gifts of grain or money. Many of the teachers in the 'pial' schools of the district are recruited from this community. The Budubudukulas, so named from the tomtoming of the little drum they carry to announce their presence, are a lower class of people altogether, possibly a sect of Mālas originally. They obtain alms by prophesying good fortune to the people, as they travel from village to village, and will accept presents of any sort, such as old clothes and lumber, for which the owners have no further use.

[1] The description of the Dāsaris is taken almost verbatim from the Anantapur District Gazetteer.

CHAPTER IV

AGRICULTURE AND IRRIGATION

INTRODUCTORY. WET CULTIVATION—Paddy—Ragi—Sugarcane—Garden crops. DRY CULTIVATION—The guntaka or scuffle—The gorru or drill—Weeding—Practices peculiar to the 'black cotton' country—The peddą madaka or big plough—Harvesting—Cattle food—Modern changes. IRRIGATION—General—River channels—Tanks—Wells. IRRIGATION WORKS—The Kurnool-Cuddapah Canal—The Chapād and Maidukūru Projects—The Sagilēr Project. ECONOMIC CONDITION OF AGRICULTURISTS—Indebtedness of the ryot.

CHAP. IV. INTRODUCTORY.

IN dealing with the physical description of the district I have already had occasion to note its want of uniformity and for purposes of convenience to regard the whole as falling into three natural divisions. From its diversity in general configuration, soils, and even climate, it inevitably follows that agricultural practice also varies. In Jammalamadugu taluk which is characterized by flat stretches of black cotton soil more than 75 per cent. of the cultivated area is grown with cholam and cotton, and the cultivation of wet crops is almost negligible, for the configuration of the country is unfavourable to the construction of tanks, while owing to the absence of a porous sub-soil and even of adequate surface drainage the land would be ruined by persistent irrigation. Eastwards these conditions gradually disappear, and in east Proddatūr, Cuddapah and Kamalāpuram taluks where the soils are predominantly loamy the cultivation of paddy is much more extensive, cholam is largely replaced by korra and ragi, and cotton to some extent by indigo. The change becomes complete in the eastern division of the district where, in Pullampet taluk, paddy is more extensively grown than any other crop, cotton is not found and cholam and korra cover less than one-third of the area cultivated with ragi and cumbu. Finally, the upland taluk of Rāyachōti is marked by features that do not characterize any other portion of the district. It contains very few irrigation sources that are not precarious though it is seamed throughout by chains of little kuntas with ayacuts of insignificant extent. Without the aid of supplemental well irrigation these sources are inadequate to

CHAP. IV. INTRODUCTORY.

secure the raising of a paddy crop, except in years of good rainfall, so that dry crops such as ragi and cholam are often grown on wet lands. The red soil in this taluk is the poorest in the district and the cereal most commonly grown is cumbu which represents more than 50 per cent. of the total cultivated area of the taluk.

WET CULTIVATION. Paddy.

In this district, as elsewhere, paddy occupies the most prominent place among the crops grown on irrigated lands. Formerly, when indigo was more extensively cultivated this crop was used in rotation with paddy over large areas much in the same way as cotton with cholam in the black cotton country. This practice, which consists in putting down indigo once in three years on wet lands and growing paddy in the other two, is still followed in the Cuddapah and Sidhout taluks, where indigo continues to occupy an appreciable percentage of the cultivated area. Indigo refuse from the vats is a very good manure for paddy and the continued growth of this crop—mostly on wet lands nowadays—must be attributed to its restorative value as much as to any profit that accrues to the growers from the declining trade in the dye. In the case of paddy the system of cultivation is very similar to that pursued in other parts of the Presidency. Formerly the practice of sowing the seed broadcast was almost universal throughout the district. Being a method that results in a great waste of seed as well as an uneven crop it is surprising that farmers, whose ingenuity evolved the seed-drill to avoid these very evils in the case of dry crops, should be so slow to abandon it. It is the prevailing system to the present day, though that of transplanting the seedlings has gained ground in late years and is exclusively followed in some parts as, for example, under the Kurnool-Cuddapah Canal. In Rāyachōti and parts of Pullampet taluk transplanting is for some reason only the rule for the *Vaisākham* or later crop. If the tanks fill during the south-west monsoon and make paddy cultivation possible earlier in the season, the grain is sown broadcast. In other parts of the district both systems prevail, except in Kamalāpuram and Pulivendla taluks where broadcast sowing appears to be exclusively practised. The saving of time under the transplanting system is an important consideration, for it may often happen that the last two weeks in the life of the crop determine its success or failure, so that the longer the cultivation season the greater the risk.

Besides ordinary cattle manure, leaf manure is extensively used, of which some five to ten cart-loads constitute the

CHAP. IV. WET CULTIVATION.

usual application for an acre. In Rāyachōti taluk the leaf invariably used is that of the *kānuga* tree (Pongamia glabra). Where neither this tree nor indigo waste is available, the ryots have generally to obtain their green manure from the forests. The manure is applied to the land after the soil has been reduced to a state of liquid mud-puddle, and the seed is sown broadcast immediately. After the seed is sown the fields are generally allowed to dry until the sprouts are about two inches high, and from that time till harvest it is considered necessary to keep two or three inches of water on the land. As the cultivators also like to keep the water in their fields constantly moving, the amount used is thus far in excess of the quantity actually required, but this waste is so general throughout the country that it demands no special notice in regard to Cuddapah district.

The uneven crop which results from broadcasting is usually remedied by crossing it with a rake when about six inches high and removing the seedlings from the thicker to the thinner patches.

Paddy has two main seasons known as *Kārtikam* and *Vaisākham*, these being the months in which the harvest is gathered. The most popular variety is *sannavadlu*, and unless the soil is of inferior quality no other sort is grown on single-cropped land; but as it takes nearly five months to mature, some other variety immediately precedes or follows it where irrigation facilities render possible the cultivation of two paddy crops in a single year. Of such other varieties the principal is the *chennangi*, while *tōkavadlu*, *lāvuvadlu* and *nallavadlu* are also grown on inferior soils.

Ragi.

Ragi is either grown as a second crop on irrigated lands which possess a good water-supply or as a substitute for paddy when the supply is insufficient for a wet crop. The crop is transplanted from seed-beds, the land being ploughed up when moistened by the rain and then manured. The depth of tilled soil does not exceed three inches. After the manure has been applied, it is not infrequently left for a few days before the water is let in, which is done immediately before planting out the seedlings. During its growth the crop is said to require watering about once in from seven to ten days, and to be weeded once.

Sugarcane.

The sugarcane grown in the old sub-division of the district, now represented only by the taluk of Rāyachōti, is exceptionally good and the jaggery manufactured therefrom is widely known. This crop occupies the land for about a year. Considerable care is exercised in the preparation of

CHAP. IV. WET CULTIVATION.

the soil for it, and large quantities of manure are applied. The land is ridged and the cuttings planted, being laid flat in lines about eighteen inches apart, four or five joints being allowed to each cutting. During the growth of the crop it is watered between every second row, so that a high ridge and a water furrow are formed. Water is applied about once in four or five days. To prevent the attacks of jackals several stems in each plant are tied up together with leaves of the cane.

Garden crops.

Highly irrigated areas are sprinkled with the usual "garden" crops, such as the plantain and betel-vine. One that deserves particular mention is turmeric, from which saffron powder is extracted. It is grown in small patches on fertile soils under the better irrigation sources. As it requires constant though not excessive irrigation and withers very rapidly if deprived of water, it is not often found on lands unprotected by wells. Large areas are grown with this plant in the taluks of Pullampet and Cuddapah as well as under the Kurnool-Cuddapah Canal. There are saffron works at Cuddapah where the powder is extracted from the turmeric by power-driven machinery.

"Cuddapah melons," which are exported to all parts of India, are cultivated in the sandy bed of the Pennĕr river, mainly at Sidhout. The fruit is raised either from seeds planted in pits dug in the sand, or from transplanted seedlings. As soon as the river dries up after the cold weather rains the cultivation of melons is begun. The only expense involved in their cultivation—which is very remunerative—is the heavy manuring required. The plants trail over the sand like creepers and are so prolific that thousands of melons can be produced on a single acre.

DRY CULTIVATION.

The guntaka or scuffle.

With the first showers that herald the approach of the south-west monsoon the ryot begins to prepare his dry fields for cultivation. When the surface is sufficiently soft to commence operations, the stubble of the last crop is rooted up, and this is usually done by means of the *guntaka*, or scuffle, which is peculiar to the Telugu country. It consists of a beam about four feet long to which the draught pole is attached, as also an iron blade, which is fixed by two wooden holders to each end in such a way as to be forced into the soil when the implement is drawn along. The driver often stands on the beam so as to ensure that the blade sinks to an adequate depth. The surface of the soil being thus prepared, the land is ready for the plough as soon as sufficient rain has fallen. If the monsoon is seasonable, ploughing operations

CHAP. IV.
DRY CULTIVATION.

will be in full swing before the end of June. Manuring, which is the next process, is often accomplished by the simple means of penning sheep and goats on the land. Otherwise manure is only applied to dry lands when the ryot has enough and to spare for his irrigated and garden lands, and then not in large quantities, ten cart-loads being considered a fair dressing for an acre. If manure is applied to the land, the *guntaka* is again used to work it in and break up the clods. Then, after more rain, the seed is sown.

The gorru or drill.

The use of the seed-drill, or *gorru*, for the sowing of dry crops is universal in the Ceded Districts. This implement has from three to six teeth. In the black cotton country six is the usual number. In other parts of the district the number of lines sown by the drill is generally five or three. The teeth are of iron, strengthened by a wooden backing, and are hollow. Connected with each of them is a hollow bamboo and the upper ends of these are brought together and fixed into a hopper called the *zadigam*. The seed is dropped into the hopper, passes down the bamboo tubes through the hollows in the teeth, and so into the miniature furrows which the teeth make as the instrument is dragged over the field by the pair of bullocks yoked to it. The seed being thus sown, the *guntaka* is again lightly used to cover it. The chief advantages of the seed-drill are that it economises seed, provided the machine is carefully fed, sows it evenly and at a uniform depth and is very well suited for the sowing of mixed crops. The commonest form of mixing is to sow two rows of some low-growing crop such as ragi or korra and then one row of a taller and wider spreading plant, such as dhall or cotton. This is effected by stopping up one of the holes in the hopper and attaching by a string, a foot or two behind the *gorru*, a separate seed-tube consisting of a separate hollow bamboo and hopper, into which a second sower drops the seed required for the third row. This seed-tube is made to run in the track left by the tooth of the *gorru* which has been put out of action and thus sows the seed at the proper distance from the other rows. By obvious variations of this system it is possible to sow the different seeds in alternate lines or in such other proportions as may be desired. To prevent dishonesty or unnecessary waste of seed the machine is generally fed by the ryot himself or one of his family. In the black cotton country the work is usually done by a woman.

Weeding.

The use of the *gorru* effects a saving of labour in the matter of weeding, which can be done by bullock power instead of by hand; for the teeth of the *gorru* are attached to it at even intervals of about nine inches or a foot, so that the field can be weeded by driving an implement so constructed as to pass between the rows made by the *gorru*. Such an implement is that known as the *metla guntaka*. It consists of three blades resembling English hoes fixed to a transverse bar at the requisite intervals, and is drawn by a pair of bullocks. This is not very serviceable on an uneven surface, for which another variety of bullock-hoe is generally used. This is known as a *danthi* and resembles the ordinary *guntaka* in shape, except that the single blade attached to it is of course less wide. Three of these, each guided by a separate man, are drawn by one pair of bullocks. In a rocky and uneven country such as Rāyachōti taluk the advantage of this composite implement lies in the independence of each of its parts, any one of which can be lifted over obstacles without stopping the work of the others.

Practices peculiar to the 'black cotton' country.

To this general description of agricultural practice in the cultivation of dry lands must be added some account of the methods which are peculiar to farming on black cotton soils. In the first place the practice of burning the stubble of the last crop on the land and using the ashes as manure, which is common in other parts of the district, is not usually followed. Firewood being very scarce, the dead cotton plants and roots of the cholam are generally collected and taken away for fuel. This is done before the rains set in. Even after the south-west monsoon declares itself agricultural operations are not begun till a month or six weeks later than elsewhere. In July or August the ryot will sow some of his lands with an early crop, which is locally known as the *mungāri pairu*. The grain thus sown is nearly always korra or ārika. The rest of his holding is reserved for one of the two principal crops of the country, namely cotton or cholam, though it should be noted that the marked predominance of the latter crop is at length threatened by the enormous increase in the cultivation of groundnut. The cotton is put down towards the end of August and in September, but only on land which has not been grown with cotton for the previous two years. The practice of mixing cotton with other crops which, partly as a substitute for rotation, often obtains elsewhere is not generally followed. The system of rotation is, however, thoroughly understood and is given full play in the very extensive holdings which are characteristic of the black cotton tracts of this district. Two-thirds of the land that remains to be cultivated apart from that sown with an early crop is, or was till the recent introduction of groundnut, grown with cholam,

CHAP. IV. DRY CULTIVATION.

which is put down a few weeks after the cotton. The figures showing the average distribution of crops in Jammalamadugu taluk for the five years immediately preceding the recent resettlement indicate how uniform was this system, under which every holding contains about twice as much cholam as cotton, for cholam represents 50·14 per cent. of the total cultivated area and cotton 25·10 per cent. The *mungāri* crop accounts for about 20 per cent. and the small remainder is mainly represented by paddy and indigo. Cholam is often mixed with various pulses by which means it is said the ryot is enabled to keep all his cholam and pay the assessment with what he gets for the rest.

As individual holdings sometimes run to two or three hundred acres and the whole extent has to be sown in a little more than two months, it follows that the ryot has no time to lose once he begins operations. Cotton especially is a crop that cannot be grown successfully unless put down at the proper time. Consequently the ryot makes no attempt to plough annually more than about one-third of his holding, the rest being merely scuffled by the *guntaka.* Very little manure is used, and that only in the neighbourhood of the village-site. Though the value of manure is well recognized it is scarce, and the amount needed for an average holding in these parts would be prohibitive. This and the natural fertility of the soil render its use uncommon.

The pedda madaka or big plough.

Although the usual system of tillage is poor the ryots are aware of the value of deep cultivation, as is shown by their use of the *pedda madaka* or big plough. It is of wood like the ordinary plough but weighs about 230 lb. and requires six pairs of bullocks and raw-hide traces to pull it. While the ordinary plough is used but once in three years, land is only very exceptionally brought under the big plough, the effect of which is however said to be observable for ten years. It was formerly chiefly used for bringing waste under cultivation and clearing land that had got foul with the deep rooted *hariali* grass. Now that there remains but little valuable waste to reclaim, its use has become more general, but the area annually operated on is very small. The crop usually taken immediately after the deep tillage is Bengal gram. It is said that in the adjoining taluk of Tāḍpatri, in Anantapur district, the *pedda madaka* has in the last fifteen or twenty years been largely superseded by iron ploughs of European pattern. This is not the case in Cuddapah district, perhaps because the black cotton tract is too remote from any convenient centre of distribution.

CHAP. IV. DRY CULTIVATION. — Harvesting.

The threshing of cholam is begun only after the entire crop has been brought in. The heads of the plant are stacked in heaps on or near the threshing floor and protected by a covering of the stalks till the reaping is over. The crop is then spread on the floor and rolled with light stone rollers drawn by bullocks. This practice is now universal in Jammalamadugu taluk, having entirely superseded the old system of treading out the corn by cattle.

Cattle food.

Besides cholam straw which is said to be excellent fodder the ryot of these parts usually feeds his cattle on cotton seed and husks of the green-gram (phaseolus mungo). Bulls in heavy work are given horse-gram. If other fodder is scarce cattle are occasionally fed with cholam picked green from the field. The cattle being of the heavy Nellore breed and very valuable demand and obtain better treatment than is accorded to the small local variety in other parts of the district.

Modern changes.

Improved varieties of the cotton plant have been introduced and are making some headway in the district, but their undoubted superiority is, it is said, counterbalanced by the fact that their seeds are, unlike the country variety, unsuitable for cattle food: so that the ryot gains little if any advantage by their cultivation. By far the most important change, which dates from only two years ago, is involved in the extensive substitution of the groundnut for cholam. It may perhaps be thought strange that the ryot of this part of the country has been so slow to recognize the advantages of cultivating this remunerative crop, which has for many years steadily gained favour in other parts of the district. At any rate his obstinate conservatism has at length given way before the growing popularity of this foreign root and he appears to have cast aside all hesitation in the matter of its adoption. There is no doubt that thousands of acres, which were grown with cholam three or four years ago. are now under groundnut. Two husking mills were opened at Kondāpuram last year, and two more at Muddanūr and one at Yerraguntla in the current year. It is impossible as yet to foresee how far groundnut will eventually replace cholam in the black cotton country. Its further extension must largely depend on whether the soil is found as suitable to a rotation of groundnut and cotton as it is to one of cotton and cholam, and whether the ryot will be content to become a purchaser of food-grain instead of raising it on his own land. This remarkable development of the groundnut in the best black cotton tracts of the district presents exactly the same features that characterized its introduction into Pulivendla taluk which,

CHAP. IV. DRY CULTIVATION.

occurring just before the resettlement, is adverted to by Mr. T. E. Moir in his scheme report as follows:—"Unrecorded prior to fasli 1316[1] it was in that year grown on 7,042 acres, while in fasli 1317 the area under it had increased to 21,448 acres or nearly 11 per cent. of the total cultivated area. Figures are not available for the present year, but I found large areas under it, more especially in the western part of the taluk, and it has evidently come to stay and in 1317 seriously encroached on both cotton and indigo . . . It is grown on soils of all kinds including fairly heavy black loams and clays. The boom may prove temporary, but if not the introduction of groundnut will greatly affect the agricultural practice of the taluk and the area devoted to food crops."

IRRIGATION. General.

Allusion has already been made to the uneven distribution of irrigated-cultivation in the district. It is also noticeable that different forms of irrigation are typical of different parts. In the low-lying taluks west of the Nallamalais, which are watered by the Kurnool-Cuddapah Canal system and the Pennēr, Pāpaghni and Chitrāvati rivers, channel irrigation prevails. In the eastern division where the most important tanks in the district are found, of which about sixty-five irrigate ayacuts exceeding 250 acres, more than 71 per cent. of the occupied wet area is tank-fed. The Badvēl and Pōrumāmilla tanks have occupied ayacuts of nearly 3,000 acres each, while those at Vontimitta and Rāmāpuram in Sidhout taluk and at Pedda Ōrampād, Pōli, Cherlōpalle and Penagalūr in Pullampet taluk each irrigate over 1,000 acres. In addition to its tanks Pullampet taluk also benefits considerably by channel irrigation from the Cheyyēr and its tributaries. This river, under the name of Bāhudānadi, also affords irrigation facilities to six villages in the south-east corner of Rāyachōti taluk which is otherwise devoid of reliable sources and depends on well irrigation to a larger extent than the rest of the district.

River channels.

The vast majority of river channels take their rise in spring heads excavated in the sandy river beds and often flow long distances in the bed or along the bank of the river before reaching their ayacuts. A few channels from the Cheyyēr in Pullampet taluk are provided with head sluices, and there are two or three anicut channels taking off from the Gunjāna river, a tributary of the Cheyyēr in the same taluk, a narrow stony bedded stream, which contracts into isolated pools in the hot weather instead of completely drying up and thus lends itself more readily to anicut irrigation than the wide sandy beds of the larger rivers. But with these exceptions the river channels

[1] 1906-07.

of the district are devoid of any permanent construction and depend for their maintenance on the spade work of the ryots whose interest it is to keep them up. Every landholder claiming irrigation from such a channel must contribute his quota of labour, or its equivalent in money, according to the extent occupied by him. If properly maintained, these river channels will ordinarily afford a supply sufficient to raise two paddy crops. Most of the river channels of the district take off from the Pāpaghni in its course through the Surabhu valley and northwards to Kamalāpuram and from the Cheyyēr in Pullampet taluk. The Chitrāvati also contains some good channels but it only touches the western fringe of the district. Owing to the steepness of its banks the Pennēr which is the largest river in the district is not so well adapted to irrigation as its tributaries.

CHAP. IV. IRRIGATION.

Tanks.

A feature of the tank irrigation of the district is the large number of good-sized tanks that depend for their supply mainly if not exclusively on the rainfall. The situation of the eastern division between the Veligondas on the east and the Nallamalais and Sēshāchalams on the west is particularly favourable to the storage of water in the rainy season. Most of the tanks of the district, notably those of Pōrumāmilla and Badvēl, were constructed some hundreds of years ago. The large tank at Pōrumāmilla was built by one of the earliest of the Vijayanagar princes, in the first quarter of the 14th century A.D., and the Badvēl tank by a raja of the Matli family at the beginning of the 17th century. It is not improbable that the principal period of tank construction in the district coincided with the apparently uneventful era, corresponding roughly to the 15th century, which marked the heyday of Vijayanagar supremacy, when diamond mines were being worked at the foot of the Nallamalais. The practice of granting dasabandham inams to the principal ayacutdars on condition of maintaining a tank in good condition was particularly prevalent in this district, and, if we may rely on an inscription discovered in Pulivendla taluk, dates back at least to the 14th century. These inams were always confirmed by subsequent governments, but in the last sixty years many of them have been resumed owing to the conditions of the grant not being fulfilled. They are particularly numerous in Rāyachōti taluk where they generally take the form of money remissions.

Wells.

The distribution of wells throughout the district is largely determined by the nature of the soil and the adequacy of other means of irrigation. There are naturally but few wells to be

CHAP. IV. IRRIGATION.

found in the heavy black soils of the western taluks which are generally unsuited to irrigation and present unusual difficulties in the matter of excavation. In the neighbourhood of Cuddapah, the prevalence of well irrigation indicates a high order of farming rather than the necessity of protection against drought. The soil is for the most part a fine free loam and the water level is usually near the surface, while the town affords large supplies of manure. As land endowed with such advantages of situation and natural fertility can be brought to an excellent condition at a comparatively low cost, want of capital, which is the chief obstacle to good farming, is less felt here than elsewhere. With this exception the largest number of wells are to be found in the poorest tracts. Rāyachōti taluk contains about 5,700 wells, of which nearly half were till recently dasabandham wells. In extending to wells the policy of granting dasabandham inams for their upkeep, former governments evidently placed but little value on private enterprise. This view may have been justified at a time when all well lands were assessed at a much higher rate than ordinary "dry" lands. But with the recognition of the principle that ryots' improvements should not be taxed and the assimilation of "garden" or "well" lands to "dry," the holders of dasabandham wells, under which the wet rates, though diminished by the dasabandham allowances and remission for lift, still greatly exceeded the dry rates, laboured under disadvantages from which owners of private wells were free. Consequently many hundreds of dasabandham wells throughout the district were abandoned in the last half century, and their loss is but just balanced by private enterprise, so that the total number of wells in the district at present differs but little from that recorded prior to the original settlement. As dasabandham wells were with the consent of the inamdars converted into private property, the inams resumed, and the ayacuts assessed at dry rates at the recent resettlement, it is believed that the tendency to allow wells to fall into ruin has been to a large extent arrested, though their abandonment is also in some cases to be attributed to the divergence of the sub-soil water or the drying up of springs. The taluks of Badvēl, Sidhout and Pullampet contain in the aggregate but one thousand more wells than Rāyachōti, their frequency in the latter taluk being, as already observed, due to the necessity of supplementing in all ordinary years the inadequate irrigation afforded by its insignificant tanks. Many of the wells in the eastern taluks are doruvu wells which are constructed by revetting the river banks. The Pennēr,

Sagilēr and Gunjāna rivers are specially adapted to the construction of these wells.

The only water lift in general use in the district is the single mhote or *kapila*. The picottah is scarcely known. Two pairs of cattle are generally employed to work the single mhote, one walking back up the slope while the other is raising the water bucket. A man unhitches the rope from the yoke of the cattle as soon as the bucket is empty and returning quickly up the slope attaches it to the yoke of the second pair which is waiting ready. This is an improvement on the method by which one pair of cattle is used and made to back up the steep slope every time the bucket is let down into the well. The system however involves a waste of cattle power, which is enhanced by the universal use of leaky leather buckets and inferior pulleys.

Irrigation works.

To this general description of the irrigation of the district must be added a more detailed account of the great irrigation works which have been undertaken at different periods with the object of bringing large portions of the district under effective protection. The most important of these is the Kurnool-Cuddapah Canal.

The Kurnool Cuddapah Canal.

This project owed its inception to the policy inaugurated in the middle of the last century of introducing into India British capital and enterprise in the construction of irrigation works. The canal forms only a section of the original ambitious design undertaken by the Madras Irrigation and Canal Company which was incorporated in 1858. The capital of the company was to be £1,000,000 on which Government guaranteed 5 per cent. interest. The Madras Government was not in favour of the work being undertaken by a private company, but the Government of India was desirous of attracting private capital to such enterprises and the highly successful results of irrigation work in the delta tracts as well as the views held by the late Sir Arthur Cotton and other irrigation experts contributed to the decision of the Secretary of State to accept the company's proposals.

The canal takes off from an anicut, seventeen miles above the town of Kurnool, on the river Tungabhadra, which skirts the district of Bellary and joins the Kistna in that of Kurnool. The anicut supplying the canal is built across the Tungabhadra at Sunkēsula. It is fifteen hundred yards in length, is founded on rock, has a clear overfall, and is furnished with a set of under-sluices. The canal enters the Cuddapah district at Suddapalle in Jammalamadugu taluk and passing through the Proddatūr taluk crosses the Pennēr at the 182nd mile and finally discharges into a stream a few miles west of Cuddapah town. Its continuation parallel to the Pennēr as far as the Pulicat lake was originally contemplated but never carried out.

Owing to a threatened famine, work was commenced in the Kurnool section in 1860. As a result of hasty procedure, engineering difficulties and mistakes, and extravagance and carelessness in the management, the guaranteed million was expended by 1866, by which time only half of the section had been completed. Fresh contracts were made in that year by which operations were restricted to the canal between Sunkēsula and Cuddapah and new financial arrangements were made. By 1871 the canal was finished throughout its length, though its capacity and efficiency were by no means satisfactory. Even then very little use was made of the water by the ryots and with the exception of the famine years 1877-78, the working of the canal resulted in an annual deficit which was met by the Government. In view of the increasing loss thus entailed, Government purchased the canal and assumed charge on July 1, 1882, at a cost which, including direct payments and claims surrendered, amounted to £3,018,758.

The total length of the canal which thus came into the possession of the State is 190 miles, of which about 62 lie in this district.

Prior to the assumption of control by the Government there had been considerable friction between the ryots and the company's officers and it had been thought for many years before the transfer actually took place that applications for water would be made more readily if the canal were managed by Government agency. Permanent causes operating against the financial success of the canal were however recognized, such as the sparseness of the population and the large tracts of heavy regada soil commanded by the canal, which really needed no irrigation. As soon as Government took over its management, the irrigation rates were considerably lowered; but in spite of this concession and the change in administration little improvement was shown either in the area irrigated or in the revenue realized. In reviewing the Administration Report of Irrigation Works in the Madras Presidency for 1887-88, the Government of India remarked as follows:—"The financial position of this canal is in the last degree unsatisfactory; not only did the revenue fall off during the last year and the irrigated area decrease, but at no time since the canal was bought by Government has it been worked except at a heavy loss. There is a loss both in navigation and irrigation and, while the irrigation return is Rs. 2·5 per acre irrigated, the cost of working expenses falls at Rs. 6·5 per acre, and there is no prospect of any material improvement. The total estimated value of the crops raised under irrigation, Rs. 2,48,330, does not largely exceed the sum which it cost Government to supply the water. The revenue expenditure on works and repairs alone (Rs. 1,11,780) is nearly double the income earned by the canal. It would appear that it might be economical to close the canal as an irrigating system merely keeping it in repairs so as to be ready to be put in working again, if a season of drought should create a sudden demand for the water. The Governor-General in Council trusts that the Government of Madras will consider the question and formulate such proposals as may seem to them expedient with a view to putting a stop to the constant drain on the treasury, which the maintenance of the canal on its present footing entails."

In August 1890, the Government accordingly sanctioned the appointment of a Special Deputy Collector for nine months to enquire into the possibilities existing for the further extension of irrigation under the canal.

The report of this officer contained a number of suggestions, the most important of which was the appointment of a Special Revenue Officer on the canal. As a result of this report the appointment of a Special Deputy Collector to be in revenue charge of the canal for two years from the 16th March 1894 was sanctioned by the Government and this appointment was, by subsequent extensions, continued till the end of March 1907. This measure met with a very considerable amount of success, and inaugurated an era of improvement in the financial history of the canal. From 1894 to 1903 the excess of revenue over expenditure increased fourfold. The canal has been a greater success in Cuddapah than in Kurnool, chiefly owing to the fact that the proportion of the commanded area adapted to irrigation is higher in the Cuddapah district. Statistics of cultivation under the canal for the five years ending June 30, 1913, show that the average extent annually irrigated in this district is 28,702 acres, of which nearly 5,000 acres are cropped twice in the year.

The Chāpād and Maidukūru projects.

Connected with the Kurnool-Cuddapah Canal system are two important irrigation works known as the Chāpād and Maidukūru projects, which came into operation in the last decade. The Chāpād channel and its distributaries benefit a tract of country extending about 12 miles south-eastwards from Gōpavaram, a village three miles north of Proddatūr, to

CHAP. IV. IRRIGATION.

the junction of the Kundēr with the Pennēr, and lying wholly between these rivers with a maximum breadth of about 6 miles. The project was first sanctioned as a famine relief work in 1897 at an estimated cost of about three and a half lakhs, and was put in hand in the year 1900 when work was needed for relief purposes. In the course of execution it was found that the provision made for some of the works was inadequate and that some additional works were necessary for the completion of the scheme, with the result that the estimate was revised and the total expenditure incurred, including indirect charges, actually amounted to nearly six lakhs. The channel was opened for irrigation in 1904 and has at present five distributaries. It is however intended to construct a sixth distributary, for which purpose land is now being acquired. The Maidukūru project takes its name from the village of Maidukūru the northernmost of some nine villages situated along the Cuddapah-Kurnool road which are benefited by the project. The names of these villages are given in the margin. The Maidukūru channel takes off from the left bank of the Kurnool-Cuddapah Canal at 171 miles, 40 chains, and the project was designed to improve this channel for a distance of a little over three miles, extend it for a length of 11 miles, to provide the necessary branch channels and masonry works so as to irrigate an extent of 8,000 acres in all, and in seasons of drought to supply tanks in the nine villages above mentioned. The project, originally estimated to cost about Rs. 2,30,000, was finally completed at an outlay of a little over three lakhs, and the area which it was intended to operate, namely 8,000 acres, has in fact been brought under irrigation, so that it may be regarded as a successful enterprise.

Maidukūru.
Sivapuram.
Pullūr.
Rāvulapalle.
Duppalagatta.
Chemūllapalle.
Chennamakkapalle.
Buddayāpalle.
Bōyanapalle.

The Sagilēr project.

This project takes its name from the Sagilēr river which rises in the Nallamalai hills in Kurnool district and, draining the narrow valley between these hills and the eastern ghāts, enters the Bādvēl taluk at its extreme north end and after traversing the Badvēl and Sidhout taluks falls into the Pennēr. It is not a perennial stream but a jungle torrent which in an ordinary year flows for about twenty days. The project, which was designed to improve the supply to the Pōrumāmilla tank, consists of an anicut across the Sagilēr about three miles north of Kalasapād and a main channel taking off at this point and extending a distance of ten miles to the

Pōrumāmilla tank. By means of head sluices at various points in its course the channel affords a supply to the four smaller tanks of Kalasapād, Pendlimarri, Pidugupalle and Akkisetti-palle and between the 8th and 9th mile passes through the Chintalapalle tank before finally crossing the Cumbum road and tailing into the Pōrumāmilla tank. Including establishment and indirect charges the total cost of the work amounted to rather more than four and a half lakhs. Operations were begun in the year 1898, and the construction estimate was closed on March 31, 1907. Judging from the additional revenue realized in the five years succeeding the completion of the project, it cannot be regarded as very remunerative, as the return on the capital outlay represented less than one per cent. per annum.

ECONOMIC CONDITION OF AGRICULTURISTS.

The average extent of ryots' holdings as indicated by the assessment they bear constitutes an important factor in the economic condition of the agricultural population as a whole. There are but few great landholders and they are chiefly found in the black cotton country. More than 70 per cent. of the holdings in the district are assessed at less than Rs. 10, while those bearing over Rs. 50 do not exceed three per cent. As about five-sevenths of the population of the district are agriculturists the small ryot accordingly represents by far the majority of its inhabitants, and it is on his economic condition that the prosperity of the district largely depends.

It is a truism that in this class of people material progress is least to be expected. They are, it seems, incapable of bringing their minds to bear on the problem of bettering their condition. Their horizon is bounded by the next harvest, their stereotyped habits and universal respect for old customs as such induce a positive fear of innovation, while that element of intelligent self-interest which western economists predicate of the 'ordinary man' is in their case curiously ill-developed. Their mental habit is stagnation, and the difficulty of educating them out of it can scarcely be exaggerated. A system of education which embraces from the beginning the special consideration of their peculiar educational needs as agriculturists would seem to offer the best promise of ultimate success. If the education of this class of people has hitherto failed in its object, such failure must be attributed to its being usually divorced from all the interests of their life work. At any rate it is difficult to point to any change of practice or modification of manners in the last three decades in any way indicative of the progress of enlightenment, and I cannot do better than quote the following description of these people, contained in

CHAP. IV. ECONOMIC CONDITION OF AGRICULTURISTS.

an official report [1] of thirty-five years ago: "In this district (Cuddapah) the cultivators are as a rule altogether illiterate, despising and rejecting all education for their sons, as being likely to unsettle them and lead them in turn to despise the vocation of their forefathers. They ask 'of what use is writing, if our sons cannot plough and work on our fields properly?' This objection is one which has been met with amongst the rural populations of nearly all countries. At the same time the adherence to custom, which is so strongly developed in this country is, I think, more powerful in this district than in the south. The obstruction which this feature has presented to agricultural progress in all countries is well known, and it might almost be said that the persons in the old story, [2] which is often quoted to exemplify this in England, could have been a Government official advocating the use of a European plough, and a ryot of this country replying to him. But no doubt to a certain extent it is, as Wren Hoskins says, 'a mistake to attribute these things to obstinacy or any unwillingness to adopt an improvement that *can be perceived;* it is in the perceptive faculty that the impediment lies—a faculty which will not act of itself without exercise,' and one which the circumstances of the life of the ryot do nothing to develop, but much to deaden. Causes and effects follow so slowly in agriculture, that the difficulty of following out the teaching of experiments is very great. If we add to those agencies the extreme poverty, the manifold superstitions and other influences affecting the ryot, it is difficult to reasonably expect that in the longest life of effort for agricultural improvement much can be effected in the modification of his present practices, unless pressure is brought to bear on the cultivators by their landlord—the State.

"The amount of capital which the ryot possesses is generally extremely small; and were he willing, he would not be able to make many experiments with changes of his system, which he has at least found to bring him means of subsistence in ordinary seasons. If by any means new men—men not born and bred in it—can be induced to embark in agriculture,

[1] Report of a tour in the Cuddapah and North Arcot districts made in August 1879, by C. Benson, M.R.A.C., Acting Superintendent of Government Farms.

[2] This well-known story is that a certain nobleman, seeing a man ploughing a light soil with four horses in a line, got off his horse, unhooked the two leaders, harnessed the two others abreast, and ploughed a few furrows out with his own hands, intending to show how easily it might be done with a pair. "Ah! it's all very well for you that can afford it," said the man; "but those newfangled improvements are too expensive for a poor man."

and to bring to it such a reserve of capital as will enable them to attempt things which the ordinary ryot cannot from his circumstances adventure on, then can more rapid progress be expected, for such men 'often form the most intelligent of husbandmen.' As an old writer on English agriculture observes: 'They have more zeal and fewer prejudices to surmount than those who have been brought up in it from their infancy. Their closer attention and freedom from the influence of habit make amends for their first ignorance of minutiæ; and being driven to the pains of really *studying* their pursuit, they form their ideas upon its guiding principles.' . . .

"Thus it is, I believe, almost hopeless to attempt to influence the present race of ryots, or even their children, as long as they resist their being educated even to the slightest degree. . . . The diffusion of agricultural information amongst the educated ryots through the schools, and by means of employing in the subordinate revenue posts only such men as are acquainted with the true principles of agriculture, will do much. But if any marked improvement is to be effected, it must be from the infusion of new blood into the cultivating classes, and how this is to be done it is difficult at present to see."

Nowadays there is of course but little active opposition to education, but it is at least doubtful whether the ryot considers it to have any *practical* bearing on his after-life. How the remedies advocated in this report are to be applied, namely, the infusion of new blood into the cultivating classes and the attraction of capital to the land, is still an unsolved problem. If the "new men . . . who often form the most intelligent of husbandmen" are furnished by the agricultural colleges in sufficient numbers it may be that they are destined to become the pioneers of a forward movement in agriculture, to which at any rate they may be calculated to bring knowledge, brains and enterprise; and that capital in such a case would not be slow to take advantage of the new conditions might be predicted with tolerable certainty.

In the Census report of 1911 it is recorded that nearly 38 per cent. of the cultivable area of the district is waste. If for the sake of argument half of this is regarded as land of the worst kind the cultivation of which under present conditions is scarcely remunerative, it is still clear that of pressure of population on the land, in the sense of a dense population on a restricted area, there is no indication whatever. The sparseness of the population is out of all proportion to the

CHAP. IV. ECONOMIC CONDITION OF AGRICULTURISTS.

resources of the district, were they properly exploited. At present they are inadequate to maintain the population because the occurrence of a famine or a series of bad seasons paralyses agriculture. Capital cannot be attracted to the land till something is done to combat the disadvantage of the position of the district in the famine zone. The conditions of much of the district, apart from this liability to drought, are by no means unfavourable. For example the soils of the black cotton country are good and very retentive of moisture, while the ryots are industrious and not unacquainted with some of the rudiments of good farming, yet they have made no effort to protect themselves against the effects of a prolonged drought. In seasons when the rain fails, the crop fails, and they find themselves face to face with starvation. That such failure and distress are unnecessary there is no room for doubt in face of the latest agricultural achievements in other parts of the world where the conditions of soil and rainfall, if not of climate, do not largely differ from those obtaining over large areas of this district. The success that has there[1] attended scientific dry-farming is measured in the following words: "[2]The last romance of agriculture, the most daring of its many triumphs, is the conquest of the desert. Pictured in the winsome song of the Psalmist, the sonorous prose of the Hebrew prophet, and visioned in the pages of a modern seer, it has remained for the latest science, the deep-set share and the diligent harrow to complete the ancient prophecy and to produce a harvest of corn from a rainless land."

But while there is thus reason to believe that the rich black cotton soils can be made to withstand the effects of prolonged drought, the case is different with the barren red soils of the upland, and much of the dry land in the east of the district. Even horse-gram, the last resource of the poorest lands, cannot be made to grow without at least one good shower of rain. But it is reasonable to suppose that under improved methods of agriculture these lands could in good and average years be made to yield an outturn so far in excess of what is now the case as largely to enable the ryot to tide over the bad years with the surplus of the good. As it is he has no means of mitigating adverse conditions, and in a series of bad years many a small ryot will sink under the accumulation of his indebtedness and disappear.

South Africa.

[2] See "The Nineteenth Century and After" June 1913: "A rainless wheat.'

CHAP. IV. ECONOMIC CONDITION OF AGRICULTURISTS

Indebtedness of the ryot.

By this it is not implied that indebtedness is peculiar to the small ryot or confined to periods of scarcity. The ordinary operations of agriculture depend to a considerable extent on borrowed capital, and indebtedness is common among all grades of ryots. The small ryot trying to establish himself borrows the use of cattle, seed grain, or enough to keep himself till the harvest season; the bigger ryot buys cattle on the instalment system and borrows money for a marriage festival or other special occasion while at the same time he possibly has money or grain out at interest himself, for the extent to which the large landholders finance the small holdings is rather noticeable in this district. From one point of view it is perhaps advantageous that these transactions should be in the hands of the big ryots, who are at least likely to time their demands with more intelligence than a merchant living in a distant town. On the other hand the greed of land in the rich black cotton plains is such an overpowering passion that landholders of means are only too anxious to accommodate the smaller ryots, in the hope of eventually adding acre to acre. They but seldom accept any security but the land itself, the usual rate of interest in this case being 12 per cent. per annum. It is said that they decline to take back small instalments of the principal, and wait for years on the chance of the borrower failing to meet the interest, when they immediately foreclose. If land were only mortgaged to raise loans for agricultural improvements there would be nothing unsound in ryots' indebtedness. It is unproductive debt and the borrowings necessitated by caste and social customs to which exception must be taken inasmuch as they constitute a burden on the land which the land should not be called upon to bear. It is this aspect of the ryot's indebtedness that renders his position so precarious, as a succession of bad seasons, the immediate effect of which he has no means of avoiding except by further borrowing, quickly strains his resources to the breaking point.

CHAPTER V.

FORESTS.

FORESTS—Their situation and area—Administration. CHARACTER OF THE FORESTS—The Red sanders tree—Its uses—Summary. CONSERVANCY—Prior to the Madras Forest Act of 1882—Subsequent operations. RECENT WORKING PLANS—Fuel—Timber. WORK IN PROGRESS—Fuel operations—Timber operations—Sandal-sowing—Minor forest produce—Grazing and goat-browsing—Forest offences—Fire protection—Stream-bunding—Cart-tracks and bridle-paths—Demarcation—Planting and sowing.

CHAP. V. FORESTS.

Their situation and area.

THE district of Cuddapah contains some large and important forests, the systematic conservancy of which dates from the passing of the Madras Forest Act of 1882. They are mainly situated on the principal hill ranges, namely, the Veligonda, Sēshāchalam, Pālkonda, Lankāmalai and Nallamalai hills. Many of the isolated blocks of rocky hills which are scattered throughout the district and occur most frequently in the western taluks of Rāyachōti, Pulivendla and Proddatūr have also been constituted reserved forests; but they are clothed for the most part with thorny scrub jungle of an inferior quality and are, from a sylvicultural point of view, of little value. The district contains 1,817 square miles of reserved forests, representing about 31 per cent. of its total area and the figures in the margin give particulars of their distribution.[1]

Block.	Extent in square miles.
Veligonda	221
Sēshāchalam	327
Pālkonda	358
Lankāmalai ...	212
Nallamalai	193
Isolated blocks	506
Total ...	1,817

Administration.

Prior to 1911 the district as then constituted was divided into three forest charges, known as East, North and South Cuddapah, the latter corresponding to the old revenue subdivision of the district, the headquarters of which was at Madanapalle. With the transfer of Kadiri, Madanapalle and

[1] Since writing the above an extent of about 30 square miles of reserved forest in the Sēshāchalam hills have been added to this district from that of Chittoor.

Vāyalpād taluks to other districts the number of charges was reduced to two, which are still known as East and North Cuddapah, though they should more properly be termed East and West.* At the same time the administration was rendered more effective by increasing the number of ranges, of which there had hitherto been three in each division. The east division now contains five ranges, Kōdūr, Rājampet, Sidhout, Badvēl and Pōrumāmilla; and the north division four, namely, Rāyachōti, Cuddapah, Pulivendla and Proddatūr. The boundary between the two divisions accordingly runs north and south along the watersheds of the Sēshāchalam, Pālkonda, Lankāmalai and Nallamalai hills.

CHARACTER OF THE FORESTS.

The two great classes of evergreen scrub and deciduous forest are found here as elsewhere. The former, which is confined to the bottom and sides of ravines and to moist localities at the foot of the hills, comprises the following among its principal trees and shrubs. The description of these trees and shrubs is taken from Gamble's "Manual of Indian Timbers":

Diospyros chloroxylon (Ullinda).—A large shrub or small tree, useful for fuel.

Maba buxifolia (Uti).—A small tree, useful for fuel.

Erythroxylon monogynum (Dêvadāri).—A small tree. The wood is strong, hard and pretty but is little used except for fuel. The leaves are said to be eaten in famine seasons.

Mimusops Indica (Pāla) and *Hexandra (Pogada).*—Fine large trees. Wood is very hard and heavy, and is valued as fuel. The fruit is edible. The bark is used for native medicinal purposes. The wood can be used as timber, but its great weight and hardness and the existence of better timber trees are against it in this respect.

Strychnos nux-vomica (Mushti).—A moderate-sized tree or shrub. Leaves, bark, fruit and especially the seeds are poisonous. The latter yield alkaloids, strychnine and brucine. With two exceptions the tree is untouched by animals. The Langur monkey is able to eat even the seed with impunity, while the goat occasionally browses and may even make a hearty meal off the very young shoots.

Strychnos potatorum (Chilla).—A moderate-sized tree. Not poisonous. The seeds are used to clear muddy water by rubbing the inside of the vessels with them. It is known as "clearing nut" tree. The pulp of the fruit is edible and is made into preserve. The wood is good and is used for ploughs, building purposes and cart wheels.

* This alteration has since been carried out.

CHAP. V. CHARACTER OF THE FORESTS.

Eugenia jambolana (Nēredu).—A good timber tree. Useful for building timber and also for agricultural implements. The bark is used in native medicine as a specific for dysentery.

Pterospermum suberifolium (Tada).—A moderate-sized tree. The wood is used chiefly for fuel but also for making carts.

Sapindus emarginatus (Kunkudu).—A large tree. The fruit is used for washing as a substitute for soap, and is known as the "soap nut." The wood is good but is not much used.

Vitex altissima (Nemaliadugu).—A good timber tree used in building and cart-making.

Webera corymbosa (Kommi).—A large shrub.

Ixora parviflora (Kurivi).—A shrub. The green branches are used for torches.

Carissa carandas (Kalivi).—A shrub. Extremely thorny. The branches are used for fencing. The wood is used for fuel.

Dodonæa viscosa (Bandāru).—A shrub. Its branches are used to support the earth of a flat roof.

Marraya Konigii (Karēpāku).—A small tree. The wood is used for agricultural implements. The leaves are used to flavour curries.

The Red sander tree.

The deciduous forests are very open and have a luxuriant undergrowth of grass. The dominant and most valuable tree is *Pterocarpus santalinus* (Red sanders—*Chandanam*). It is a very pretty, moderate-sized tree, with an upright clean bole and rounded crown. The wood is dark claret red in colour, and is extremely valuable. The red sanders, or "redwood" tree as it is also called, deserves more than passing mention, as it is said that there is probably no important Indian tree the distribution of which is so limited in range, and it is on the encouragement of the growth of this tree that the whole work of the Forest Department is concentrated in its timber operations in this district. It is confined to the slopes of the main hill ranges of Cuddapah and to the adjoining parts of Nellore and Chittoor districts.

Its uses.

The red sanders is principally used nowadays for the construction of house-posts. An important factor in their value is that they are never attacked by white-ants. The best posts are usually bought in pairs for verandah pillars and are often sold at Rs. 40 to Rs. 50 per pair of 1½ cubic feet each, or in other words at Rs. 15 per cubic foot. Such posts are known as 'specials.' The dimensions of a 'special' are 15 to 18 inches in mean girth and 12 feet long. This represents the measurement of the heart-wood after removal of the bark and sap-wood. A tree capable of yielding a 'special' post measures as it stands in the forest from 3 to 4 feet in girth at a

CHAP. V. CHARACTER OF THE FORESTS.

Redwood posts.

height of 4½ feet above the ground. In addition to the required dimensions a 'special' post must be without defect and must taper uniformly from base to top. Since they are usually sold in pairs, the more alike it is possible to find two posts the greater will be their value. A defective post, which, but for the defect, would be classed as a 'special,' falls into the first class. The figures in the margin show the average prices obtained in auction for posts of each class. The rates obtained, it will be observed, fall very rapidly. The charcoal obtained from this tree is excellent, and fuel of the best quality is provided by the branches of badly formed and diseased trees. Small pieces of the heart-wood are carved by the Settigunta doll-makers into dolls or idols, which are in great demand among pilgrims to Tirupati. The wood is also used for agricultural implements and the leaves for fodder.

		Price of each.		
Class of timber—		RS.	A.	P.
Special	...	10	15	9
1st class	...	5	0	8
2nd ,,	...	2	13	11
3rd ,,	...	2	2	4
4th ,,	...	1	5	8

In former days the wood of the red sanders tree was chiefly valued for its red colouring principle, "santalin," which is soluble in alcohol and ether but not in water. It was very extensively used as a dye, and large quantities of redwood were exported to Europe for this purpose. The shipments continued until comparatively recent times, when this natural dye was entirely superseded by the introduction of artificial substitutes. The earliest account of this trade was brought to light by the editor of 'Nature' (Calcutta), who published an interesting article in the issue of May 4, 1911, of which the following are extracts :—

"During the preparation for the press, in 1895, of the 'Diary and Consultation Book of the Agent, Governor and Council of Fort St. George,' for 1682–85, Mr. A. T. Pringle, the editor, inquired if I could throw any light on the origin of caliature, a name for redwood (Pterocarpus santalinus), frequently referred to as an article of trade in Madras. Presuming the name to be that of a port on the east coast, it has evidently disappeared from nearly all the available gazetteers and modern atlases. Inquiries were made in London, Holland and Java with no results; but recent researches in the libraries of Calcutta have been more successful, and the following notes on the early trade of the country form an interesting chapter on the history of red sanders wood :—

"To Rumphius belongs the credit of giving the origin of the term 'caliture.' In 'Herbarium Amboiense,' 1750, vol. ii, 48, he speaks of 'Santalum rubrum' being known in his country and in

CHAP. V. CHARACTER OF THE FORESTS.

Europe, and as coming from a tree from which 'lignum calitour' is derived. The wood is very hard, solid, and dull red, which he says could be obtained in great abundance from the northern parts of the Coromandel coast. Various kinds of furniture were made of it, as benches and elegantly carved chairs. Only the mature trees afforded good sandal-wood, as was shown in letters sent to him in 1689. The wood was also used as a tincture in the arts, and the Armenians in Shiraz and Ispahan added it to distilled spirit of wine to give it a beautiful and intense red colour. The identity of the town by Rumphius I will quote in the original Latin :—

'Hisce addo ex iisdem litteris locum Caliatour quondam dictum, hodie in ora Coromandelensi hoc nomine non amplius esse notum, sed tempore mutatum fuisse in Krusjna-Patanum, seu Kisjna-Patan, ita ut primi nominis memoria inter Europeos tantum conservetur.'

"The town of Kistnapatam, referred to in this paragraph is in the Nellore district of the Madras Presidency. It is now a village, situated at 14° 17′ north latitude, 82 miles north of Madras; it has a fine backwater of great depth, and is a shelter for native craft during the monsoon. In an old glossary it is said to be the Greek Sopatma, and 'title otherwise Calitore.' In a map accompanying 'A True and Exact description of the most celebrated East India Coasts of Malabar and Coromandel' (1672), by Philip Baldeus, Callerture is shown between Armagon and Penne (Penner river). In a map of the 'Peninsola deli India' (dated 1683), by Giacomo Cantelii da Vignola, a Portuguese, the town is indicated as 'Caletur.' It is evident that while the town was known to foreigners as Calitore or Caletur, it was not recognised by that name by the British factors . . .

"The earliest English factory was planted in 1625 at Masulipatam, where trade was carried on with varying fortune for several years. In 1628 the agent, pressed by the Dutch rivalry, migrated southwards to Armegam. In 1639 Armegam in its turn gave way to Fort St. George, Madras, which in 1653 was raised to the rank of an independent presidency. Between this young growing factory and the Court of the Honorable East India Company there was considerable correspondence, and interesting extracts are made in the Diary and Consultation Book of the Agent and Governor. In their despatch dated February 8, 1681, the Court wrote as follows :—

'And we do further order that you make the like provision of 300 tons redwood for our next year's shipping. The Dutch called this redwood by the name of Calliature wood, and we do p̄ the Nathaniell and Williamson send a pattern thereof which came from India. We are informed that it costs about 2½ Pag° p̄ candy, they are usually in pieces of about 3 yards long but you may have it sawed into pieces of about 2 feet more or less as the Commanders shall desire for conveniency, it being to be ground to powder here and used in dyeing.'

"Contracts for the supply of the wood were negotiated by the Governor, and the question of advances was settled with merchants. In September 1682, the following entry in the Diary occurs:—'The Calliature or Redwood merchants having made a contract with ye Agent, etc., for-candy of redwood, declared that without they might have half the money before hand they could not comply with their contract w[ch] upon their promise of giving security was granted them.'

"Redwood was frequently used as ballast in homegoing ships. A specific case is recorded in the Diary for 1682:—'Captain Willshaw of the Resolution complained that he would not be able to ride out ye storm without sufficient Quintelage (ballast) therefor ordered that the warehousekeeper doe lade on board him 100: Tonns saltpetre and what Calliature wood can be got to stiffen his ship and inable him the better to ride out ye storm.' . . .

"In 1685 as much as 1,337 pagodas were paid to the local redwood merchants in 7 instalments during the year. Calculating the pagoda at 9*s*., this amounts to £605. This, however, indicates only a portion of the trade for the year.

"Reference to 'The Private Diary of Ānanda Ranga Pillai from 1736 to 1761' proves that the trade in red sanders wood was still brisk. In 1753 the ship 'Fleury' sailed for France with 1,000 candies (candy = 500 lbs.) and the 'Phenix' with 2,000 candies of redwood. It might be mentioned that the 'James and Mary,' that gave its name to the dreaded sandbank in the Hughly, and was wrecked on September 24, 1694, carried a cargo of redwood taken up at Madras.

"In the 'Letters received by the East India Company from its Servant in the East, 1602–1617,' there are numerous references to the various kinds of sanders wood, but they are easily distinguished The red sanderswood always came from the Madras coast, and was sent to Europe for dyeing purposes. . . ."

Further particulars about the red sanders are given by the District Forest Officer[1] as follows: "It flowers from April to June, seeding the following February and March. The seedlings die off annually during the hot weather, while the root system increases until the shoots are large and strong enough to resist the heat of the sun and at times also fire. It prefers the eastern aspect of stony hills and is to be found at altitudes between 900 and 2,000 feet. It forms the greater percentage of the growing stock on the lower slopes, where it is in places

[1] Mr. T. A. Whitehead, who has furnished all the material for this chapter. Other quotations in this chapter, when no authority is mentioned, are from Mr. Whitehead's note.

CHAP. V. CHARACTER OF THE FORESTS.

found pure. As the altitude increases the percentage of red sanders decreases, but the quality improves: The largest and best trees are to be found in the upper limit of the red sanders zone." Owing to its valuable properties and the fact that it received no protection in the past, the drain upon the forests of the district "has," says the District Forest Officer "been enormous and has continued until quite recent times. Gamble in his 'Manual of Indian Timbers' records: 'In the five years ending with 1882–83, 12,782 tons were exported to the United Kingdom, 1,116 tons to France, and 1,687 tons to other Indian and Ceylon ports, the whole valued at five and a half lakhs of rupees.' Not only the stems and branches but also the roots were extracted, and it is to be wondered at that the tree has survived total extermination. The unmerciful treatment meted out to it in the past is apparent from the present degenerated state of the forest. A mature red sanders tree is difficult to find, a large proportion of the growth is in a pole stage and a great many trees have been mutilated by fire and man. It, however, reproduces itself vigorously in coppice, by suckers and from seed, and to this innate vigour it owes its existence. A local tradition maintains that a red sanders tree, after attaining a girth of 40 inches becomes rotten at the heart. This no doubt is at present true, but it is not due to old age and over-maturity as is generally supposed. It is, I believe, entirely due to injuries received during the period of its life, resulting from repeated scorching. There are two or three trees in the Kōdūr red sanders plantation which are now over 50 inches in girth and which are still quite sound. No fire has occurred in this plantation since its formation in 1865. Another tradition maintains that there are two distinct varieties of red sanders trees. One variety which has a comparatively smooth bark and a light heart-wood is known as the 'female,' the other with the rougher bark and darker heart-wood as the 'male.' Botanically there is no difference, and the variety is not due to a difference in the quality of the soil since the two kinds are found mixed. The contention that the smooth-barked tree generally has a lighter coloured heart-wood appears to be true. The scientific explanation is still to be discovered.

"A seedling commences to form heart-wood at the age of about 18 years or when it has attained a girth of 6 to 9 inches at breast height, while a coppice shoot shows signs of forming heart-wood at the age of 15 years or when it has attained a girth of 9 to 15 inches. Pseudo-heart-wood or a premature deposit of the red colouring principle 'santalin' is found around natural wounds and artificial injuries. A red sanders tree of 70 to 80 years of age, which as a rule averages 4 feet in girth at breast height, may be said to have attained an exploitable age or, in other words, an age at which it is capable of yielding a 'special' post."

CHAP. V. CHARACTER OF THE FORESTS.

Summary.

The general character of the growth on the five main blocks in the district may accordingly be summarised as follows:— First come "the fuel forests along the foot of the hills. These are as a rule overgrazed and degraded. Along the outer boundaries the growth often consists chiefly of thorns which gradually disappear and give place to more valuable growth as we penetrate deeper in towards the hills. The species found in the fuel forests are:—Hardwickia binata, Anogeissus latifolia, Albizzia odoratissima and lebbek, Eleodendron glaucum, Buchanania latifolia, Sapindus emarginatus, Canthium didymum, Mimusops hexandra and elengi, Terminalia chebula and tomentosa, Pterospermum suberifolium, Odina wodier, Atlantia monophylla, Albizzia amara, Memecylon angustifolium, Adina cordifolia, Cassia fistula, Gardenia turgida, Gardenia gummifera, Vitex pubescens, Strychnos nux-vomica, Diospyros chloroxylon, Butea frondosa, Ixora parviflora, Shorea tumbuggaia, Gelonium lanceolatum, Hemicyclia sepiaria and Maba buxifolia."

Next, at a greater elevation, occurs the red sanders forest, to which allusion has already been made. "Important timber trees with which the red sanders is generally found mixed in various proportions are, in the lower elevations, Anogeissus latifolia and, at a higher altitude, Terminalia tomentosa, Chloroxylon swietenia, Buchanania latifolia, Diospyros ebenum, Shorea tumbuggaia and talura and Anogeissus latifolia. The red sanders belt is irregularly cut up by the evergreen growth along stream beds. In parts within its zone it entirely disappears, Anogeissus latifolia being as a rule found in its place.

"Finally, above the red sanders belt the predominating species is Eugenia alternifolia, which is found pure in large patches especially on the plateaux. It is associated with Terminalia tomentosa, Anogeissus latifolia and Chloroxylon swietenia in the lower elevations and with Terminalia pallida and chebula and Shorea tumbuggaia and talura in the higher elevations. The ridges above the plateaux mostly support Shorea tumbuggaia, with Eugenia alternifolia and Gardenias as auxiliaries and wild date and cycads as under-growth.

"This may be said to be more or less true of all the five large blocks, but the three distinct belts as described above

CHAP. V. CHARACTER OF THE FORESTS.

are most marked in the Sēshāchalam, Pālkonda and Lankāmalai hills. In the Veligonda and Nallamalai hills the red sanders is not nearly so common. In the northern portion of the Veligonda range, *i.e.*, in the Badvēl taluk, the fuel forests at the foot of the hills sometimes give place to a very fine pure Hardwickia binata forest as well as a mixed forest of Anogeissus latifolia and Hardwickia binata."

CONSERVANCY. Prior to the Madras Forest Act of 1882.

Conservancy operations were first begun in 1860 and were chiefly confined to the south-east portion of the district. From a report[1] dated January 25, 1877, submitted by Colonel Beddome, Conservator of Forests, much may be gleaned of the results obtained up to that time and of the previous history of the plantations and fuel reserves controlled by the department. The following are extracts from the report:—

"*Plantations.*—These are five in number, viz., the red sanders plantation at Kōdūr and the four fuel plantations at Upparapalle, Pullampet, Reddipalle and Kamalāpuram.

"*The Red sanders plantation.*—This is close to the railway line near the Kōdūr station; the extent is 50 acres, surrounded by a ditch and aloe fence; over an area of about 20 acres there are some twelve or fifteen thousand red sanders trees growing very straight and well. . . . The largest tree now measures 41 feet 2 inches in height and has a girth of 27½ inches, but many others are nearly as large. . . . The rest of the area does not seem adapted for the growth of red sanders, as the tree has failed when it has been tried, but almost the whole of this has been planted up with various other trees. . . . The plantation was commenced in 1865; the expenditure up to date has been Rs. 5,839; receipts nil; the expenditure is now limited to Rs. 8 per mensem, the pay of one gardener. . . . . .

* * * * *

"*The Pullampet fuel plantation.*—Close to the railway line, 4½ miles from Rājampet railway station. This is an area of 402 acres; . . . . Nurseries commenced in 1871, planting out in 1872; it was intended as a mixed fuel plantation. . . . . As far as it has gone this plantation is a failure, and the planting of the vāghi, nim, bābul and other trees, hitherto attempted at great expense in trenches and pits, will never pay.

"*Reddipalle fuel plantation.*—Commenced in 1869-70; 924 acres fenced in. . . . The Bābul has utterly failed. The other trees have grown fairly in some instances, but are not likely to pay as fuel. . . .

[1] Contained in G.O. No. 1974, Revenue, dated 13th June 1877.

CHAP. V. CONSERVANCY.

" *Fuel reserves.*—There are seven in number . . . . all situate along the north-west line of railway between Tirupati and Nandalūr. . . . .

" *Bālapalle No. 1 reserve.*—Area about 2,000 acres . . . . taken up and fenced round in 1867, since which the growth has rapidly improved. . . . The value of timber on the reserve at the seigniorage rate is about Rs. 70,000."

The other fuel reserves mentioned by Colonel Beddome are Bālapalle No. 2 (1871), Vāgatikōna (1874), Kōdūr (1871), Thunakonda (1874), Yerraguntakōta (1873) and Gāthala (1874).

In their order on this report the Government observe that the condition of the fuel reserves is more satisfactory than that of the plantations.

From what has already been said of the red sanders tree and its past history it may readily be inferred that the forests of Cuddapah district received but little protection prior to the passing of the Madras Forest Act of 1882, and that operations were mainly directed towards the realization of revenue. It should, however, be remembered that the establishment at the disposal of the department during these years was so small and the areas under its control so extensive that no scientific forest work could be attempted with any hope of attaining many successful results.

Subsequent operations.

From 1882 to 1901, some improvement took place, but timber, fuel and minor forest produce was still extracted by contractors for the department. This, of course, was detrimental to the forests since little supervision could be exercised by the department over the contractors. They were permitted to work over extensive areas and helped themselves to the plums. With one exception, the mistake to attempt to deal with large extents of forest was again made, the Act of 1882 was not vigorously enforced and the deterioration of the forest continued. The one exception is to be found near Balapalle in the forests to the east and west of the railway line. Here an attempt to work the area systematically for fuel was made with gratifying results. A working circle was selected in the forests on either side of the line in about the year 1880. The two working circles are known as Balapalle East and West. They were each divided into thirty coupes and one coupe in each working circle was worked annually. The fuel extracted was sold to the Railway Company. The first rotation in both the working circles has been completed and five years ago the second rotation was begun. The coupes are being worked under the 'coppice with standards' system. Thirty standards per acre are selected and marked

CHAP. V. CONSERVANCY.

departmentally. The annual coupe (50 acres to 150 acres) is then put up to auction. The actual felling and extraction of the fuel and such small timber as is available, is done by contractors under departmental supervision. The success of operations in the past is evident from the fact that at the present day (*i.e.*, in the second rotation) an average of Rs. 12 to Rs. 18 is obtained per acre for coupes which were originally felled some thirty years ago. There is little doubt that these working circles will afford a perpetual fuel supply in future.

"There are one or two small plantations in the Pullampet valley which were planted with red sanders in 1865. The most important and most successful of these is the Kōdūr Red sanders plantation. The trees here are now 48 years of age and have long since attained their full height growth. The largest tree in the plantation measures 4 feet 4 inches in girth at breast height and is about 60 feet high. This is probably the largest red sanders tree in existence. Some useful work was also done in the North division in planting palmyra on the banks of the Pennēr, Pāpaghni and other rivers. The most successful of these is the Idupulapāya palmyra plantation which in the near future will become invaluable in the supply of building timber to this part of the district where it is so badly needed.

RECENT WORKING PLANS.

"In 1908 the following batch of working plans for the supply of fuel was sanctioned:—

Fuel.

Fuel Working Circles.

East Cuddapah : Bālapalle (East and West series), Kōdūr (East and West series), Rājampet, Pullampet, Badvēl (East and West series), Lankāmalais, Pōrumōmilla (North and South series), Sancherla, Nandalūr Vontimitta, Pālkonda Bullmen, Lankāmalai Bullmen, Sidhout and Kanamalōpalle.

North Cuddapah : Pālkonda (Maddimadugu East and West and Māmillapalle series), Lankāmalais[1] (Bainapalle and Pattur) and Nallamalais[1] (Dāsari palle North, East, South and West).

"The 'coppice with standards' system for these fuel working circles has been prescribed. The coupes were originally worked departmentally, but in 1912 the work of felling, extraction and disposal of the produce was handed over to contractors. The demarcation of the coupes and the selection and marking of standards still remain in the hands

[1] Also timber working series.

CHAP. V.

RECENT WORKING PLANS.

Timber.

of the department. The department also supervises the work of the contractors.

"In 1909 a timber working plan for the Sēshāchalam hills in the East division was sanctioned. An attempt to work it was made until 1912. It was then proved to be unworkable owing to the impossibility of carrying out its prescriptions with the inadequate staff sanctioned. In addition to the timber fellings conducted under this working plan unregulated timber fellings were carried out in the Veligondas, Pālkonda, Lankāmalai and Nallamalai hills. Owing to the weakness of the establishment, inadequate supervision and the excessive extents of the coupes the work was not evenly distributed over the whole area. The fellings degenerated into the extraction of only the best trees from the most promising and accessible localities. Such inadequately controlled work would soon ruin any forest. The fellings were put a stop to in the years 1912 and 1913.

WORK IN PROGRESS.

Fuel operations.

"Operations for the supply of fuel are chiefly confined to the terai forests. With but one or two exceptions all the fuel working circles in both divisions are doing well and the working plans at present require no revision. The 'coppice with standards' system continues to be in force.

Timber operations.

"Timber compartments were without exception worked under the "selection" system in the past. The failure of this system which provides for the removal of a number of trees of each age class every year, was due not so much to the fact that it was inapplicable to this class of forest but chiefly to the fact that the prescriptions of the working plans were never conscientiously enforced. The areas allotted for annual treatment were far too large (1,500 to 6,500 acres) for the executive establishment to deal with, or for the controlling staff to supervise. The result might perhaps have been foreseen. Each compartment had been estimated to yield a certain quantity of material. The quantity was extracted, but from only a very small portion of the compartment; this means that the small portion from which the material had been extracted was hopelessly overworked while the greater portion remained untouched. It was impossible for a responsible officer, in addition to his other duties, to adequately check and supervise the work in these enormous timber compartments. They were often mismanaged or entirely neglected by the irresponsible executive staff who knew that their neglect or dishonesty would probably not be brought to light. Even had the areas been satisfactorily worked a rigid protection of them after treatment would have been impracticable. In the

CHAP. V. WORK IN PROGRESS.

East division these compartments were worked departmentally but in the North division the further error was committed in the last year or two of handing them over with but little restriction to contractors. In 1912 unregulated timber extraction in the East division was stopped. In 1913 the old system in tracts both under sanctioned and unregulated working was put a stop to throughout the district and a new system was introduced. Under the new system the realization of revenue by the extraction and sale of timber-yielding trees is not the main consideration. It provides for the improvement and subsequent rigid protection of areas sufficiently small to ensure detailed work and thorough supervision. The system was primarily devised to encourage the growth and to protect the existing stock of sound red sanders trees, and work is therefore confined within the limits of the red sanders belt or zone. Under this system the area of the annual coupe in each working circle is at present limited to about 100 acres, and with the object of producing mature red sanders timber the rotation has been fixed at seventy or eighty years, so that each working circle will include a block of red sanders forest of 7,000 acres to 8,000 acres. It is necessary to retain and protect all the best and soundest trees which are at present in a young pole stage, and to cut back, for the purpose of obtaining a re-growth of healthy coppice shoots, all trees which have been pollarded, injured or damaged in such a way as to be crippled for the production of sound and valuable timber. The trees selected for retention are marked by departmental agency. Each tree so marked is entered in a register with its girth measurement. The coupe is then sold in auction and a contractor removes, under detailed departmental supervision, the inferior growth which has not been marked for retention. While the coupe is being felled over by the contractor a stone wall 3½ feet in height is erected by departmental agency around the coupe so that when the work of felling and extraction has been completed, the ring wall is also completed. By this means the sound trees left standing and the re-growth within the coupe will be protected from cattle and fire and it is hoped will also arouse the better feelings in man. Three working circles in the East division and some half dozen in the North have been roughly located and the first coupes demarcated on the ground. Work has already commenced in the East division and in two cases is in full swing in the first coupe. As this system is being introduced in the red sanders areas throughout the whole district no sound timber will, except illicitly, be extracted from

CHAP. V. WORK IN PROGRESS.

the Cuddapah forests for some years to come. It has already been pointed out that this course is absolutely necessary on account of the present degenerated state of the forests.

Sandal-sowing.

"Sandal is being introduced into the plateau forests at an elevation of 2,500 feet and above. Small areas are sown and then demarcated with narrow lines and coupe stones.

"It will thus be seen that the three classes of forest mentioned above, *i.e.*, the terai fuel forests, the red sanders belt and the plateau forests are being worked for the production of fuel, timber and sandal respectively.

Minor forest produce.

"As hitherto, the right to collect minor forest produce and bamboos from certain blocks of forest is usually auctioned, and the free removal of grass is permitted except when it has a market value, in which case the right to remove it is leased by Government.

Grazing and goat-browsing.

"Grazing on permit is allowed in all reserves except in plantations and worked areas. The rates at which permits are issued per head per annum are given in the margin."

	RS.
Sheep	1½
Cow, bull, ass, etc. ...	3
Buffalo	6

Grazing has hitherto been permitted in the valuable hill forests of the district, and the cattle have been penned in long established "pentas" or cattle kraals, which are situated in the heart of the forests. A large proportion of these cattle come from Nellore, but the valuable stock of that district is not sent over, and the animals that are grazed are usually of a very inferior class. Considerable damage has been done to the forests by these annual incursions of cattle, for not only have the red sanders and all other valuable timber disappeared from the sites of the "pentas" but the forest in the vicinity has suffered from theft, mutilation and fire caused by the graziers. Under these circumstances the hill forests of Cuddapah are being gradually closed to grazing and the cattle that resort to them are being provided for elsewhere. Goat-browsing was hitherto permitted in certain selected reserves. An attempt has recently been made gradually to exclude the goat from all reserves, and Government sanction has been obtained to close permanently the few blocks that still remain open to the goat from 1st July 1914.

Forest offences.

"Theft of timber and fuel and offences of illicit goat-browsing have made the proper protection of the reserves extremely difficult. Settigunta is the home of the doll-makers. These dolls are made out of red sanders timber and the forests in this locality have suffered and are still suffering from the raids made upon them by these people. The so-called

CHAP. V. WORK IN PROGRESS.

"Bullman," a low caste Muhammadan timber thief, who makes use of his bull for the extraction of illicitly felled timber and fuel, has been very troublesome in the past. His sphere of operations has been confined to the Pālkonda and Lankāmalai hills. It was chiefly to keep him out of mischief and to afford him a chance of obtaining an honest livelihood that the Pālkonda and Lankāmalai Bullmen fuel working plans were introduced. He was employed by the department to extract the fuel felled departmentally on the hill slopes, and is now being employed by the contractors who are working the coupes under departmental supervision. Every village along the foot of the Nallamalai hills can boast of gangs or portions of gangs of men that have for a great many years earned a livelihood by the sale of stolen timber. Vanipenta harbours a crowd of brass-workers. These men required first-class charcoal with which to feed their furnaces and have for many years helped themselves to red sanders and Hardwickia binata fuel from the adjoining reserves to satisfy their demands.

"Though determined attempts have been made in the past to put a stop to the destruction of reserves, results so far show that still more thorough steps must be taken for the protection of the forests against timber theft. With this view the Government have recently sanctioned the introduction of a revised set of timber transit rules. They are considerably stricter than the old rules, but no honest man need fear them. The existence of a large number of shrotriem forests wedged into the large blocks of Government reserves had made protection of the latter extremely difficult in the past. It is hoped that the present rules, if properly and fairly enforced, will largely mitigate this evil.

Fire-protection.

"A new work of fire lines over the more important blocks is, as elsewhere, the system of protection adopted. So long as grazing is permitted within the reserves and especially within large blocks of hill forest absolute and permanent protection against fire cannot be expected. This is an additional argument for the exclusion of foreign cattle.

Stream-bunding.

"The upper affluents of the more important forest streams are being bunded with small dams from their sources downwards in order to hold up the water for a greater number of days after heavy rainfall and to prevent torrents and rapid erosion.

Cart-tracks and bridle-paths.

"A network of cart-tracks and bridle-paths is being constructed in the large Sēshāchalam, Pālkonda, Lankāmalai and Nallamalai blocks in order to open up the forests and facilitate work under the new system described above under 'Timber operations.' All bridle-paths are being aligned at a gradient not steeper than 1 in 20 so as to facilitate their conversion into cart-tracks when necessity arises.

Demarcation.

"A permanent form of demarcation for reserves was commenced in 1913 and will be continued until all reserves have been completely and accurately demarcated. The particular form adopted is:—Planting numbered stone pillars at all turns, building a cairn around each pillar and placing a row of large stones from cairn to cairn along the outer edge of the cleared 12 feet boundary line. In cases where the reserve line at present in existence was wrongly cut, the errors are being rectified as the permanent demarcation proceeds. It will take many years to complete the work.

Planting and sowing.

"With the exception of the sowing of sandal seed in a few selected areas in the plateau forests no sowing or planting is being done. It is considered more important to protect and revive the forest at present in existence than to attempt to create more forest when that which exists is not yet adequately controlled."

CHAPTER VI.

OCCUPATION AND TRADE.

AGRICULTURE. ARTS AND INDUSTRIES—Textile—Condition of weavers—Cotton-weaving—Silk-weaving—Blankets and rugs—Cotton printing and dyeing—Shoe-making—Wood—Metal—Stone—Other occupations. FACTORIES. TRADE—Exports and imports. WEIGHTS AND MEASURES—Table of weights—Grain measures—Liquid measures—Lineal measures--Measures of time.

CHAP. VI. AGRICULTURE.

WHILE agricultural and pastoral pursuits constitute the livelihood of about five-sevenths of the population of Cuddapah district, there still remains an appreciable proportion which may be termed partially agriculturist. Under this head must be included the village artizans who customarily hold land on favourable tenure in consideration of their services to the community. The last census returns also show that of those engaged in the textile industry some 9 per cent. representing probably the Māla community who are agricultural labourers as well as weavers of coarse cloths, rely partly on agriculture for their living. In a wider sense the welfare of nearly the entire population is dependent upon agriculture, for the industries mainly followed in the district deal with the products of the earth in their natural state, obtained locally. The market for the finished article is also no less restricted. The effect of a bad season on the industrial worker is therefore twofold, in that it raises the price of raw material and reduces the purchasing power of the agriculturists, who are his principal customers.

ARTS AND INDUSTRIES. Textile.

Excluding agriculture, weaving provides employment to a larger proportion of the population of the district than any other industry. The castes of weavers who carry on their hereditary occupation in this district are the Togatas, Sāles and Dēvāngas, in the order of their numerical importance. Many Muhammadans are also engaged in this industry and, as already mentioned, Mālas are employed, especially in the black cotton country, in the weaving of coarse fabrics. The industry is carried on entirely with hand-looms. In the year 1900 there were only three districts in the Presidency containing a larger number of hand-looms than Cuddapah, in which there were 11,500. The area of the district has been largely reduced since then, but it is not thought probable that there has been much change in the number of hand-looms in the whole Presidency since that date.

Condition of weavers.

Though it is often assumed that the condition of the hand-loom weavers has steadily deteriorated owing to the effect of competition, the conclusion drawn from certain facts and figures recorded at the last census is that on the whole the industry is holding its own, and that the general increase in prosperity is leading to an increased demand for its finer products. The weavers have on the whole responded to the stress of competition and work harder nowadays, turning out a larger amount of finished goods than was formerly the case. The cleverest weavers are to be found in Pullampet taluk, and their high class products command very good prices. It is here that the use of the fly-shuttle slay has principally developed, by which the output of each loom is said to be increased on the average by not less than 50 per cent. On the other hand less skilful workers in the backward parts of the district have failed to hold their own, as the demand for their coarse goods has steadily decreased with the raising of the standard of comfort. With this contraction of the market and the general increase in the cost of living it is doubtful whether a family that depended entirely on the weaving of coarse country cloths could maintain itself in these days: in fact, they invariably supplement their earnings by other labour.

Cotton weaving.

Formerly in the black cotton country every process from the picking of the cotton to the manufacture of his dress was carried out under the eye of the Kāpu himself, with the possible exception of its cleaning by the Dūdēkula caste of professional cotton-cleaners. The ginning, on which his womenfolk were employed, was performed by propelling stone rollers over the cotton up and down the verandah of his house. He would also spin the yarn at home and supply it to the weavers to make up into such cloths as he and his family required. Nowadays very little yarn is homespun and if the ryot still patronises home-made stuffs he buys his yarn in the bazaars of the bigger villages and towns which get their supply from the spinning mills in Madras and elsewhere. Meanwhile the cotton that he grows finds a ready market in the ginning and pressing factories of Tādpatri and Proddatūr. It is the country cloths worn by the women of the black cotton country that are now mostly manufactured by the Mālas. They are sometimes coloured, but generally white with red or black borders. The thread for these cloths is

CHAP. VI. ARTS AND INDUSTRIES.

bought ready dyed. In other parts of the district softer fabrics are worn, and these are woven by the Togatas and Sāles, who use the best imported yarn. The Dēvāngas are numerically unimportant. These weaving castes are found throughout the district but are most numerous in Proddatūr and Pullampet taluks. Red is the prevailing colour of the *sāris* and *ravikas* which they make, and they occasionally dye the thread themselves. They also weave good white turbans and white or coloured upper cloths for men, for the latter of which a common pattern is red chequered with narrow white lines. Whether white or coloured, the ends of the cloths are often embroidered with gold or silver thread. Some of the best embroidery of this kind is done at Pullampet.

Silk-weaving.

The best silk-weaving in the district is done at Mādhavaram in Sidhout taluk, a village near the confluence of the Cheyyēr and Pennēr rivers, and at Uppalūr in the taluk of Kamalāpuram. The weavers of the latter village are Togatas, and some account of their work is given below in the gazetteer. The inhabitants of Mādhavaram number less than two thousand, and seventy-five per cent. of them are Padma Sāles. They make coloured *sāris* of silk, the colours, usually red and black, being in alternate squares, and silk upper cloths for men, which if not white are coloured pink, pale blue or red, the weavers usually dyeing the thread themselves. These are generally more richly embroidered than the cotton variety. The best silk cloths cost between Rs. 100 and 150. These weavers also make *sāris* and *ravikas* of mixed silk and cotton, which, from the origin of the pattern, are known as Kornād cloths. A *sāri* of this kind costs about Rs. 15 and is of the same colour and design as the silk, but the squares are smaller. The weavers of Mādhavaram are, as elsewhere, largely in the hands of capitalists who advance them money or grain and supply them with the materials of their industry, paying them piece-work wages for the cloths they turn out. One of these merchants, who has from time to time exhibited samples of the excellent workmanship of the Mādhavaram weavers, obtained a silver and a bronze medal at the Industrial and Arts Exhibition in Madras in 1903 for embroidery and two silver medals from the Industrial and Arts Exhibition of Mysore in 1911 for silk work.

Blankets and rugs.

Rough blankets which are made from the wool of the small black and white sheep found in Rāyachōti taluk are woven by Kurubas. This breed of sheep is much commoner in the higher altitudes of the plateau, and the industry employs very few people in this district, where the blankets woven are only sufficient for local requirements. In Pulivendla taluk the same shepherd caste of Kurubas make coarse hair rugs from the fleeces of the other kinds of sheep. These rugs, which the Kurubas dye red, are brought in large quantities from Pārnapalle and other places in the west of the taluk to the weekly fair at Pulivendla.

Cotton printing and dyeing.

White cloths intended for *sāris* or children's skirts are sometimes printed in black or red colours by hand by the Marathi caste of Rangarāzus or Rangaris. The printing is effected by stamping the cloth with wooden blocks engraved with various floral designs. *Sāris* of this kind are dyed red or black to a length of about two feet at each end. The Rangaris are said to be skilful dyers, and the colours do not easily fade.

Shoe-making.

Recent statistics show that "Industries of dress and the toilet" afford employment to nearly as many persons in the district as do weaving and its allied occupations. Under this comprehensive head are included barbers and washermen, cleaners and dyers, who in the aggregate number more than half of the total, but these are not of exceptional numerical importance in proportion to the population of the district. On the other hand the number of those engaged in the making of shoes, boots and sandals shows that this is one of the more important industries of the district. It is chiefly carried on by Muhammadans, and the largest number of workers are found at Badvēl and Cuddapah. There are only two districts in the Presidency, namely, Guntur and Nellore, where the proportion of shoe-makers to the total population is so high. From the large development of the industry at Badvēl it seems probable that it was to a great extent introduced from Nellore.

Wood.

Under the major head of "workers in wood" the latest census tables include basket-makers, of whom we find the proportion in Cuddapah district exceeds that for the Presidency and most other districts. The followers of this industry are mostly to be found in villages adjoining the forests at the foot of the Sēshāchalams in Pullampet and Rāyachōti taluks and also include Yerukulas and other wandering tribes. Fewer in number but of more importance are the carpenters, joiners and turners who utilize the abundant material afforded by the forests of the district for making agricultural implements, cabinets and the different kinds of household furniture for which there is a steadily increasing demand. At Settigunta, in the south of Pullampet taluk, there are some clever wood carvers who specialize in the mythological figures, generally

CHAP. VI. ARTS AND INDUSTRIES.

made of redwood, which are sold as votive emblems to pilgrims who visit the sacred hill of Tirupati.

Metal.

At Vanipenta in Proddatūr taluk, at the foot of the Nallamalais, workers in brass, copper and bell-metal have attained considerable reputation. The industry, if not confined to this village, is at any rate very highly localized. The workers are of various castes and include a large number of Musalmāns. They make cattle-bells, rings, copper pots, drinking vessels of copper and brass and various household utensils. As in the case of the weavers of Mādhavaram, this industry is financed by capitalists who supply the workers with metal and give them advances, paying them for their labour. It is said that the industry has suffered of late years by competition with vessels of foreign make and materials such as aluminium and german silver. Formerly these metal-workers consistently drew on the neighbouring reserved forests for the means of making the charcoal which their process of manufacture renders necessary in large quantities, and it is possible that the improved protection of the forests has added to their difficulties.

Stone.

The stone-carving of many modern temples in the district has been carried out by some expert sculptors who call themselves *Silpis*, but are locally known as the Gumpramānu-dinne people, from the name of their village in the Sirvel taluk of Kurnool district. A Muhammadan of Peddamudiyam in Jammalamadugu taluk acquired the art of stone-carving from these people and transmitted the knowledge to his son. With this solitary exception Cuddapah district does not appear to contain any professional stone-carvers, though in several places Balijas and Muhammadans can carve ordinary rough figures on stone. Workers in stone claim our notice rather on account of the large number of unskilled labourers who obtain employment by quarrying the famous Cuddapah slabs. These are obtained from the sub-crystalline limestone of the Cuddapah rocks and are so excellently adapted for building purposes that they are exported to various parts of the Presidency. The best kind is described as a regular-bedded, compact, dark-grey, semi-splintery rock, which, being well jointed at right angles to the bedding, is easily obtainable in blocks and thin slabs. The colour is so dark at times as to give almost a black marble when the stone is polished. As the group in which this limestone occurs underlies the 'great Cuddapah plain' and crops up to the surface on either side of it, it follows that good varieties can be obtained anywhere along the base of the Nallamalais, as also to the westward of a sinuous line drawn from Chintakommadinne, some five miles south of Cuddapah, through Kamalāpuram and Proddatūr to Peddapasupula, a few miles north-east of Jammalamadugu. The best quarries are therefore very favourably situated for transport by rail. The largest quantity of slabs are entrained at Yerraguntla station.

Other occupations.

Other industries, which account for small numbers of the population, present no exceptional features and are in no way peculiar to the district. 'Labourers and workmen otherwise unclassified' represented at the last census about 15 per mille of the total inhabitants. To the rest, of whom thousands are petty shopkeepers, occupation is mainly provided by trade.

FACTORIES.

The district of Cuddapah has not been unaffected by the industrial tendency exhibited since the beginning of the century in the direction of the supersession of hand labourby power-driven machinery. Using the term 'factory' to signify every installation of such machinery, the figures in the margin show the number of factories in the district as at the last census and at the present time. Excluding the application of motive power to the raising of water for irrigation, which is largely encouraged by Government, the growth in the factory movement during the last few years appears remarkable in what must be regarded as a conservative district. The recent boom in groundnut cultivation is responsible for the establishment of nine husking mills in the taluks of Jammalamadugu, Kamalāpuram and Cuddapah. Cotton is both ginned and pressed by motive power at Proddatūr, and there are now also five gins in Jammalamadugu and two in Pulivendla. The weaving factory at Cuddapah is temporarily closed pending the construction of new buildings.

	1911	July 1914.
Weaving factory	1	1
Municipal water-works	1	1
Cotton pressing or ginning factories	6	11
Saffron works	1	1
Irrigation	6	...[1]
Groundnut factories	...	9

The saffron factory at Cuddapah deserves special notice as it appears to be the only one in the Presidency.[2] The machine used is 'Carter's Disintegrator' and is fitted with two sets of plates which enable the operator to grind the powder coarse or fine as may be required.

TRADE.

As the manufactures of the district are few and for the most part satisfy local requirements, trade assumes but little

[1] Number not reported.

[2] See Census Report, 1911, Chapter XII, Appendix II.

CHAP. VI. TRADE.

importance and merely consists of the collection of the various products which it exports and the distribution of its imports. As in other districts, there are one or two recognized centres at which this collection and distribution are mainly carried on. The principal trade centre in the district is, without doubt, Proddatūr, though some eight miles distant from Yerraguntla, the nearest railway station. Cuddapah comes next, after which we must probably rank Rājampet, which is situated in the busiest part of the eastern division of the district and is easily accessible from Madras, the port from which are conveyed such of the products of the district as find their way to other countries.[1] Business is also brisk in Badvēl and Pulivendla, the former providing a link with the coastal district of Nellore and the latter attracting by means of its weekly market much of the merchandise of Rāyachōti taluk and the Kadiri taluk of Anantapur district. It is through such weekly markets, established at most villages of importance throughout the district, that egress is afforded to the industrial output of less accessible places. The big traders of the district are Kōmatis, the principal caste of hereditary merchants in the Telugu country. Much of the retail trade is also in their hands. Excluding these, the Muhammadan community probably contains a larger proportion of shopkeepers than any others. Numbers of Hindus of various castes are also engaged in retail trade.

Exports.

The principal export of the district is raw cotton, most of which, to the aggregate value of about 10 lakhs a year, is dealt with by two large firms in Proddatūr. Tādpatri, in Anantapur district, is, however, nearer to the south-western villages of Jammalamadugu taluk, the ryots of which, dispensing with middlemen, often put up their cotton in bags and cart it to the Tādpatri mills themselves. It is said that about twice as much cotton finds its way from Proddatūr to Madras—mainly for export to Europe—than to other parts of India. After cotton the chief exports appear to be food-grains, Cuddapah slabs, minor forest produce, indigo, turmeric and, in recent years, groundnuts. The food-grains mostly consist of cholam and ragi. Cuddapah slabs, which have already been referred to, are exported to all parts of the Presidency. Of minor forest produce the toothsome nut known as *sārapappu* is obtained in large quantities from the Pālkonda hills and is exported to Madras and elsewhere both by way of Cuddapah and Rājampet. The trade in indigo, as is well known, has fallen

[1] A very limited quantity is also exported from Pondicherry.

CHAP. VI. TRADE.

on evil times, but it is still exported to Madras and Rangoon and parts of the Central Provinces and Bombay Presidency. Turmeric which is largely grown in parts of Proddatūr, Cuddapah and Pullampet taluks, also has a wide market, including such distant places as Bombay, Delhi and Amritsar. Groundnuts are generally sent to Tiruttani, Madras or Pondicherry. Other local products that deserve mention are the melons grown in the bed of the Pennēr river, especially at Sidhout, the silk goods of Mādhavaram and the oranges of Vēlpula in Pulivendla taluk. The latter are not exported in very large quantities, but the melons of Sidhout are famous and bring a large profit to their growers. It is said that some 15,000 melons can be raised on an acre of river sand, with but three manurings. They are exported to Hyderabad, Bombay, Calcutta, Madras and even to Tanjore. The silk cloths of Mādhavaram are chiefly sent to neighbouring districts, but also find their way to Raichūr and the Nizam's Dominions.

Imports.

In exchange for these products the district mostly obtains such household requisites as salt and kerosine-oil, and, in lesser quantities, sugar, spices and rice, the latter principally from Nellore: whence also come the agricultural cattle used in the black cotton country. European piece-goods and yarn are largely imported. Finally there is a growing demand for coffee and wheat owing to the recent popular habit of taking coffee and wheat cakes as morning refreshment. The increased consumption of wheat is also partly due to the supposed injurious effects of a rice diet on people who are predisposed to diabetes.

WEIGHTS AND MEASURES.

The weights and measures in popular use are not uniform throughout the district. Variations even occur in the same taluk. The following is an account of the standards most generally accepted:—

Table of weight.

The ordinary table of weights is as follows:—

20 tolas	=	1 seer.
6 seers	=	1 pānch seer.
12 seers	=	1 dhadiyam.
4 dhadiyams	=	1 maund (about 26 lb.)

The reason, it is said, why a weight of six seers is called "pānch seer," which literally means "five seers," is that the old maund weighed 40 seers instead of 48 as at present. One-eighth of a maund then represented five seers. Early in the 19th century the weight of the maund in the Ceded Districts was changed to 48 seers, but though one-eighth of this new maund now weighed six seers it was still called "pānch seer." A seer of gold or silver weighs, as elsewhere, 24 tolas and is

CHAP. VI. WEIGHTS AND MEASURES.

designated in parts of the district "pedda althi" to distinguish it from the ordinary or "chinna althi" seer. It may be mentioned that a weight of 60 maunds of raw cotton is called a *kantlam*, and the same term is used to signify 15 maunds of pressed cotton or 45 maunds of cotton-seeds.

Grain measures.

The seer generally used for measuring grain is one which will hold 88 tolas weight of second sort rice when heaped. There is however another seer known as the "pakka seer" which weighs 132 tolas and is sub-divided into two *padlu*. *Padi* is the word commonly used for the lowest unit of measure or seer. The largest measure of grain in use is called a *putti*, but the number of seers it contains varies in different parts of the district. In the black cotton country it is generally 640 seers, and in Rāyachōti taluk 500 seers. Elsewhere it may be 320, 480 or 560 seers. The measures below the putti are generally the following:—

2 kunchams	=	1 irasa.
2 irasas	=	1 thūmu.
5 thūmus	=	1 ēdum.
2 ēdums	=	1 pandum.
2 pandums	=	1 putti.

Between the seer and the kuncham is the muntha, but the number of seers to a muntha varies to such a bewildering extent, that it is best excluded altogether. In the above table it will be seen that the putti contains twenty thūmus. In some parts of the district, however, the thūmu is one-eighth of a putti.

Liquid measures.

The seer of measure and its sub-multiples, half, quarter, eighth and sixteenth, are used in retailing liquids, except that oil and ghee are sold sometimes by measure and sometimes by weight.

Lineal measures.

The English yard and, less frequently, the foot and inch are in use, but the popular standards of measurement, which are derived from the hand and the arm are as follows:—

A *vēledu* is a finger's breadth, and

4 vēledus	=	1 bethedu (breadth of the four fingers closed).

The distance between the tips of the thumb and forefinger when fully extended is called a *jittedu*, and that between the tips of the thumb and little finger fully extended is a *jānedu*; then

2 jānedus	=	1 mūredu (cubit, *i.e.*, the length from the elbow to the tip of the middle finger).
4 mūredus	=	1 bāredu (the distance between the tips of the two middle fingers measured across the chest with the arms extended).

CHAP. VI. WEIGHTS AND MEASURES.

The depth of wells is calculated in terms of a unit of measurement called *mattu*, roughly corresponding to a man's height. In Kamalāpuram taluk and places where wells are revetted with Cuddapah slabs the term *gudhi* is used to denote an excavation of three feet deep and two yards wide, these being the dimensions of the slabs in use. In other parts an excavation of a cubit in depth and width is known as a *kunta*.

The common measures of distance are the *paragu*, or 2½ miles, and the *ámada* which is equal to four paragus or ten miles.

Measures of time.

Now that watches are much more used than formerly, the English measures of time are pretty well understood, but the popular measures are—

60 vighadias	=	1 ghadia (24 minutes).
2 ghadias	=	1 muhūrtam.
7½ ghadias	=	1 jāmu (three hours).

Besides these terms certain expressions are used by the country people to indicate particular times of the day, for example *rèpitàla* means the period between 6 and 9 A.M., *payitāla* is the time from 12 noon to 2 P.M., while *pedda yesulla* and *chinna yesulla poddu* correspond roughly to the periods from 2 to 4 P.M. and 4 to 6 P.M. respectively. *Māpitayāla* is also used to express the evening up to about sunset, from which time till about 8 P.M. is the period known as *sandhakada*.

CHAPTER VII.

MEANS OF COMMUNICATION.

ROADS—In 1854—Extension during famines—Present administration—Avenues—Travellers' bungalows and choultries. THE CANAL. RAILWAYS—Projected lines—Accidents.

CHAP. VII. ROADS. — In 1854.

THE roads of the district received but little attention prior to the middle of the last century. In the early fifties we find the districts of Cuddapah and Nellore comprised, for the purpose of Public Works, in the second division of the Presidency. The Civil Engineer in charge of this division reports, in 1854, "The Government are fully aware that up to the commencement of the present year little had been effected for this division under the first of the above headings (*i.e.*, Communications) further than in the formation of the great north road running through the whole length of the Nellore district." From the same report we gather that a small amount had recently been expended in improving the "direct Cuddapah and Madras road" and that the Superintendent of Roads had in progress the important line of communication joining Arcot with Cuddapah. With the exception of these two roads the district was practically devoid of communications. In this year, however, an important new road was in course of construction, namely, that leading from Badvēl eastwards through Atmakūr to Nellore and Krishnapatam on the east coast, and sanction had been obtained to the extension of this road westwards to Proddatūr. The programme of operations for 1855 and 1856 was ambitious and included among the roads to be commenced all those noted in the margin. Of these projected lines two, namely, the road from Pōrumāmilla to Rāmayapatnam and the 'direct road from Cuddapah to Nellore' on the south side of the Pennēr, never materialized. Both these roads were to be constructed with the avowed object of

Pōrumāmilla by the Thākūr ghāt to Rāmayapatnam on the east coast.
Extension of Badvēl and Proddatūr line to Bellary frontier north of Pennēr.
Khājipet to Kurnool frontier.
Rāyachōti to Chitvēl.
Cuddapah and Madras Road (Trunk No. 13).
Cuddapah to Vēmpalle.

CHAP. VII. ROADS.

Kadiri to Vēmpalle.
Rāyachōti to Vēmpalle.
Kadiri to Pulivendla.
Rāyachōti to Gurramkonda.
Direct Road from Cuddapah to Nellore on south side of river.
Badvēl to Pōrumāmilla.
Completion of Cuddapah and Cumbum line.

"opening up the coast to the interior," to which considerable importance was attached. Special emphasis was laid on the feasibility of the direct route from Cuddapah to Nellore, south of the Pennēr, and the advantages of its proposed alignment, which is reported to be "so clearly advantageous for adopting the first 15 miles of the direct Cuddapah and Madras road as far as Vontimitta, and leaves only 70 miles to be constructed, making a total distance of 85 miles in lieu of 103 by the present road, to say nothing of crossing only one river (Cheyyēr) in lieu of the Pennēr, the Sagilēr" and other streams in Nellore district. The section from Vontimitta to the Veligondas was never laid, and the country which this road was intended to traverse is to the present day probably the most inaccessible in the district, while the road through Badvēl and Ātmakūr is, and is likely to remain, the only passable route from Cuddapah to Nellore.

Extension during famines.

All the other roads included in the list exist at the present day, though many of them, notably the road from Kadiri over the Kurli ghāt to Pulivendla, a branch of which extends also to Vēmpalle, were only completed during the great famine. In the famine of 1891-92 relief works were opened in the main division, but, as concerns roads, were confined to repairs. In Rāyachōti taluk, however, a serviceable road was constructed from Gālivedu to Kōnampet through Nūlivedu. More lasting results were obtained from the relief works instituted in 1897, when the marginally-noted important roads among others, were constructed or improved.

Proddatūr-Jammalamadugu.
Maidukūru-Pōrumāmilla.
Yerraguntla-Vēmpalle.
Yerragudipād-Kōkatam.

Present administration.

As in other parts of the Presidency, the maintenance and construction of roads entirely devolved on the Local Fund Boards in the year 1879-80, from which date the District Board has employed its own engineering establishment directly responsible to itself. The maintenance of existing communications constitutes the heaviest charge on Local Funds and the annual allotment for new works often amounts to about half the maintenance charges. The district is well provided with metal and in the greater part of it good gravel is obtainable, but the lack of water often renders successful maintenance a very difficult task, and in seasons of scanty

CHAP. VII. ROADS.

rainfall many miles of important roads are perforce left unmended. Presumably this mainly accounts for the considerable surrenders of allotments under repairs to communications in past years, and in face of this difficulty it may be thought unreasonable to urge a further expenditure on existing roads in preference to opening up new communications. On the other hand the utility of even the best roads of the district is so impaired by the difficulty of crossing the rivers which intersect all but one of the main roads, to say nothing of the swollen hill streams that periodically wash away the minor roads and cart-tracks, that the question of bridging the rivers on the most frequented routes is, especially in view of the rapid development of motor traffic, assuming considerable importance. The Pennēr, Pāpaghni and Cheyyēr all interpose wide barriers of sand between some of the most important towns in the district, to cross which a loaded cart often requires two or three pairs of bullocks. There are but few ferries that are regularly maintained, so that during heavy rains cart traffic is not infrequently held up for days together, and foot passengers who cannot swim are wise if they stay at home.

Avenues.

As a whole the district is not well off in respect of avenues. In the eastern division they only occur in the southern parts of Pullampet taluk. There are some well-grown trees on the Cuddapah-Guvvalacheruvu road and others passing through the central taluks of the district. Elsewhere one only observes a few tender shoots and young trees for short distances along the road-side, which afford evidence of recent attempts to render less irksome the journeys of a future generation of travellers by road. But the want of water largely frustrates these good intentions, and in many places the greatest difficulty must be experienced in bringing the trees to maturity. At present therefore the district is mostly devoid of effective avenues, and an occasional tope by the road-side generally affords the only shade obtainable.

Travellers' bungalows and choultries.

A list of travellers' bungalows maintained by the Public Works and Forest Departments, with particulars of their accommodation, will be found in a separate appendix.[1] At Cuddapah one is maintained by the Municipality. The Local Boards provide three bungalows in this district, and keep up fourteen choultries for the use of Indian travellers.

THE CANAL.

Some account of the Kurnool-Cuddapah Canal has already been given in connection with the extensive irrigation which it affords. It is also a waterway and attracts a certain amount

[1] See Volume II.

of traffic, mostly in the shape of heavy goods. Cuddapah slabs are conveniently transported in this way. The estimated values of cargoes up and down the canal in the year 1912–13 exceeded three lakhs of rupees. Sixteen boats ply for cargo and eight for passenger traffic. The number of passengers on the canal did not exceed thirteen hundred in 1912–13. Navigation receipts for the same year amounted to a little less than fifteen hundred rupees. These figures are for the whole length of the canal in Kurnool as well as Cuddapah district.

CHAP. VII. THE CANAL.

RAILWAYS.

The north-west line of the Madras and Southern Mahratta Railway enters the district at Bālapalle in its south-east corner, and runs diagonally across it to the north-west boundary whence it continues through the Anantapur district. The principal railway stations are Kōdūr, Nandalūr, Cuddapah, Kamalāpuram, Yerraguntla and Kondāpuram. This line was opened in 1854–66. About 120 miles of its length falls within Cuddapah district. This solitary line of railway is inadequate to the needs of the district. Not only are there towns of secondary importance such as Rāyachōti and Pōrumāmilla situated more than thirty miles from any station, but Proddatūr and Jammalamadugu—the former probably the wealthiest town in the Ceded Districts—are as yet unconnected with any railway system. The importance of opening up more of the district to railroad communication has for a long time been recognized by the Government and is constantly receiving the attention of the local authorities.

Projected lines.

In the year 1898, after the second famine of the last decade of the century, the Government selected certain lines as being best suited for construction as famine protective railways. One of these was a line from Kalikiri, a station on the metre-gauge line in Vāyalpād taluk, to Rāyachōti. The line was surveyed and a report on its proposed construction, together with an estimate and plans, was made ready by the end of 1900. In April 1902 this line was considered along with five others and was placed last in order of relative urgency because, in the opinion of the Government, "a reconsideration of the conditions that prevail in the district to be served by this branch has led to some doubt as to whether its possible utility is sufficient to justify the expenditure which would be incurred on its construction." In November of the same year the Government says of this project: "The conclusion now arrived at is that the conditions of the district with regard to the population, the roads and the routes of communication that have become established for cart traffic

CHAP. VII. RAILWAYS.

are such as would prevent Rāyachōti from becoming a really efficient centre of distribution; so that its connection with the railway system would not accomplish the principal object sought for—that of facilitating and cheapening the transport of grain in a time of scarcity." The Government therefore no longer advocated its construction as a famine protective line and it was definitely withdrawn from the programme.

This line was however only part of a bigger enterprise formulated by the Board of Revenue in 1897, which contemplated the construction of a line from Kalikiri to Nandyāl, traversing the whole of the district from south to north and passing through Rāyachōti, Yerragudipād, Proddatūr and Jammalamadugu.

In 1905 the Collector of the district urged a reconsideration of the abandonment of the Kalikiri-Rāyachōti line which he represented should be regarded as a segment of the more ambitious project of connecting Kolar with Nandyāl by a line taken from Bowringpet station through Punganūr to Kalikiri, Rāyachōti and Vēmpalle, and thereafter to Yerragudipād whence the formerly projected line would continue through Proddatūr and Jammalamadugu. The Government however adhered to their decision to abandon the Kalikiri-Rāyachōti line.

In the following year the Government suggested that it was desirable "to include in the programme of protective railways a line for the protection of the Cuddapah and Kurnool districts, which will connect the north-west line of the Madras Railway with the Bezwāda-Guntakal line: for example, a line from Cuddapah to Giddalūr *via* Badvēl, or Cuddapah to Nandyāl *via* Sirvel." The Collectors of Kurnool and Cuddapah were requested to report on the relative advantages of these alternative lines. As the proposed route *via* Badvēl would not greatly benefit the Kurnool district, a line through the north of Cuddapah district to Nandyāl was advocated.

As a result of the correspondence that ensued the Government of Madras addressed the Government of India in 1910 to sanction the construction of the Yerragudipad-Nandyāl Railway as a protective line, funds for which should be provided from the Famine Insurance Grant. But the Government of India, while recognizing its importance, declined to sanction the execution of the project from this grant as all the money available therefrom was likely to be required for some time to come for the carrying out of "even more important irrigation projects."

CHAP. VII. RAILWAYS. — Accidents.

Within the last few months the District Board has passed a resolution in favour of levying an additional cess for the construction of this branch line. The papers are said to be before Government at the time of writing,[1] and it is hoped that the project may have a better chance now of being carried out.

Several railway accidents have unfortunately occurred within the limits of this district, the majority being due to the weakening of some one of the numerous bridges which span the various rivers and streams over which the line has to pass. The district appears to be peculiarly liable to periodical bursts of rain, of a violence quite out of proportion to the average annual rainfall, and at such times the rivers and streams of the district—which receive most of the drainage of the Mysore plateau—rise with alarming rapidity and endanger both life and property. The annals of the district show that the most dangerous floods are to be expected in the latter part of October, when the north-east monsoon sometimes first makes its appearance with the burst of a cyclonic storm. Such an instance occurred on the night of October 20, 1870, when the Cheyyĕr rapidly rose to full flood, and an arch of the bridge gave way before the violence of the torrent and the débris which it brought down and wedged against the piers. Whether the section was actually carried away before the train arrived or the train itself brought down the bridge was never ascertained. As the mail passed over the bridge with slackened speed, though without any warning of danger, the engine and the two front carriages were precipitated into the river. Three passengers were killed, two of whom were Europeans, as well as five railway employees. The bodies were recovered and buried on the south bank of the river. Owing to the slow pace at which the train was going the hinder wagons were stopped in time by the brake, the couplings between the front wagons and the rest of the train having snapped.

In June 1874 there was another serious accident. An inspection train going over the bridge at Kamalāpuram at a rapid pace got off the line, came into collision with one of the piers, and then leapt down into the sandy bed of the river. It is a matter for surprise that every person in it was not killed. Mr. Robinson, the Permanent Way Inspector, and Mr. Haworth, the Assistant Traffic Manager, escaped with slight injuries, but a subordinate who was in the same carriage was cut to pieces, and another employee was so injured that he afterwards died. The other occupants of the train escaped with few injuries.

[1] 1st July 1914.

CHAP. VII. RAILWAYS.

But these accidents, serious enough as they were, are dwarfed by the magnitude of the disaster that occurred near Mangapatnam in 1902. Between the hours of midnight and 3 A.M. on the early morning of September 12, a sudden deluge of rain in the nature of a waterspout fell and flooded the country on the south side of the railway line, sweeping away the second and third spans of bridge No. 664 near the 206th mile a little beyond Mangapatnam railway station. The mail train, which was unusually full as it carried homeward bound passengers and the Europe mail, passed through the station without stopping shortly after 3 A.M., and, on reaching the bridge, was, with the exception of the rear brake-van, precipitated into the gap. The disaster was unfortunately attended with lamentable loss of life; seventy-one dead bodies were subsequently recovered either at the scene of the accident or at various points down stream where they had been carried by the current. Seventy-seven persons escaped, and eight only remained unaccounted for to complete the total of 156 who were in the train according to the calculation made by the committee of enquiry. The collapse of the bridge was found to be due to the side pressure to which the skew piers and girders were subjected by the immense volume of water which rose above the girders on the south side: its force being augmented by large accumulations of straw and rubbish until one of the piers gave way and was bodily overturned. The Government held the accident to be due to causes beyond human control and neither attributable to negligence on the part of the railway administration nor laxity on the part of the Company's establishment.

CHAPTER VIII.

RAINFALL AND SEASONS.

RAINFALL—Liability to famine. EARLY SCARCITIES. THE GREAT FAMINE OF 1876–78—Series of bad seasons—Beginnings of distress in July 1876—Relief works opened in September—Prices suddenly rise in October–December 1876; serious famine—Deputation of Sir Richard Temple—His views in regard to Cuddapah—Distress increases in 1877—June to August 1877—Rain falls in September—The cost of the famine. SCARCITIES SUBSEQUENT TO THE GREAT FAMINE—The famine of 1891–92—The famine of 1896–97. FLOODS—In the first quarter of the 19th century—Great storm of 1851—Excessive rains in 1874—The floods in 1903.

CHAP. VIII.

RAINFALL.

THE rainfall in the Ceded Districts is lighter than in any other division of the Presidency, but of these districts Cuddapah on account of its situation derives greater benefit from the north-east monsoon than do the rest, and this advantage is measured by an excess of about five inches over the average annual rainfall of Bellary and Anantapur, and about three inches over that of Kurnool. This average is for the whole district something less than 27½ inches, but the variations between its parts are often very considerable; for example, Jammalamadugu, the least favoured taluk, has an average fall of only 21 inches while Pullampet taluk obtains as much as 35 inches in the year.

With Jammalamadugu must be ranked Pulivendla taluk, for which the average is only half an inch higher. These are the two westernmost taluks of the district and adjoin the drier districts of Kurnool and Anantapur. The central taluks of Proddatūr, Kamalāpuram and especially Cuddapah are better off. Cuddapah itself has an average annual rainfall of 31·66 inches, but is so situated amid surrounding hills that it seems to catch many showers that leave the rest of the taluk dry. Rāyachōti taluk on the plateau is better off than the black cotton tract, but here also the rain is very partial and the fall recorded at the taluk headquarters can scarcely be taken as truly indicating the condition of the whole taluk, which is so broken up into hills and valleys that heavy showers are often confined within very limited areas.

CHAP. VIII.

RAINFALL.

More rain is obtained in the eastern taluks than the rest of the district, and the fall is heavier in the south than the north where the Eastern ghats attain a greater elevation and bar the way of the north-east monsoon to the interior. The following figures show the annual rainfall based on the records of the several registering stations in the district for a series of years prior to the resettlement :—

Station.	Average.
Cuddapah	31·66
Kamalāpuram	24·80
Proddatūr	24·99
Jammalamadugu	21·05
Pulivendla	21·54
Rāyachōti	26·99
Badvel	27·08
Sidhout	32·80
Pullampet	35·13
District average ...	27·34

The rainiest months for all the district except the eastern division are August and September. In Badvēl, Sidhout and Pullampet more rain often falls in October than in either of the two previous months. In these three taluks the north-east monsoon occasionally continues into December; but with this reservation December and the first three months of the year are generally very dry. More showers are received in April and May and some heavy rain is usually recorded before the end of June after the south-west monsoon sets in. Wet weather should then continue till the end of September in the western half of the district and till the end of November in the eastern division. The following figures give the average monthly distribution of rain at Cuddapah :—

Months.	Rainfall in inches.	Number of rainy days.
January	0·33	1
February	0·10	...
March	0·9	...
April	0·43	1
May	1·64	3
June	2·96	5
July	3·82	6
August	5·91	8
September	6·84	8
October	5·52	6
November	3·13	5
December	0·89	1
Total ...	31·66	44

CHAP. VIII. RAINFALL.

For the district as a whole the heaviest fall on record is that in 1874, just before the commencement of the series of bad seasons that led to the great famine of 1876-78. In that year each of the taluks of Cuddapah, Proddatūr and Jammalamadugu received approximately twice their annual average, and the fall in Pullampet taluk which bore the brunt of the cyclone that raged over much of the district from October 23 to 25 reached the abnormal figure of 67¼ inches. Ten years later unusually abundant rains borne in by the north-east monsoon in 1884 brought the year's rainfall in this taluk to within four inches of the same figure. Throughout the whole district the minimum rainfall was recorded in 1876, when Jammalamadugu received but four and a half inches, Cuddapah nine and a half, and Pullampet six and a half. The marked variations between these two extremes, of which the records of the last forty years are eloquent, show how uncertain is the supply from year to year. Moreover, agricultural practice is so stereotyped that if the heavy rains are not obtained at certain definite periods dry crops will fail over large areas: so that the prosperity of a year cannot be gauged merely with reference to the total rainfall received. This is also no true criterion of the relative economic conditions of two such dissimilar tracts as are represented, for example, by the Jammalamadugu and Rāyachōti taluks. The heavy, fertile soils of the former require but a scanty rainfall to produce bumper crops of cholam and cotton, while the coarse red soils on the plateau are incapable of retaining moisture and need a more copious and better distributed rainfall to obtain a satisfactory harvest.

Liability to famine.

Agriculture is so predominant a factor in the life of the population and the area effectually protected by irrigation is so small that the prosperity of the district may be said to depend almost entirely on an adequate rainfall and its timely precipitation. That it is nevertheless subject to marked vicissitudes of seasons necessarily entails its liability to periods of more or less acute distress. By far the most serious of these was the great famine of 1876-78. But both prior and subsequent to this widespread disaster there have occurred visitations which, though less calamitous in their intensity, were of sufficiently exceptional severity to deserve mention.

EARLY SCARCITIES.

The only famine previous to the cession of the Deccan districts, of which any particulars have come down to us, is that of 1791-92. The Northern Circars were chiefly affected, but the famine was also intense across the whole breadth of the Peninsula to the southern districts of the Bombay Presidency,

CHAP. VIII.

EARLY SCARCITIES.

and the whole of the Deccan was therefore involved. It was on this occasion that relief-works were first opened by the Madras Government for the support of those affected by the famine. In writing about this famine some ten years later Munro says: "Had the officers of Government lowered the assessment, or even let it remain as before the effects of the famine would probably only have been felt while it lasted but as they raised it nearly 50 per cent. wherever there was a crop, this addition to the high price necessarily occasioned by the scarcity rendered grain so dear that very little could be purchased by the lower classes of the inhabitants, and great numbers of them perished in consequence." The first scarcity after the cession was in 1802, when Munro reported that the crop outturns were below the average throughout his charge. In 1806 again there was a widespread failure of rain, but the Deccan districts were less heavily visited than other parts of the Presidency, notably the Carnatic and the neighbourhood of Madras. The distress however was very severe and Munro considered the season worse than had ever been known. There was much discussion as to the proper measures to be taken by Government on the occasion of this famine. In deprecating interference with the grain trade and suggesting that distress could best be alleviated by remissions of revenue Munro adumbrated principles that have been accepted in all subsequent famines.

In 1833 occurred the Guntur famine, so called from its severity in the old Guntur district where thirty per cent. of the population were estimated to have perished from want. In Cuddapah district the black cotton tract seems to have suffered worst. But in writing in 1874 of this famine as well as the subsequent visitations of 1854 and 1866 which had occurred well within the memory of the great majority, ryots and officials, then living, Mr. Gribble, the author of the "Cuddāpah Manual," states as follows: "Famines do not ever seem to have seriously affected this district. Even during the celebrated *Nandana*[1] year, though there was considerable distress and severe pressure, there was never an actual famine. . . . In 1866 there was distress but no actual famine. Several relief works were then put in hand, and notably roads, but the distress was not so general that very large numbers availed themselves of this offer of labour." It should also be mentioned that numbers were employed on the construction of roads during the famine of 1854, when, as already recorded,[2] the task of improving

[1] The Hindu cyclic year corresponding to A.D. 1833. [2] See Chapter VII.

CHAP. VIII. EARLY SCARCITIES.

communications first received serious attention. Mr. Gribble's rather optimistic view of the comparative immunity of the district from famine was destined to receive a severe shock, for within two years of writing the words here quoted he was himself, as Sub-Collector of the sub-division, engaged in combating the worst visitation of the kind ever recorded.

THE GREAT FAMINE OF 1876–78.

In respect of the area and population affected and the duration and intensity of the distress, the great famine which prevailed for more than a year and a half over most of the Madras Presidency from 1876 to 1878 was the worst calamity of its kind experienced in British India since the beginning of the century. Fourteen districts were affected, eight of them severely, and the famine is calculated to have caused the death of three and a half millions of people. The expenditure incurred by the State on account of famine during the two years ending March 1878 is officially estimated at nearly Rs. 625 lakhs, to which must be added a further sum of Rs. 191 lakhs on account of loss of revenue. Cuddapah district was unfortunately included in the tract that suffered most.

Series of bad seasons.

The continued series of unfavourable seasons which led to the establishment of famine conditions began in 1874 when a part of the crops throughout the district suffered from excessive rains. In the following year the south-west monsoon was late and brought but a scanty rainfall, while the north-east monsoon was a complete failure. In April 1876 Collectors whose districts were regarded as likely to suffer from this failure were called on by the Board of Revenue to submit lists of relief works proposed to be put in hand should necessity arise. Cuddapah was one of the districts so dealt with, but it was then thought possible that no exceptional measures would be called for.

Beginnings of distress in July 1876.

This hope was frustrated in July when the Collector, Mr. J. R. Daniel, reported that the taluks of Pulivendla and Badvēl as well as the country round Kamalāpuram were in distressed conditions and apprehended that it would shortly be necessary to undertake some work in those parts for the relief of the poorest: to provide for which he asked for Rs. 25,000 to be placed at his disposal. The Board remarked that previous reports had not shown the danger to be so imminent, and recommended a provision of Rs. 10,000 to meet emergencies. The Government accordingly placed this sum at the disposal of the Collector.

In the early part of August there was 'a fair fall of rain,' and agricultural operations were begun. Conditions in

CHAP. VIII.
THE GREAT FAMINE OF 1876-78.

Kamalāpuram and Pulivendla had improved and the danger zone had shifted to the black cotton taluks and Badvēl, where the Collector reports an increase in crimes of housebreaking and mischief by fire for the purpose of obtaining grain.

Relief works opened in September.

By the middle of September conditions were everywhere much worse, no rain having fallen since the beginning of the previous month. In Jammalamadugu taluk the labouring classes were in great distress. Dry crops had not been sown except in a strip of country within a five miles' radius north of Jammalamadugu. A sum of Rs. 2,000 was accordingly sanctioned for opening relief works in this taluk. The people themselves were very apprehensive of the future. Merchants and such of the ryots as had stores of grain would not offer it for sale, expecting to need it for their own requirements. In this month also parts of the sub-division began to suffer severely, and the Sub-Collector, Mr. Gribble, was allotted Rs. 2,500 for commencing a relief work in Kadiri taluk.

Prices suddenly rise in October.

During October prices rose suddenly, and the rates of wages paid to relief workers had to be enhanced. Towards the end of the month the Board of Revenue drew up a forecast of the probable requirements per month of each district affected by the famine, on account of expenditure on relief works, the calculation being made at two annas per head per day. There were then upwards of 25,000 persons employed on relief works in Cuddapah district, and the monthly expenditure was estimated at Rs. 2,12,000.

December 1876; serious famine.

The absence of rain throughout November rendered the outlook still more gloomy, and by the beginning of December all hopes of a favourable monsoon had to be abandoned. A famine of some months' duration now became inevitable. The numbers on works and gratuitous relief steadily increased and by December 16 reached the following figures:—

	Men.	Women.	Children.	Total.
Relief works	42,078	46,833	13,429	10,2,340
Gratuitous relief ...	1,292	1,514	502	3,308

This large increase together with the uncertainty of supply of food led the Government to order the establishment of grain depots in the districts of Bellary, Kurnool and Cuddapah. Mr. Thornhill was constituted the first Government grain agent for these districts, with his headquarters at Bellary, and divisional officers were ordered to indent on him for grain for their depots and to pay special attention to providing adequate means of transport from the railway stations to the several depots. At the same time they were to obtain such grain as the local trade could supply.

The condition of cattle about this time began to cause grave anxiety, and the advisability of utilizing prickly-pear as fodder was commended to Collectors. The experiment was only partially successful.

Officers of other departments were, towards the end of the year, largely employed to assist the revenue officials to cope with the immense amount of additional work entailed upon them by the famine. A few days before the new year Mr. Puckle, the Deputy Director of Settlement, acting on the instructions of Government, temporarily broke up the Cuddapah Settlement Party and distributed it over the Ceded Districts for the supervision of relief works.

Deputation of Sir Richard Temple.

At the end of 1876 the Governor of Madras (the Duke of Buckingham and Chandos) left the Presidency to take part in the ceremonies at Delhi in connection with the proclamation of Her Majesty Queen Victoria as Empress of India. His departure at this critical time was looked upon with some disfavour in Madras, but the visit was attended by good results in that it afforded an opportunity for a personal conference with the Governor-General and enabled the Government of India to realize for the first time the full measure of the calamity from which the Southern Presidency was suffering. At the Council which met at Delhi on January 5 the policy hitherto adopted to combat the famine in Madras was discussed and subjected to some adverse criticism, the fear being expressed that expenditure was more profuse than it need be, and that stricter economy was necessary. The outcome of these deliberations was the deputation of Sir Richard Temple, who had had famine experience in Bengal in 1874, to the Madras Presidency.

His views in regard to Cuddapah.

Sir Richard Temple lost no time in setting out. He first visited Kurnool, which he reached *viâ* Hyderabad, and then toured through Bellary and Cuddapah. In the latter district, one-fourth of the crop having been saved, the distress was in Sir Richard Temple's opinion not so great as in Bellary and Kurnool. At the time of his visit there were 200,000 persons on relief out of an estimated total population of 1,350,000. This was held to be too large a proportion to be satisfactorily accounted for. Under the Collector, near headquarters, the management was stricter than at Madanapalle where Sir Richard states he believed an excessive expenditure was being incurred as to which reconsideration was urgently called for. So far as this district was concerned the visit of Sir Richard Temple had three main results, a reduction in the scale of wages paid to relief workers, the

CHAP. VIII.
THE GREAT FAMINE OF 1876–78.

Distress increases in 1877.

exercise of greater stringency in admitting persons to the works and the discontinuance of the purchase of grain by Government.

From the beginning of the year the intensity of the famine steadily increased, the distress being augmented by a severe visitation of cholera which claimed 564 victims in the second week of January. In the same week the official returns show that 1,460 head of cattle succumbed through privation or disease. The course of the famine in the ensuing months may be seen at a glance in the following table:—

Month.	Numbers in receipt of State relief at the close of each month.			Total per cent. of the district population.	Average price in seers per rupee of	
	On works.	Gratuitously.	Total.		Ragi.	Rice, 2nd sort.
1877.						
January ...	170,704	893	171,597	13	8·00	7·00
February ...	67,728	1,705	69,433	5	9·26	7·14
March ...	78,902	6,129	85,031	6	10·04	7·81
April ...	51,192	24,988	76,180	6	9·60	8·10
May ...	94,961	33,629	128,590	10	8·35	7·76
June ...	120,053	56,362	176,415	13	8·41	6·92
July ...	146,682	118,328	265,010	20	6·18	5·90
August ...	148,903	133,688	282,591	21	6·46	5·54
September ...	109,994	155,015	265,009	20	8·25	{ 4·98[1] 6·22
October ...	43,609	78,798	122,407	9	{ 7·90 14·22	6·22 9·13
November ...	12,560	8,265	20,825	2	{ 8 15·00	5·60 9·13

The large reduction in the number of relief workers in February must be attributed to the change of policy that followed Sir Richard Temple's visit to the district. Every effort was henceforth made to restrict expenditure as far as was compatible with the safety of the people. Large numbers from Cuddapah and the adjoining districts were drafted to work on the Buckingham Canal on the East Coast. Attempts in this direction had been made in the previous year, but many of the labourers had come back again. The plan was now attended by greater success as the more stringent administration of famine relief offered the workers but little inducement to return to the district till prospects improved. Meanwhile matters grew worse as new difficulties arose. Cattle for grain transport became very scarce and the Collector's

[1] Bracketed figures show the highest and lowest prices, averages not being available.

CHAP. VIII. THE GREAT FAMINE OF 1876-78.

proposal that the feeding of cattle with prickly-pear for fodder should be sanctioned as a relief work was approved by the Government. In Cuddapah taluk the Special Assistant Collector, Mr. MacCartie, was very successful in conducting this experiment, by which means numbers of useful beasts which would have otherwise certainly perished were preserved. The great danger that while the bread-winners were at relief works their families at home would die of starvation led to the necessity of making house to house visitations in all villages that had not been deserted, and village officers were held responsible for bringing to notice all cases of dangerous want. This contributed to the large increase in the numbers admitted to gratuitous relief.

June to August 1877.

The failure of the south-west monsoon once more intensified the distress. Its immediate effect was a still further rise of prices, and an enormous increase in the numbers dependent on State relief. Towards the end of July the Collector[1] wrote as follows in regard to the very critical condition to which the district had been brought: "It is with the greatest reluctance, and after waiting until what I consider to be the last safe moment, that I have the honour to apply to Government for assistance, in order to meet the rapidly increasing distress. I have, in previous reports, both official and demi-official, stated my opinion that a failure of the south-west monsoon would entail the most serious consequences, and have observed that in this case Government must be prepared to meet a very heavy outlay. I and those under me have worked on in the hope that rain would come and all would be well. I now see but little chance of its falling, except by a special dispensation of Providence. Day after day clouds come up only to disappear with the sunset; the crops are beginning to wither and the grass to dry up. Village relief is assuming gigantic proportions, and prices are steadily and surely rising. Rain may come, but from the accounts from Bombay and the West Coast which I see in the newspapers, there is but very little chance of its making its appearance. A fortnight more of the present weather will certainly end in the destruction of nearly the whole of the dry crops of the district. It is not necessary for me to say what the effect of this will be."

Reviewing its resources the Government apprehended that with the depletion of local stocks of grain they might in the near future have whole populations on their hands without the prospect of being able to carry food enough to keep them

[1] Mr. (afterwards Sir Frederick) Price.

CHAP. VIII.

THE GREAT FAMINE OF 1876–78.

alive. The Supreme Government was notified of this danger, and early in August the Viceroy determined to visit Madras and to take such measures as might be necessary to ensure the provision of adequate transport to convey food to the inland districts. The Viceroy left Simla for Madras on August 16. At Poona, where he halted to consult with Sir Richard Temple and the officers of the Great Indian Peninsula Railway, arrangements were made for pouring grain into the Madras Presidency by railway at the rate of from 1,000 to 1,200 tons per day. All other traffic was to give way to the conveyance of grain. The main result of the Viceroy's tour was a reorganization of the famine administration, which was placed under the immediate control of the Governor, with a Personal Assistant accredited by the Government of India.

Rain falls in September.

The climax of the famine had, however, been reached. Rain fell early in September and was seasonably distributed through that and the following month. But though the crisis was passed the effect was not immediate. The numbers on gratuitous relief in the district reached the highest figure in September, about 11½ per cent. of the total population; but in October there was a marked fall in prices and thousands of people on relief were enabled to return to work in the fields. Thenceforth the distress steadily abated, though the effect of a famine of such unexampled intensity necessitated the continuance of relief throughout the following year, and that mainly gratuitous.

The cost of the famine.

The district of Cuddapah as then constituted, being the largest of those principally affected by the famine, it follows that the expenditure incurred on account of relief operations was enormous. The loss of revenue it is impossible to estimate with any exactitude, but the charges directly due to relief and excluding expenditure on extra establishment amounted to nearly sixty lakhs of rupees.

SCARCITIES SUBSEQUENT TO THE GREAT FAMINE.

During the thirty-five years that have elapsed since the great famine many seasons have been far from satisfactory, but famine conditions have never since prevailed over the whole district at any one time. In 1891 it was Rāyachōti and the other taluks of the old sub-division now belonging to other districts which suffered most severely. Over the rest of the district distress was only apparent in parts of Badvēl and Sidhout and the south-east of Cuddapah. On the other hand the famine of 1896–97 was far heavier in the main division than in Rāyachōti and the rest of the sub-division, where distress was not acute. More recently, the years 1898

CHAP. VIII. SCARCITIES SUBSEQUENT TO THE GREAT FAMINE.

to 1901 were markedly unfavourable, and again in 1904-05 the rainfall in the black cotton country was very defective. Finally, seasonal remissions were very considerable in all parts of the district in 1908-09 and 1911-12.

The famine of 1891-92.

The rainfall of 1890, especially in the sub-division and particularly in the latter portion of the year, was very scanty, while both the monsoons of 1891 were almost total failures. The prices of the principal food-grains began to exceed the normal rates about the end of July 1891, and many of the working classes soon felt the pinch. With the failure of the south-west monsoon in 1891 distress became prominent in Rāyachōti taluk, where the scarcity of drinking water was severely felt, as also in Badvēl. In August 1891 relief operations were opened in Rāyachōti and a kitchen was started at the taluk headquarters for the distribution of cooked food to the deserving poor. By the middle of December prices reached famine rates, and relief works were opened about the middle of January 1892 in the taluks of Badvēl and Sidhout, and some four months later in that of Cuddapah. It was during this famine that operations were begun on the Sagilēr project[1] in Badvēl taluk, some four thousand people being employed daily thereon from April till the end of August 1892. Prior to the latter date all other relief works in the district had been closed with the favourable opening of the south-west monsoon, the promise of which was not belied, in the month of June. A plentiful rainfall soon allayed all anxiety, and normal conditions were rapidly re-established.

A notable feature of this famine was the large measure of relief afforded, especially in the sub-division, by the numerous advances made to the owners of land under the Land Improvement Act, for the sinking of wells. Nearly four and a half lakhs of rupees were disbursed on this account in the sub-division alone, from January 1891, and by the end of the following year nearly seven hundred wells had been completed, and some four thousand were reported to be under construction.

The famine of 1896-97.

In fasli 1306 there was again distress amounting to famine. Both monsoons were very defective, especially in the black cotton country and adjacent tracts, where the total rainfall amounted to scarcely more than half the average. Conditions were not so serious in the eastern division of the district, but in the following fasli the persistence of the bad season necessitated the grant of dry remissions in more than forty villages of the Badvēl taluk. The "sub-division," now represented only

[1] See Chapter IV.

CHAP. VIII. SCARCITIES SUBSEQUENT TO THE GREAT FAMINE.

by the taluk of Rāyachōti, suffered least. In the Jammalamadugu, Proddatūr and Cuddapah taluks it was estimated that the crop was entirely lost on 33 per cent. of the total area sown and on 22 per cent. the yield was "from 1 to 4 annas." Stocks appear to have been sufficient, but those in the hands of merchants had been largely depleted to meet the demand which had arisen earlier in Bombay and the Central Provinces. Very heavy exports were made up to November 1896. Then when local conditions declared themselves unfavourable the merchants refused to sell, while the ryots also would not bring their surplus stocks to market owing to the general apprehension that a three years' famine was impending. Prices were thus artificially inflated and the labouring and non-agricultural classes were greatly pinched by the dearness of grain as well as the lack of labour in the fields owing to the failure of the north-east monsoon. In November 1896 relief works, comprising mainly road-construction, were opened in each of the taluks of Proddatūr, Jammalamadugu and Pulivendla. There was a heavy fall of rain at the end of November, and as agricultural operations were begun the numbers on relief works fell rapidly. But the drought quickly set in again and the month of February saw the end of all hopes of a satisfactory harvest. Relief works were accordingly opened at six more stations in March 1897, and the numbers employed at the end of the month amounted to eleven and a half thousand as against two and a half thousand at the end of February. In April the average daily number of relief workers in the taluks principally affected is noted in the margin. There were practically no agricultural operations in May, and no crops were on the ground except here and there under wells. The numbers on relief works therefore steadily increased, and from June to August eight more works were opened in the affected taluks. Private charity contracted considerably and those incapable of work suffered from acute distress. Relief kitchens were accordingly opened in May 1897. During this and the following month the famine reached its climax. The south-west monsoon broke in June, and the rainfall was well distributed over the next four months, being heaviest in August. By the end of September the rainfall throughout the district was much above the average and almost all the irrigation sources had received plentiful supplies. These favourable prospects were accompanied by the gradual cessation of relief, and normal

Proddatūr	4,447
Jammalamadugu	6,164
Pulivendla	8,654
Cuddapah	7,088

CHAP. VIII. SCARCITIES SUBSEQUENT TO THE GREAT FAMINE.

conditions were practically restored by the end of October. Taking account of the liberal remissions and suspensions of revenue as well as direct expenditure, the famine in the four taluks mainly affected cost the State more than fourteen lakhs of rupees. Relief was undoubtedly generous and the Collector stated that no change had been wrought by the distress in the economic condition of the people. A later Collector referred to the famine as the "fat cooly famine," and stated that he "feared the famine of 1897 had demoralised the people."

FLOODS.

The position of the district in the valley of the Pennĕr and its tributaries, many of which drain the upland of the Mysore plateau, render it specially liable to sudden inundations following on an excessive rainfall. Many such have been recorded since the beginning of the 19th century.

In the first quarter of the 19th century.

The earliest of which particulars have come down to us is that reported by Munro to have destroyed in October 1804 most of the tanks over the Ceded Districts from Harpanahalli in the west to Chitvĕl in the east. As much as Rs. 6½ lakhs were spent on repairing the damage done to tanks and river channels in the four districts by this storm.

Thirteen years later, in September 1817, a very heavy fall of rain occurred, causing damage principally in the taluks north of the Pennĕr. The river itself burst its banks and is said to have extended in some places to a width of about three miles. No sooner had the district recovered from this inundation than the north-east monsoon broke with a torrential downpour on the night of October 13 and continued for two days, when the rain became lighter. Again on October 25 it began to rain more heavily than ever and lasted well into November. Every taluk seems to have suffered, especially Sidhout. On this occasion Badvĕl tank, the finest in the district, nearly breached in three places, but was saved by the Tahsildar who put the whole village to work and kept them labouring for three days. Fifty-three tanks in Rāyachōti taluk breached or suffered serious damage. The next year, 1818, proved very unhealthy owing to the excessive rain which fell almost without cessation during the rainy months of both monsoons. The floods of these two years caused considerable damage to the crops and remissions of revenue were extensively granted.

On May 8 and 9, 1820, there was another violent storm which damaged over a hundred tanks in Rāyachōti taluk and caused the loss of a number of cattle and the death of twenty persons in Pullampet taluk.

CHAP. VIII.
FLOODS.

Great storm of 1851.

It was also in May that the heavy rains fell which occasioned such extensive damage in the year 1851. The Pennēr and Chitrāvati came down in full flood and the village of Chautapalle which lies between the two rivers near their confluence was swept away. Pārnapalle, situated on the bank of the Chitrāvati in the extreme west of Pulivendla taluk, was also partially destroyed. The destruction of these villages was attended with the loss of hundreds of lives, as the rivers rose so rapidly that the inhabitants had no time to escape.

Excessive rains in 1874.

The year 1874 is remarkable for an excessive rainfall in both monsoons. A violent storm occurred in the first week in May and from the following month till nearly the end of September the black cotton taluks received about twice their normal supply of rain. But the heaviest downpour took place at the bursting of the north-east monsoon in the second half of October. In parts of the district the rain that fell from the 23rd to the 25th amounted to as much as twenty inches. Considerable damage was done to the railway bridges, and traffic between Rājampet and Kondāpuram was suspended for some weeks.

The floods in 1903.

The last occasion of an abnormal fall of rain was in November 1903. The rain began on the early morning of November 6. A fall of four inches was registered during the morning and rain continued all day. By sunset the Bugga Vanka at Cuddapah was within three feet of its banks when, owing to the breach of some tanks higher up, it suddenly rose six feet and flooded the greater part of the town. The waters began to subside at 8 o'clock, but only after many of the less substantial houses had been washed away. The water rose to the foundations of the Sessions Court and the Collector's cutcherry, and the Gunta bazaar between these two buildings suffered very severely. It was reported two days afterwards that 461 houses had been destroyed and 756 badly damaged. The loss in house property was estimated at Rs. 30,000, and in moveables at another Rs. 25,000.

Outside Cuddapah town the principal damage was in Pullampet taluk where the railway line was washed away to a length of three quarters of a mile owing to the breaching of the Utukūr tank. Large numbers of small tanks also burst in Rāyachōti taluk.

The standing crops were so much damaged that remission of revenue on this account was granted to the extent of twenty-five thousand rupees.

CHAPTER IX.

PUBLIC HEALTH.

GENERAL HEALTH — Plague — Cholera — Small-pox — Malaria— Infirmities — Vaccination. MEDICAL INSTITUTIONS — Public— Private.

CHAP. IX. GENERAL HEALTH.

IN the matter of public health it is probable that Cuddapah district has reaped some advantage from the recent contraction of its limits. In the years 1903 and 1904 the introduction of plague into the district is recorded to have been due on both occasions to importation from Mysore into Madanapalle taluk. Malaria is also more prevalent in Kadiri taluk and the Pīlēr division of Vāyalpād taluk than in any part of the Cuddapah district as now constituted.

Plague.

The nine taluks of which the district is now formed have been practically free of plague during the present century, except for the outbreak in Cuddapah town in 1912. Two imported cases from Ādōni were recorded in 1902. In the year 1903 a very few imported cases occurred in the taluks of Proddatūr, Badvēl and Pullampet, and in the following year there was a single suspicious case, also imported, at a village in the vicinity of Cuddapah. Again in 1905 a case of the same sort occurred in Buddayāpalle in Cuddapah taluk. With these exceptions the only recent visitation of plague to be recorded is that which affected the municipality in 1912. The disease broke out on August 31. It began to abate at the opening of the new year and, largely owing to the effective measures taken to stamp it out, finally disappeared in February. During the three months immediately following its outbreak the plague was virulent, but the destruction of rats and the inoculation of the people, to which they readily submitted, served to mitigate its ravages. The number of deaths was one hundred and twenty-two.

Cholera.

Cholera is an annual visitant to the district, and seems to affect Pullampet taluk more seriously than other parts. Rājampet suffers regularly every year and other towns and populous villages in the vicinity of the railway are very prone to receive and spread the disease. Probably not much improvement is to be looked for until the principles of sanitation are

CHAP. IX. GENERAL HEALTH

better apprehended by the general public. With all the will in the world to remedy defects pointed out by the sanitary authorities little can be effected by the presidents of taluk boards and chairmen of unions in the face of general apathy, if not opposition. Another difficulty is that really effective steps in the direction of sanitation entail heavy expenditure such as the local boards are often unable to meet. During the last decade the heaviest mortality from the disease was in the year 1908-09, when the number of deaths amounted to more than 6,500. The year 1906-07 was nearly as calamitous, when the figure reached 5,746. The municipality used to be subject to terrible epidemics of cholera, but since the introduction of pipe water in 1890 mortality from this cause has very markedly decreased.

Small-pox.

Fewer victims are claimed by small-pox, which is much less feared by the people than cholera owing to the larger proportion of recoveries. But deaths occur from this disease every year, and the annual figures show that the worst visitations synchronize with the severer outbreaks of cholera. If recrudescences of these diseases are referable to the same cause, it is probably to be found in some climatic vagary, such as a defective rainfall or unseasonable weather, to which a people accustomed to time meteorological changes with exactitude cannot easily adapt itself. The virulence of small-pox has been considerably abated by the extension of vaccination in recent times. Fatalities from this disease number but a few hundreds in a year when cholera claims thousands.

Malaria.

The number of annual admissions to medical institutions owing to fever affords no very reliable criterion of its prevalence in the district. On the other hand, after making every allowance for the inaccuracy of village registration as to the causes of death and a propensity to describe as fever all disorders not clearly assignable to some other origin, it must be admitted that malaria is endemic in many parts of the district. Cuddapah itself has an unfortunate notoriety in this respect and the unsparing efforts made during the last forty years to improve the health of the town by paying greater attention to sanitation and prohibiting wet cultivation within municipal limits have only been partially successful. In recent years it is doubtful whether the improvement has been fully sustained, and the problem of freeing Cuddapah from malaria continues to engage the attention of the authorities. Outside the municipality parts of Pulivendla taluk are very feverish. In the eastern division malaria is chiefly prevalent in the south of Sidhout taluk and the north of Pullampet while the most unhealthy parts of Badvēl and Proddatūr are at the foot of the Nallamalais. CHAP. IX. GENERAL HEALTH.

Infirmities.

Of incurable maladies or infirmities statistics were obtained at the last census in respect of insanity, blindness, deaf-mutism and leprosy. It is questionable if the returns relating to leprosy and insanity are of much value in point of accuracy. The number of lepers in the district is recorded as ninety-six, of whom, as we have seen above,[1] some thirty or forty are inmates of the Leper Asylum at Krupapalle. The figure given is almost certainly below the mark, as the average number of leper patients annually treated in the Cuddapah hospital in the first decade of this century amounted to forty-four, which one would suppose can only be a fraction of the total numbers afflicted with the disease. As to insanity, even admitting its relativity, the numbers returned, which amount to less than two per ten thousand of the population, appear to fall far short of the reality. Even among that portion of the ryot population of about half the district, with which the present writer came into personal contact during the recent resettlement, cases of insanity, ranging from weak-mindedness to idiocy, were sufficiently numerous to appear remarkable. As the census included in the category of blindness only the completely blind, and in that of deaf-mutism only those entirely devoid of speech or hearing, their classification presented less difficulty, though it lacks scientific value in the absence of any distinction between those congenitally defective and others. In Cuddapah district as in most others the deafmutes are more numerous than the blind. The figure recorded at the census are given in the margin.

District population,	893,998
Deaf-mutes	797
Blind	603

Vaccination.

Vaccination is compulsory only in Cuddapah town and the fourteen unions of the district. Outside the municipality the staff employed consists of three deputy inspectors and twenty-four vaccinators, the cost of the latter establishment being, as elsewhere, debitable to local funds. Under recent orders the vaccinators now work under the immediate direction of the taluk boards and not, as previously, under that of the district board.

MEDICAL INSTITUTIONS. Public.

The Municipal hospital at Cuddapah is the only public institution of its kind in the district. It was built in 1872 and is controlled by the municipality, an annual contribution being made from Local funds towards the expense of its upkeep. A maternity ward and septic sheds have recently

[1] See Chapter III.

CHAP. IX. MEDICAL INSTITUTIONS.

been constructed from funds allotted by Government. There are eight dispensaries in the district maintained by Local funds, which are located at the following places: Proddatūr, Jammalamadugu, Pulivendla, Vēmpalle, Rāyachōti, Rājampet, Sidhout and Badvēl. The total number of patients treated at the local fund dispensaries during the year 1912–13 amounted to 65,274. The Railway Company maintains a dispensary at Nandalūr.

Private.

The only private bodies which control medical institutions in the district are the Protestant Missions, of which a general account has already been given.[1] The principal institution of this kind is the Jammalamadugu hospital, which belongs to the London Mission, and was constructed in 1896. The mission had associated itself with medical work since 1891 and this branch of its activities extended so rapidly under the able direction of Dr. T. V. Campbell, that the construction of a hospital for the accommodation of patients and their more effective treatment became in a few years a paramount necessity. Additions and improvements to the hospital have since been made from time to time and it is now a very commodious building. The medical staff of the mission comprises a European doctor in charge, and a lady nursing superintendent. In 1905 the mission started a medical school, in which the course of instruction lasts four years. By recruitment from among such students as emerge satisfactorily from this training the mission has been enabled to establish branch hospitals, of which there are now four. Particulars of their location and the years in which they were respectively established are given in the margin.

Kamalāpuram	1909
Kantalam	1909
Simhādripuram	1910
Mayalūr	1914

The Lutheran Mission maintains a small dispensary at Kōdūr, as well as the Leper Asylum at Krupapalle to which reference has already been made. There is also a busy dispensary at Kalasapād belonging to the S.P.G. Mission.

[1] See Chapter III.

CHAPTER X.

EDUCATION.

Census Statistics—Progress since 1901—Education according to religions. Educational Institutions—High schools—Lower secondary schools—Education by the missions.

CHAP. X. Census Statistics.

In regard to education the foundation of the formidable structure of statistics elaborated at the census is 'literacy,' defined as the ability of a person to write a letter and read a reply thereto. Measured by this standard the Deccan is educationally the most backward division of the Presidency except the Agency, but within this division Cuddapah district is the most advanced.

Progress since 1901.

Of the male population of the district more than ten per cent. are literate, but of women and girls only sixty-four in every ten thousand. The educational progress of the total population in recent years is marked by an increase of eight per thousand over the number returned as literate in 1901. Though not a remarkable advance it may be regarded as satisfactory, for it compares favourably with that made by six other districts of the Presidency outside the Deccan.

Education according to religions

As elsewhere, the Christians comprise a larger proportion of literate persons than any other religious community. Secular instruction constitutes so important a branch of the Christian Missionary's activities that the acceptance of Christianity practically brings the convert within reach of education. It also secures to women educational advantages as yet denied to their Hindu and Musalmān sisters, so that the proportion of Christian women and girls who can read and write is more than nine times that of the total female population of the district. As in most of the Deccan, the percentage of Musalmāns who are literate is somewhat below the corresponding figure for Hindus. In other parts of the Presidency the reverse is generally the case.

Educational Institutions. High schools.

The district contains only two upper secondary schools. One of these is the Municipal High School at Cuddapah. This institution, which was founded in April 1858, was originally known as the Government Zillah School and was for many years maintained and managed by Government.

CHAP. X. EDUCATIONAL INSTITUTIONS.

When a proposal was made later on that the municipality should assume the management and support of the school, that body pleaded inability to bear the whole cost of maintenance but agreed to defray a moiety thereof. The school accordingly came under the management of the municipality in 1885, but half the cost continued to be met by Government. Some years after this arrangement had come into force the municipality, owing to the increase of its expenditure in other directions of public utility, contrived to divest itself of all pecuniary obligations in regard to the school, so that its upkeep again devolved entirely upon Government, though the management was retained as before in the hands of the municipality. Some two hundred and thirty boys are educated in this school, to which is affiliated an elementary institution (infant to fourth standard) known as the 'branch secondary school.' This latter, which contains 243 pupils, is both managed and maintained by the municipality.

The other upper secondary institution is the National High School at Proddatūr. This is under private management and has recently come under the control of the Theosophical Society.

Lower secondary schools.

There are two lower secondary schools in the district, namely, at Proddatūr and Nandalūr. They are under the management, respectively, of the Proddatūr and Sidhout Taluk Boards and contain in the aggregate about two hundred and fifty pupils. The Campbell Memorial School at Jammalamadugu is also an incomplete secondary school, but being of recent institution it has not yet actually received Government recognition.

The district contains one training school for elementary teachers, namely, the Government institution at Rāyachōti which was opened in 1912.

Education by the missions.

In Cuddapah district, as elsewhere, education is an important branch of the activities of the Protestant Missionary Societies. Reference has already been made to the Campbell Memorial School at Jammalamadugu. This institution was founded in 1913 as a permanent memorial of the labours of the late Rev. W. Howard Campbell on behalf of the London Mission in this district. The same mission also maintains a caste girls' school in Jammalamadugu, which has been so well patronised that its premises are being extended. The Mission Boarding School which accommodates one hundred and forty Christian girls drawn from all parts of the district was originally situated in Cuddapah, but was removed to Jammalamadugu in 1898 whither the lady missionaries

CHAP. X.
EDUCATIONAL INSTITUTIONS.

migrated owing to the unhealthiness of the former station. The school first started in the district by the London Mission was their first-grade elementary school which is situated in the part of Cuddapah town known as Nāgarājupet. It dates from the early attempts of the mission to spread education in the town and neighbourhood in the middle of the last century. In connection with this institution there is a boarding school for Christian boys. These belong mostly to the Māla community and are selected from the most promising material in the Christian congregations of the villages. They remain generally for two or three years, after which they are drafted to other schools of the society in Bellary or Gooty for further instruction.

In its Kalasapād district the S.P.G. mission maintains about forty elementary schools, to the principal of which, situated at Kalasapād, are attached two hostels, in which thirty Christian boys and thirty-nine Christian girls are boarded. Of the total number of pupils on the rolls of the S.P.G. schools more than thirty per cent. are girls.

The Lutheran Mission established at Kōdūr maintains eight primary schools containing in the aggregate some two hundred and twenty pupils.

CHAPTER XI.

LAND REVENUE ADMINISTRATION.

REVENUE HISTORY—Under Vijayanagar—In the 17th century under the Muhammadans—In the 18th century—The village settlement of 1800-01—Ryotwari settlement of 1801-02—Triennial leases proposed—Munro's views thereon—He proposes to reduce existing ryotwari rates—Early operations of the Settlement Department. THE RESETTLEMENT—Mr. Moir's Reports —Dry lands—Wet lands—The sub-division—Dasabandham wells—Financial results. EXISTING DIVISIONAL CHARGES.

CHAP. XI. REVENUE HISTORY.

FOR information as to the early revenue history of Cuddapah district we are almost entirely dependent on Munro's report, dated 12th August 1801, in which he himself complains that almost all accounts and records had been destroyed during the constant disorders. "The land," says Munro, "seems at all times to have been regarded as the property of the State, no traces can be discovered of its ever having been that of the cultivators or renters. The Enam Sunnads of the Bijanuggar[1] Rājas, as well as those of more ancient princes, universally grant the soil as well as the rent, a convincing proof that it belonged to the sovereign."

Under Vijayanagar.

The Hindu systems of land revenue, however, never concerned themselves with definitions of landed property or State rights. On the one side the privileged position attaching to the man who first cleared the soil or to the leader of the band of colonists who first expropriated the aborigines was more or less conceded to their descendants, on the other the State passed no self-denying ordinances as to shares, increments, or taxation on improvements. In its best days the Vijayanagar Empire showed considerable activity in making improvements, building tanks and channels and in opening up new country. To this period of settlement probably belongs the rise of the Visapadi villages, a curious feature of the Cuddapah province referred to by Munro, who describes them as follows: "There are many villages in which the ryots settle among themselves the exact proportion of the whole rent that each individual is to pay. These are

1 Spelled in this book Vijayanagar.

called visapadi or 'sixteenth' villages from the land and rent being divided into sixteen shares, and they compose a considerable part of the Cuddapah province, besides being scattered, though more thinly, over other parts of the country. When the season of cultivation draws near all the ryots of the Visapadi village assemble to regulate their several rents for the year . . . . They ascertain the amount of the agricultural stock of each individual and of the whole body, and the quantity of land to the culture of which it is adequate, and they divide it accordingly, giving to each man the portion which he has the means of cultivating and fixing his share of the rent, and whether his share be one or two-sixteenths he pays this proportion whether the whole rent of the village be higher or lower than last year." This would seem to point to bands of colonists originally settling on the land in a sort of agricultural partnership, and doubtless the joint interest and responsibility were retained in later times as a means of resisting and of bearing up against the heavy assessments imposed. The question of property in the land and to whom it belongs can hardly be said to arise when holdings are interchangeable or subject to redistribution. The really important thing is the division of the produce which as far as the ryots are concerned under the visapadi system was regulated by the contribution made to the common stock. The State, however, also asserted its right to a share, the extent of which the State itself determined. Where it was moderate enough to allow the ryot something over and above the cultivator's expenses and profit of stock, the feeling of attachment to and of private property in his holding would naturally arise. This implied, however, a limitation of the State share, but the State recognized no limitation except such as arose from its own exigencies and the ability of the ryot to pay. "According to tradition," says Munro, "it was paid in kind in the proportion of half the produce, and this half was converted for money at a price unfavourable to the cultivator, a circumstance which must have been an insurmountable bar not only to the establishment of private property in land but also to every kind of agricultural improvement."

In the 17th century under the Muhammadans.

It was not likely that the Muhammadan conquerors would lessen the State demand and we find that the kamil assessment introduced under the Golconda kings about the beginning of the 17th century was based on the same principle of the equal division of the crop between Government and the cultivator. It was founded upon an actual survey which took

CHAP. XI. REVENUE HISTORY.

four years to complete. As all rents were to be paid in money the equivalent of the half produce in kind was found by taking the estimated gross produce of the different sorts of dry and wet land and converting it into money at the average price of the preceding ten years. The cultivator also had to bear the burden of certain rusums to the revenue officers such as the *desmukh* and the *despande.* The seeming rigour of this settlement under which, as Munro says, the ryot could not have extended his cultivation was modified by the action of the revenue authorities who allowed the ryots to hold more land than was entered in the accounts, their own rusums being proportionately increased thereby. The survey was thus gradually obliterated or rendered inoperative, and the revenue system really had no other principle than that of taking the maximum possible. Aurangzebe adopted the kamil but had to make allowances for loss. This was doubtless due to the depredations of the poligars who took advantage of the decay of the Golconda power and to the opportunities for the falsification of accounts which the change of governments afforded to the karnams. It is to be regretted that we have no account of the actual collections made under this revenue system. The proportion they bore to the extravagantly high assessment was probably ludicrous enough, for the political history of the time testifies to the absolute lack of any effective central authority.

In the 18th century.

During the weak administration of the Nawabs of Cuddapah who were constantly exposed to Mahratta attacks from without and the insubordination of poligārs within the district much revenue could never have been realized. Their political successors, Haidar Ali and Tipu Sultan, were of a different calibre. Munro frequently alludes to their administration in laudatory terms. Of their more vigorous measures we may note the resumption of rusums and unauthorized inams, the discovery and speedy repression of frauds and, most important of all, the partial reduction of the poligārs who, generally in collusion with the local revenue officials, had always contrived to defraud the paramount authority. By this means the kamil standard was gradually restored. Under the Nizam (1792–1800) misgovernment resulted as usual in decreased cultivation and loss of revenue. The managers were perpetually being changed, rents were raised, supplementary assessments were imposed and various other means adopted of raising the revenue. These violent methods, however, defeated their own object. "It was not so much the sum raised as the unskilful mode of doing it that has exhausted the country," said Munro. Finally when the intended transfer of the Ceded Districts to the Company became known, the Nizam's managers resorted to every form of exaction, so much so that many of the head farmers abandoned their villages.

Of the districts or taluks specified by Munro in his report those of Chennūr, Chintakunta, Kamalāpuram, Dhoor and Jammalamadugu correspond roughly to the north-west and central taluks of the present district excluding Pulivendla. The following table compares the kamil assessment on this tract with the assessment and collections at different times, in Kantarāya pagodas:—

Date A.D.	Name of Ruler.	Amount in pagodas.
1610	Golconda Kings (Kamil assessment).	316,763
1750–60	Cuddapah Nawabs (assessment).	208,184
1782	Haidar (collections)	255,752
1788	Tipu (collections)	269,499
1799–1800	Nizam (assessment)	258,994

The village settlement of 1800-01.

Munro took charge of the Ceded Districts so late in the season of 1800–01 that he had no time to do more that year than conclude in haste a settlement *mouzawar* or by villages for fasli 1210. The lump assessment to be paid by each village was roughly arrived at by assembling the headmen and karnams and questioning them as to the value of their own and the adjoining villages. This done, these officers were made "severally responsible for the rent (assessment) of their own villages and jointly for those of the district (taluk)." The Ceded Districts had been handed over by the Nizam in return for a subsidiary force to be stationed in his territory, and not unnaturally the Directors of the Company expected them to bring in a revenue equal to their scheduled value. Munro therefore had to face the difficult problem of meeting these expectations—a task rendered more difficult by the fact that Tipu had placed an excessive value on the districts surrendered by him in 1792—and at the same time of securing to the ryot a regular system of assessment and a proprietary interest in the soil.

Ryotwari settlement of 1801-02.

In the following year, fasli 1211, the first step was taken by introducing the "kulwar" or ryotwari settlement by which each ryot held his land immediately from the Government under a patta, and in fasli 1212 the natural complement of a fieldwar survey and assessment was commenced and completed in 1806. Logically this should have resulted in each field bearing a fixed assessment, and Munro drew up a scale

CHAP. XI. REVENUE HISTORY.

of rates for the different classes under which the fields were classified. Under the modern system the individual assessments would have been totalled, and the beriz of a village or taluk arrived at after comparing these totals with previous collections and such other checks as might be available. This doubtless was what Munro desired. A standard revenue, however, was expected to be secured, and the procedure actually followed was the exact reverse of this. As each taluk came up for settlement the total revenue was first fixed. This was done by a comparison of the collections made under the native Governments and the Company, modified by the existing circumstances of the tract and expert opinion. This total was then distributed over the villages. If a village complained of over-assessment, the claim was referred to the principal ryots of other villages for arbitrament and, if allowed, the amount remitted was assessed on other villages. The village total thus determined was then distributed among the ryots in accordance with the classification of the fields they held. It was thus only in the last stage of the assessment process that the results of the classification were employed and it consequently lost much of its value. It did not serve to correct inequalities in the assessments of adjoining villages and even in individual villages the nominal rates could not be preserved. If the financial results of the application of these rates to the classification fell short of the village total, the defect had to be met by increasing them and as the increase could only be imposed on the better lands, the nominal highest rates were often greatly exceeded. As far as possible, however, Munro carried out an equalization of assessments, while his vigorous and sympathetic administration inspired confidence and encouraged agriculture.

For the next seven years the annual revenue was settled on the ryotwari principles thus inaugurated. Loans were freely given and cowles granted for waste land, and we find that by fasli 1215 (1805-06), in spite of the series of bad seasons that immediately followed the paimash, the revenue of the whole of the Ceded Districts amounted to more than twenty lakhs of Kantarāya pagodas, which was the standard Munro had set himself to reach.

Triennial leases proposed.

In 1804, however, the desirability of a reversion from the ryotwari to a permanent settlement began to be discussed. The Governor-General in that year sent down instructions that in settling new districts the "Oudh Regulations" should be followed with such modifications as local circumstances required. Under these each village was rented out as a whole for three years at a fixed annual sum to zamindars or other proprietors of land, and the renter was solely responsible for the payment of the fixed rent. Munro, among others, was ordered to report on the proposal to extend this system to the Ceded Districts.

Munro's views thereon.

His reply embodied an able defence of the ryotwari settlements he had been at such pains to introduce. He showed that in the Ceded Districts, where there were no zamindars, the only people with whom permanent settlements could be concluded were the ordinary heads of villages and that they were totally unfit for the position into which it was desired to thrust them. He considered that so far from promoting any improvement by assisting the poorer classes with advances or allowing them to participate in the remissions granted by Government, they might rather be expected to press heavily on the ryots and reduce them to a worse state than that in which they had found them. He also foresaw the even worse mismanagement and oppression which would ensue if a speculator or adventurer were allowed to come between the Government officer and the cultivator. A settlement direct with the cultivators appeared to him more suited to the manners and prejudices of the inhabitants, because it was the system which had always been followed; more adapted to the narrowness of their circumstances in that it did not insist on the same amount of revenue being paid every year but limited it by the actual extent of cultivation; more likely to reclaim them from their wandering habits and fix them to their fields by giving them an interest in the improvement of these; less liable to embarrass the Government by considerable failures; and more calculated to promote the general prosperity of the country and the people. Believing also that the system of great estates would raise less produce from the soil than that of small farms; that it would be far more liable to failures and afford less security to the revenue; that it would be less agreeable to the inhabitants; and that it could not be permanent because their laws and customs continually urged on the rapid division of landed property, he recommended that the ryotwari system, or settlement with the cultivators, should be continued as a permanency.

He proposes to reduce existing ryotwari rates.

Before proceeding on furlough in 1807 Munro repeated his unqualified condemnation of the proposal to introduce a permanent settlement, but at the same time pointed out that as the full advantages of the ryotwari system could not be realized unless the ryots acquired a proprietary interest in their holdings a saleable value should be given to the land.

CHAP. XI. REVENUE HISTORY.

The existing rates according to the settlement he had himself conducted represented about 45 per cent. of the gross outturn, and Munro held that to give the land a saleable value they should not exceed one-third. He therefore recommended a reduction of 25 per cent. on all rates with an additional 8 per cent. on lands under wells and small tanks on condition that the ryots kept them in repair; the ryots were further to be given the proprietary right and within certain limits the right of relinquishment. He believed that the initial loss of revenue would soon be counterbalanced by the extension of cultivation induced by these measures.

Meanwhile the controversy started in 1804 continued for four years until with the departure of Munro and afterwards Lord William Bentinck, the strongest supporters of the ryotwari system, it was ordered early in 1808 that villages should be leased out to the village headmen and chief cultivators for a term of three years from fasli 1218 upon such terms as might be considered moderate and equitable, subject to the condition that no reduction in the rental would be made on account of adverse seasons. Munro had left the country in October 1807 before these instructions reached the Ceded Districts. His services to the State during his seven years' tenure of this charge received handsome acknowledgments from the Directors at home as well as from the local Government in India.

On the departure of Munro the Ceded Districts were divided between two Collectors. Mr. W. W. Chaplin, the Subordinate Collector at Cumbum, appears to have first taken charge of the Cuddapah district, but to have been transferred in the following year to Bellary, the other collectorate, while Cuddapah was assigned to Mr. G. Gregory. Sidhout was fixed on as the headquarters of the new district and continued as such for several years. The triennial lease was not a success. The headmen fearful of being ousted by new-comers accepted higher conditions of rent than they could meet. As many of them were indifferent managers, the ryots were unduly oppressed and cultivation fell off. The Collector of Cuddapah spoke strongly against the system. "I believe," he said, "that few or none have been benefited by their bargain; nearly all have been losers and some have been ruined." To the Board, however, the failure appeared to be attributable to the shortness of the lease and the excessive rents, and with the expiry of the three years' term an attempt was made to remedy these defects.

The result was the introduction in fasli 1222 (1812-13) of a decennial lease, the rents being calculated on the collections

CHAP. XI. REVENUE HISTORY.

of the seven preceding years. It resulted in even a worse failure. The renters oppressed, mismanaged, absconded with the collections, or fell into arrears; the ryots intrigued and combined against the renters, and under oppression and extortion resorted once more to the migratory habits from which Munro had tried to wean them. Cultivation decreased and many villages reverted to Government. Finally the results of a bad season in fasli 1226 made the abandonment of the renting system inevitable. The Directors with whom Munro had been in communication while at home had ordered a return to the ryotwari system at the conclusion of the lease, and Munro who had returned in 1816, when consulted, advised that these orders should be anticipated by encouraging the remaining renters to surrender their leases and that the ryotwari system should be re-established after carrying out the reductions of 25 and 33 per cent. he had formerly proposed. Final orders to this effect were passed by Munro himself as Governor in 1820, and the new settlement was introduced in 1821 in the Dhoor and Chennūr taluks where not a single renter remained solvent. The reductions in the assessment were under Munro's orders to be immediate, but the Collector in some cases did not give effect to them and in others they were saddled with the condition that waste to the extent of half the remission should be taken up. This the Board put a stop to when discovered, but the unsatisfactory way in which the reductions had been carried out was not known till Munro toured in the district in 1824, when the Collector, Mr. Hanbury, was transferred and full effect given to the intentions of Government by his successor, Mr. J. W. Russel.

The assessment thus arrived at remained in force for upwards of fifty years. The evils arising from the triennial and decennial leases could not be immediately eradicated, but the fact that the revenue of the district reached before very long the figure at which Munro's early administration had left it shows how large an increase in cultivation must have followed the percentage reductions which he finally effected. This is an uneventful period in the revenue history of the district, being marked only by the removal of a few glaring inequalities of assessment and the reduction of some exceptionally high rates, considerable relief being thus given to double crop lands. Remissions on waste and on lands under ruined irrigation sources gradually became more liberal. But the most important changes were made in regard to lands irrigated by wells. It has already been noticed that Munro granted a special reduction of 8 per cent. on the old

CHAP. XI. REVENUE HISTORY.

assessments of these lands in addition to the general reduction of 25 per cent. But in spite of this the assessment was still found to be oppressive in individual cases, and in 1824 the Collector was empowered to reduce the assessment on occupied lands in exceptional cases, and on unoccupied lands when the rates kept them out of occupation, and also to transfer lands to dry where the wells had fallen into disrepair. The question continued to occupy attention from time to time in subsequent years, and finally in 1868 and 1869 the Government ordered that the assessments on all such well lands should be reduced to the highest dry rates of the villages in which they lay. The amount of assessment so foregone in the whole district represented about a lakh of rupees, but the ultimate effect cannot be considered as otherwise than beneficial, in that it did something to arrest the wide spread neglect that had left so many wells to fall into disrepair and ruin.

Early operations of the Settlement Department.

Meanwhile the operations of the new Settlement Department had been extended to the Cuddapah district, and demarcation was commenced in Jammalamadugu taluk in 1864. The years in which the new rates were respectively introduced in the various taluks that now constitute the district are given in the margin. The Deputy Directors of Settlement responsible for the schemes submitted to Government were Mr. Cox, whose work during his long sojourn in the district is still spoken of with appreciation by the people, and Major Stuart, who dealt in one report with the three eastern taluks of the district. Though the method adopted was uniform throughout, there are variations in the resulting rates, as slightly different grain values were assumed in different taluks and the allowances made on account of cultivation expenses were not always the same. With this reservation a summary of any one of these schemes will serve to indicate how the settlement of the district was carried out. All lands, both dry and wet, were classified under the two main series of 'regar' and 'red ferruginous.'[1] In

Taluk.	Date.
Cuddapah ... }	
Jammalamadugu } ...	1873
Proddatūr ... }	
Sidhout	1877
Badvēl	1878
Pulivendla ... }	
Pullampet ... } ...	1879
Rāyachōti	1881

[1] This takes no account of the exceptional series in which were placed "permanently improved" lands. These represented a very small area, were placed on the same footing as other lands in 1893, and at the resettlement were reclassified and brought into one of the two ordinary series.

rating dry lands, villages were divided into three groups, the grouping being based mainly on a consideration of the varying fertility of different tracts; in regard to wet lands villages were similarly distributed among two or three groups, according to the advantages of irrigation enjoyed. Cholam on regar soils and cholam and korra in equal proportions on red were taken as the standard crops on dry lands—except in Rāyachōti taluk where the standard dry crop was cumbu—paddy being as usual the standard for wet. The grain values adopted were, as has been said, not uniform throughout the district. The figures in the margin * show the number of Madras measures assumed in the black cotton country to represent the outturns on an acre of the best and worst lands. The commutation rates—generally based on the prices of the preceding twenty non-famine years—were, over most of the district, based by the orders of Government on the prices of the twenty years ending with 1864. The resulting values after making allowances varying from 10 to 15 per cent. for cartage and merchants' profits are shown in the margin.† A further deduction of 25 per cent. was made for agricultural risks, as also allowances for the expenses of cultivation. The net outturn remained, and half of this was taken as the Government share. The resulting rates, rounded off to the nearest quarter rupee, ranged in the various taluks as shown below:—

* Standard crop.	Values ranging From	To
Cholam ...	400	80
Korra ...	280	100
Paddy ...	1,450	360

†	Per garce. RS.
Cholam	139
Korra	100
Paddy	126

——	Jammala-madugu, Proddatūr and Cuddapah.		Pulivendla.		Badvēl, Sidhout and Pullampet.		Rāyachōti.	
	From	To	From	To	From	To	From	To
	RS. A.	RS. A.	RS. A.	RS. A.	RS. A.	RS. A.	RS. A.	RS. A.
Dry ...	5[1] 0	0 4	4[1] 0	0 4	5[1] 0	0 4	3[1] 0	0 4
Wet ...	12[1] 0	2 8	9 0	2 0	10 0	2 0	9[2] 0	2 0

[1] These rates apply to 'permanently improved' lands in first class villages.

[2] As the whole of Rāyachōti taluk was classed in the red ferruginous series, the highest wet rate actually found therein was Rs. 7.

CHAP. XI. REVENUE HISTORY.

There were from ten to twelve rates under each head of dry and wet, the number slightly varying in different parts of the district. Munro's paimash took account of some fifty rates in all, including those on 'garden' lands. With the assimilation of garden lands to wet or dry as the case might be, and the elimination of the highest wet rates the settlement effected a considerable contraction in their range, which made for simplicity. That in spite of these measures the settlement resulted in an increase and not a reduction is largely attributable to the excess area found by the survey. What the settlement mainly effected was for the administration a simplification of the accounts and for the ryots a more equitable incidence of assessment. Its financial results represented an increase in the land revenue of a little over 9 per cent.

THE RESETTLEMENT.

The rates thus introduced were in force for a period of thirty years which expired in the early years of this century, when the district came up for resettlement. The tract was dealt with in four scheme reports, the first of which related to the taluks of Cuddapah, Proddatūr and Jammalamadugu, the second to Pulivendla, the third to the taluks of the eastern division, and the fourth to Rāyachōti and the other taluks of the old sub-division. The proposals embodied in the first three reports were formulated by Mr. T. E. Moir, I.C.S.,[1] the scheme for the sub-division being submitted by his successor, Mr. R. W. Davies, I.C.S. Mr. Moir left the party shortly before the conclusion of operations in Cuddapah taluk, and the resettlement of this taluk and Pulivendla was subsequently carried on under the direction of Mr. Davies. The latter officer, on his departure at the end of 1910, was succeeded by the present writer who continued to be in charge till the resettlement of the district was completed. The following table shows when the new rates were introduced in the various taluks, which are grouped according to the four scheme reports above mentioned:—

Jammalamadugu and Proddatūr.	Cuddapah.	Pulivendla.	Badvēl and Sidhout.	Pullampet.	Rāyachōti.
1908	1909	1911	1911	1912	1912.

Mr. Moir's reports.

The Scheme report relating to the first three taluks was submitted in September 1906. In reviewing the economic condition of this tract the Settlement officer, while giving due weight to all indications of material progress, points out that the steady recovery from the effects of the great famine—

[1] As Special Settlement officer No III Party.

CHAP. XI.

THE RESETTLEMENT.

which had occurred some three to five years subsequently to the original settlement—had received continual checks owing to the frequency of unfavourable seasons in the latter half of the settlement period. He says "The district has just passed through an extraordinary series of lean years which have checked progress and to some extent crippled the resources of the ryots. There are, further, several points with regard to the prices which urge caution." At the time this report was written it could not have been divined that the high prices which ruled in 1905 were not occasioned by causes of a local or temporary nature, but marked the commencement of the great economic change which has intensified ever since and persists to the present day.

Dry lands.

In discussing the price of cholam, the standard dry crop of the black cotton taluks, the Special Settlement officer predicts in regard to the future that "the prices of ordinary years will probably range between Rs. 150 and Rs. 190 . . . This does not admit of any increase on the score of prices." Three years later the Settlement officer, when submitting his scheme for the resettlement of the eastern taluks, had to weigh the significance of the continued rise in prices in the normal years that followed 1905. The figures in the margin show that in 1907-08 the price of cholam had reached a cent. per cent. higher figure than that held by the Settlement officer in 1906 as likely to prove the average price of ordinary years. "The seasons," says the Settlement officer, "are quite inadequate to account for the prices of the last three years . . . The question of course is no longer a local one, and as financial experts disagree as to the solution it lies beyond the province of the Settlement officer . . . Apart from vicissitudes of the seasons the high prices of the last three years are attributed to two main causes, the rise in gold prices in other parts of the world and the enormous increase in the rupee coinage, the latter being by far the most important according to the latest pronouncement on the subject in the March[1] issue of the Economic Journal. The extent to which this has been due to permanent influences is doubtful but it is clear that, depending as it does on the currency policy of the Government, it is subject to remedial action . . .

Fasli.	Price of cholam per garce.
	RS.
1314	257
1315	268
1316	305
1317	347

[1] 1909.

CHAP. XI. THE RESETTLEMENT.

Where so many uncertainties exist it seems to me better to confine attention to the period up to fasli 1314 to which these unknown factors do not apply." The conclusion drawn was the same as in the case of the western taluks, namely, that no enhancement of the dry rates was justified on the score of prices.

In dealing with the Settlement officer's proposals for the resettlement of the western taluks the Board had urged that an enhancement of 6¼ per cent. was at least justified. This was, however, negatived by the Government "in view of the smallness of the rise in prices and the economic history of the taluks." This concession to the "more prosperous western taluks" was accorded in due course to the rest of the district, and the dry rates remained unchanged.

Wet lands.

Fluctuations in the prices of paddy being less marked than in those of cholam over the same period, the question of enhancing the wet rates was never discussed. But the system by which, at the original settlement, villages had, as regards wet lands, been divided into three—sometimes only two—groups was found to have resulted in inequalities in the incidence of assessment, while the number of sorts provided under each class of soil was found to be too few to ensure a sufficient elasticity in the rates. For these among other reasons the abolition of the "wet grouping" of villages, the classification of sources according to their individual capacity together with a careful revision of their ayacuts, the reclassification of soils and the imposition of a new table of rates were, in regard to wet lands, the principal features of the resettlement in the old main division. The new wet rates for "single crop" land range from Rs. 10 to Rs. 2.

The "Sub-division."

Rāyachōti is the only taluk of the old sub-division that still belongs to the district. Mr. Davies in submitting proposals for the resettlement of this tract laid some stress on the inferior economic condition of the sub-division in general, and Rāyachōti in particular, to the rest of the district. Dry rates as elsewhere remained unchanged. In regard to wet lands the grouping of villages was abolished in favour of the classification of individual sources, but as it was found that the existing money rates were suitable and assessments by no means so unequal as in the main division, the rates were retained unaltered and there was no general reclassification of soils.

Dasabandham wells.

Allusion has been made to dasabandham wells in dealing with the irrigation of the district. In regard to shamilat dasabandham wells, which, in the order of taluks taken up

THE RESETTLEMENT.

for resettlement, were first found in Pulivendla, the difficulty in applying to them the system of differential water-rate led the Settlement officer to submit alternative proposals for their treatment, one of which was to convert them into private property and to register the ayacuts as dry, discontinuing the inam remissions. The Government not only accepted this proposal, but extended the concession to khandam dasabandham wells. Though the immediate effect of this measure was a loss of revenue it was held to be justifiable in view of the protective value of the wells, the previous high assessments having led in many cases to their being allowed to fall into disrepair and ruin.

Financial results.

The resettlement of the district resulted in a net decrease of revenue by 7 per cent. which is almost entirely attributable to transfers of double crop to single crop and wet to dry, as well as the more favourable rates now allowed for composition of the double crop charge. Besides the concession granted by Government in the matter of dasabandham wells, large areas under other sources, both Government and dasabandham, were found to be totally unirrigable and had to be registered as dry. This is particularly the case in the taluks of Pulivendla and Sidhout, where it is a matter for surprise that transfers to dry were not more freely effected by the Revenue Department during the period of the original settlement. There is no doubt that the reduction in the demand is thus largely counterbalanced by a decrease in seasonal remissions. On the other hand it is equally certain that the ryots have cause to be grateful to Government for a remarkably lenient resettlement.

EXISTING DIVISIONAL CHARGES.

The Collector of the district is now assisted in the administration of the revenue by a Sub-Collector at Rājampet, and Deputy Collectors at Jammalamadugu, Rāyachōti and Cuddapah. There is, as usual, a Tahsildar in each taluk. There are also Deputy Tahsildars at Chitvēl, Lakkireddipalle and Cuddapah town, the two latter posts being new creations following on the redistribution of districts which came into effect in 1910 and 1911. Prior thereto, the taluks of Rāyachōti, Kadiri, Madanapalle and Vāyalpād formed the sub-division in charge of a Sub-Collector at Madanapalle; Jammalamadugu, Pulivendla and Proddatūr constituted another division under the Deputy Collector of Jammalamadugu, while a second Deputy Collector in charge of the eastern taluks was stationed at Sidhout, and the taluk of Cuddapah was, as it still is, administered by the Headquarters Deputy Collector. In October 1910, Kadiri taluk

CHAP. XI.
EXISTING DIVISIONAL CHARGES.

was incorporated with Anantapur district, and in the following year Madanapalle and Vāyalpād went to make up the new district of Chittoor. Rāyachōti then became the headquarters of a Deputy Collector, whose charge includes the taluk of that name and that of Pulivendla. The Deputy Collector of Jammalamadugu has jurisdiction over the taluks of Jammalamadugu, Proddatūr and the newly formed taluk of Kamalāpuram, and the taluks of Badvēl, Sidhout and Pullampet form the charge of a Sub-Collector whose headquarters are, or shortly will be, at Rājampet.

CHAPTER XII.

SALT, ABKĀRI AND MISCELLANEOUS REVENUE.

SALT—Former sources of supply—Earth-salt; method of manufacture—Its interference with monopoly salt—Its manufacture suppressed—Present sources of supply. ABKĀRI—Arrack—Foreign liquors—Toddy—Opium and hemp drugs—The preventive force. INCOME-TAX. STAMPS.

CHAP. XII. SALT. — Former sources of supply. Earth-salt; method of manufacture.

AT the time when the Company came into possession of the district the salt consumed in it was of two kinds, namely, earth-salt manufactured from saline soils by men of the Uppara caste and marine salt obtained from the Nellore littoral.

The manufacture of earth-salt was peculiar to the Ceded Districts and was carried on by means of *mótlas* or salt-mounds. A heap of earth was piled up and on the top of it were hollowed out one or more circular basins, some five feet in diameter and two feet deep. From the bottom of these basins channels lined with chunam ran down to one or more reservoirs similarly lined. Salt-earth was collected in the places where it effloresced naturally in the dry months and taken to the *móda* on pack-buffaloes. It was thrown into the basins and then a quantity of water was poured upon it. The brine so obtained flowed through the channels at the bottom of the basins into the reservoirs. From these it was baled with chatties into a set of masonry evaporating pans, carefully levelled and plastered with chunam, where it was left to be converted into salt by solar evaporation. Each lot of salt-earth which was thus lixiviated was taken from the basins and thrown outside them and this process constantly repeated gradually raised the level of the *móda* and the basins which were perpetually being remade on the top of it. Some of the *módas* gradually grew to be as much as 20 feet in height. When they became inconveniently high for the buffaloes to carry the salt-earth up to their summits, they were abandoned and others started elsewhere.

Its interference with monopoly salt.

The earth-salt made in this manner was neither so good nor so strong as marine salt, but it was much used by the poorer classes and for cattle, and thus interfered with the profits of the Government salt monopoly which was established

CHAP. XII. SALT.

in 1805. As early as 1806, therefore, it was proposed to prohibit its manufacture. The chief arguments against any such step were that it would inflict hardship upon the Upparas who made the salt and upon the poorer classes who consumed it, and for the next three-quarters of a century a wearisome correspondence dragged on regarding the course which it would be proper to pursue.[1] In 1873, Mr. G. Thornhill, member of the Board of Revenue, visited the Ceded Districts to see how matters stood. He reported that it was not possible to check the competition of the earth-salt with the Government marine salt by imposing an excise duty, as the *módas* were numerous and scattered. For similar reasons, and also because all the Upparas were very poor, a license-tax was out of the question. At the same time he calculated that the loss to Government due to the system was from eight to eleven lakhs annually and seeing that Government salt was obtainable in Cuddapah as cheaply as in other inland districts he recommended that the industry should be gradually suppressed.

Its manufacture suppressed.

Government agreed and ordered that the opening of new *módas* should be prohibited and that those in existence should be licensed, with reference to their productive capacity, at rates to increase by annual increments until 1879, when the full duty leviable on sea-salt should be imposed on their entire produce. These measures, though they checked the manufacture, were not completely successful, and in 1876 the Madras Salt Commission and the Board of Revenue concurred in recommending that the manufacture of earth-salt should be at once and entirely suppressed. The Government of India agreed, and in 1880 orders were given that the *módas* should all be destroyed, reasonable compensation being paid to their owners. Thirty-five years have thus elapsed since the manufacture of earth-salt was prohibited, but the remains of the old *módas* are still to be seen in parts of Pulivendla and Badvēl taluks where there are extensive tracts of saline soil. Cases of illicit manufacture used to occur occasionally but largely, it is said, owing to the reduction of the duty on salt in 1907—are unknown nowadays. . Saline tracts are, however, still periodically examined by the officers whose duty it is to discover and prevent such offences.

Present sources of supply.

All the salt now consumed in the district is sea-salt made in factories on the coast under Government supervision. Salt from Bombay and Goa is not unknown in these parts but is

[1] An abstract of parts of it will be found in paragraphs 271—289 of the report of the Madras Salt Commission of 1876.

said to compare unfavourably both in substance and flavour with the east-coast article. Ninety-six per cent. of the supply is obtained from the factories in Nellore and Chingleput districts. Salt is sold wholesale at the factories by weight but is retailed in the district by measure.

ABKĀRI.

Abkāri revenue is mainly derived from arrack, foreign liquor, toddy, opium and hemp-drugs. Particulars of the revenue realized under these heads in recent years will be found in the volume of appendices.

Arrack.

The supply of arrack is at present regulated by what is known as the contract distillery system, under which the exclusive privilege of manufacture and supply of country spirits throughout the district is disposed of by tender, the contract being for a period of three years. The successful tenderers—at present the Deccan Sugar and Abkāri Company, Limited—have the monopoly of supply of liquor of their own manufacture to the retail vendors within the district, the rates at which the supply is made being fixed by Government. The Company maintains a warehouse at Cuddapah, which gets its supply from the distillery at Samalkot in Gōdāvari district. Molasses arrack is obtained from Samalkot at over-proof strength and reduced to 30° under-proof at the Cuddapah warehouse before issue to the retail vendors in the vicinity of Cuddapah, who get their supply direct from the warehouse, and to the wholesale depots in the district, of which there are nineteen. About 45,000 gallons of arrack constitute the average annual issue from the warehouse. The right of retailing the liquor is annually sold by auction, separately by shops.

Foreign liquors.

The foreign liquor trade is, as elsewhere, controlled by the issue of licenses to wholesale and retail vendors on payment of the prescribed fees. There are only three foreign liquor shops in the district, one being the railway refreshment room at Cuddapah.

Toddy.

Since 1897 the toddy revenue has been managed on the tree-tax system under which a tax is levied on every tree tapped and the right to open shops for sale is sold annually by auction. The trees tapped are dates and palmyras, principally the former. Such trees are most numerous in Pullampet taluk and thereafter commoner in Cuddapah, Proddatūr and Pulivendla than other parts of the district. In the latter taluk at Idupulapāya there is a valuable Government tope of palmyra trees. Shop-keepers apply to have certain trees marked for their use and pay a tax of Rs. 2-4-0 per tree. In addition to this a fee of four annas is payable to

CHAP. XII. ABKĀRI.

the tree-owner. Where the trees are situated on poramboke, which is generally the case in this district, the owner's fee is paid to Government. The tapping of the trees is mainly done by Īdigas, whose hereditary occupation it is, but a few Musalmāns also find employment by this means. It is noteworthy that here, as in the Ceded Districts generally, cocoanut trees are not tapped. They are not largely grown and the toddy they give is not locally favoured. It is also said that the toddy-drawers of the district do not understand the art of climbing and tapping cocoanut trees and that they and the shop-keepers have consequently created a prejudice against this sort of toddy, to prevent a demand for it. The tappers in this district are generally employed by the shop-keepers on monthly wages, the collection and transport of the liquor being arranged by the shop-keepers themselves.

An elaborate set of rules has been framed by the Board of Revenue with the object of regulating the tapping of trees and preventing their death by violent treatment. A fine of two rupees is generally levied for every tree killed by over-tapping. The offence is by no means common.

For the manufacture of jaggery sweet toddy is drawn principally in Pullampet and Badvēl taluks. A few trees are also used for this purpose in Cuddapah and Sidhout. The total number of trees in the district that are tapped for sweet toddy is only about three thousand, so that the practice is not widely prevalent. Toddy is not distilled for the manufacture of arrack.

Opium and hemp drugs.

As in the case of liquor, the right of selling opium is put up to auction annually by shops. The licensed vendors of this district get their supply from the Government treasuries at Cuddapah and Proddatūr. There is a considerable demand for opium at both these places, chiefly among Musalmāns. The hospital at Jammalamadugu and some dispensaries hold opium licenses for medicinal purposes. The district supply of ganja is obtained from the storehouse at Santaravur. Like opium, it is principally consumed at Cuddapah and Proddatūr.

The preventive force.

The preventive force employed by the Abkāri Department checks illicit manufacture of salt, arrack and toddy and illicit practices regarding opium and hemp-drugs. There is at present but one Inspector of the department in the district, whose headquarters are at Sidhout. He is subordinate to the Assistant Commissioner at Vellore. The entertainment of a second Inspector, whose headquarters will be at Jammalamadugu, has recently been sanctioned.

INCOME-TAX.

Income-tax is levied and collected, as elsewhere, according to the rules framed under the Income-tax Act of 1886. The number of assessees under Part IV bears a proportion of less than one per thousand of the population of the district. For the year 1912-13 the incidence of the tax per head of the total population was eight pies while its average distribution among the assessees amounted to nearly forty-seven rupees. With the exception of Cuddapah, Proddatūr and Rājampet the district contains very few trading centres of any importance, and the fact that there are only three other districts in the Presidency which realize less by this tax than Cuddapah need occasion no surprise. The assessees under Part IV are mostly money-lenders, dealers in food-grains and piece-goods merchants.

STAMPS.

Judicial and non-judicial stamps are sold in the district in the usual manner, local stamp-vendors obtaining their stock at a discount from Government treasuries. The population being below that of any other district in the Presidency except the Nilgiris, and the condition of the people far from affluent, it follows that the amount derived from the sale of stamps is proportionately small. The love of litigation may not be less than elsewhere but the capacity for its indulgence is limited, and the sale of judicial stamps in the same measure restricted. The demand for non-judicial stamps is also not large where big transactions are rare and land is mostly owned by small ryots. Statistics show that there are but three other districts in the Presidency wherein less revenue is derived from the sale of stamps than in Cuddapah.

CHAPTER XIII.

ADMINISTRATION OF JUSTICE.

CIVIL JUSTICE—Village munsifs—District munsifs—The District Court—Litigation rare—Registration. CRIMINAL JUSTICE—Crime—Police—Jails—Some sensational crimes.

CHAP. XIII.

CIVIL JUSTICE.

THE Civil Courts of the district are, as elsewhere, of three grades, namely, those of the village munsifs, the district munsifs and the District Judge. They have the same general power and jurisdiction as in other parts of the Presidency.

Village munsifs.

In Cuddapah, as in the Ceded Districts generally, the number of suits filed in the courts of village munsifs falls considerably below the district average for the Presidency as a whole. In an ordinary year they amount in the aggregate to about twelve hundred. The majority are valued between Rs. 10 and Rs. 20. In the year 1912 only three suits were instituted of a value exceeding Rs. 20. There are no village bench courts in the district. The figures for the year 1913 show that in Pullampet and Badvēl taluks more than twice as much civil work is disposed of by village munsifs than in all the rest of the district.

District munsifs.

Before April 1, 1911, there were four district munsifs in the district, namely, at Nandalūr, Proddatūr, Madanapalle and Cuddapah, and the limits of the jurisdiction exercised by each are shown in the margin. With the reconstitution of the district in 1911 which involved the transfer of Madanapalle and Vāyalpād taluks to Chittoor and Kadiri taluk to Anantapur district as also the creation of a new taluk, Kamalāpuram, in Cuddapah district the jurisdiction of the three courts that remained underwent in every case some change. Kamalāpuram taluk was brought within the limits of the Proddatūr Court, and the

Court.	Taluks.
Nandalūr ...	Pullampet. Sidhout. Badvēl.
Proddatūr ...	Proddatūr. Jammalamadugu.
Madanapalle ...	Madanaplle. Vāyalpād. Kadiri. South Rāyachōti.
Cuddapah ...	Cuddapah. Pulivendla. North Rāyachōti.

CHAP. XIII. CIVIL JUSTICE.

portion of Rāyachōti taluk which formerly belonged to the jurisdiction of the District Munsif of Cuddapah was further split into two divisions of twenty-five villages each, one of which was added to the jurisdiction of Nandalūr while the other remained to Cuddapah. The civil district of Cuddapah was at the same time extended by the inclusion in it of the Gooty munsifi, which comprises the Gooty and Tādpatri taluks of Anantapur district and Ādōni taluk of Bellary district. Consequently the number of district munsifs' courts subordinate to the District Court of Cuddapah remained the same as before.

The following places in the district deserve mention as having, at some time or other, been the headquarters of civil courts :—

Rāyachōti	... 1816-66	Tangatūr...	... 1816-72
Nandyālampet	... 1817-70	Duvvūr	...abolished in 1860
Badvēl ...	... 1864-84	Vēmpalle...	... 1835-66

The District Court.

It is thus apparent that the District Court of Cuddapah exercises jurisdiction over an extensive area, the length of which from south-east to north-west corresponds roughly to the section of the railway line between the junctions of Rēnigunta and Raichūr. It is however by no means a wealthy tract, and the large majority of its inhabitants, being educationally backward, are unversed in the tortuous byways of litigation whose uncertain issues they are inclined to avoid.

Litigation rare.

Consequently the business annually brought before the civil courts of the district is but moderate in quantity and demands no special steps to aid them in its disposal. It has already been seen that the work of the village munsifs is light. The average number of ordinary suits annually instituted in the District Munsifs' Courts of Cuddapah and Proddatūr from 1901 to 1911 falls in each case below one thousand, while the corresponding figure for the Nandalūr Court is mucn lower Revenue suits are very rare, about twenty a year being instituted in the Court of the Divisional Officer of Sidhout, and none elsewhere. Finally, the original work in the District Court is by no means heavy. There is no Sub-Judge at Cuddapah. Statistics relating to the business of the civil courts of the district will be found in the separate volume of appendices.

Registration.

The registration of assurances is conducted on the usual lines. The revenue district of Kurnool is, however, included in the jurisdiction of the Registrar of Cuddapah. The following is a brief account of the administrative changes that have

CHAP. XIII.
CIVIL JUSTICE.

taken place from time to time. At the beginning of 1865 two sub-registry offices were opened in the taluk of Cuddapah and designated the offices of the Sub-Registrars of Cuddapah and Kamalāpuram. In 1878 the appointment of a Registrar was sanctioned and the office of the Sub-Registrar of Cuddapah was amalgamated with that of the Registrar. In the following year the office of the Sub-Registrar of Kamalāpuram was abolished and the area of this sub-district was transferred to the jurisdiction of the Registrar of Cuddapah. From January 1, 1908, a joint sub-registry office was opened at Cuddapah as a tentative measure and was ordered to be retained permanently from 1910; but in the following year it was amalgamated with that of the Registrar of Cuddapah. Finally, with effect from January 1, 1913, the registration district of Kurnool was amalgamated with Cuddapah, and the jurisdiction of the registration district of Cuddapah became conterminous with the limits of the two revenue districts of Cuddapah and Kurnool. There are at present eight Sub-Registrars' offices in the district at the stations noted in the margin.

Badvēl.	Pulivendla.
Chitvēl.	Pullampet.
Jammalamadugu.	Rāyachōti.
Proddatūr.	Sidhout.

CRIMINAL JUSTICE.

The constitution of the criminal courts of the district presents no peculiarity. Lowest in the scale are the courts of the village magistrates, who try very few cases. The bulk of the criminal work of the district falls, as elsewhere, to the courts of the stationary sub-magistrates exercising third or second class powers at Cuddapah, Proddatūr, Jammalamadugu, Pulivendla, Rāyachōti and Rājampet. In the other three taluks, namely, Kamalāpuram, Sidhout and Badvēl, there are sheristadar-magistrates, often of the third class, the limits of whose jurisdiction within their respective taluks is determined by the District Magistrate. Where there are sheristadar-magistrates Tahsildars also actively exercise magisterial powers which is not the case where there are stationary sub-magistrates. In addition to these the Deputy Tahsildars of Cuddapah town, Chitvēl and Lakkireddipalle are sub-magistrates, the area of their jurisdiction being conterminous with that of their revenue charges. The Deputy Tahsildar and Sub-Magistrate of Cuddapah town is also the President of the only bench court in the district, which exercises third-class powers and deals chiefly with cases under the Towns Nuisances Act and the District Municipalities Act. The District Magistrate and Divisional Officers are invested with full magisterial powers as elsewhere. The jurisdiction of the Sessions

CHAP. XIII. CRIMINAL JUSTICE.

Court was in 1911 extended to include the Gooty and Tādpatri taluks of Anantapur district, which formerly fell within that of the Sessions Court of Bellary. Statistics regarding the work of the criminal courts will be found in the separate volume of appendices.

Crime.

In proportion to its population the number of grave crimes committed in Cuddapah district is something less than in Kurnool but exceeds the corresponding figure for the other two of the Ceded Districts. Following the redistribution of districts in 1911 whereby the area of Cuddapah was reduced by about one-third, it is worthy of note that, while crimes of house-breaking and theft, including cattle theft, are much fewer the decrease is not very appreciable in respect of murders, dacoities and robberies. It appears to be undeniable that crimes of violence have always been commoner in what was the old main division than in the rest of the district.

Statistics show that crime is more rife in the hot weather than at other seasons. The causes of this are not far to seek. The harvest has then been gathered in and agricultural operations are at a standstill. Lacking a legitimate occupation bad characters are no longer diverted from their evil propensities, while houses are more easily entered for felonious purposes at a time when their inmates are compelled by the intolerable heat to sleep outside and thus relax due vigilance over their property. The great majority of offences against property are committed by professional criminals of whom there are large numbers in Cuddapah and the adjoining districts. Different tribes are conspicuous in different parts of the district. In Proddatūr taluk the principal habitual offenders are the Donga Woddars, mainly located at Kottāla, Vanipenta and Duvvūr; in the south of Pulivendla taluk the Donga Dāsaris of Ammayagāripalle have an unsavoury reputation; in Cuddapah taluk the Sugālis of Maddimadugu are addicted to cattle-lifting. Of criminal gangs in adjoining districts the worst are probably the Korachas of Vāyalpād taluk in Chittoor district who make periodical inroads into Cuddapah district for the purpose of committing crime. These and the Donga Woddars have been declared criminal tribes under the Act of 1911.

No account of crime in Cuddapah district would be complete without some reference to the practice, unfortunately widespread, of employing hired assassins for the commission of murder. The gang whose misdirected energies are devoted to this nefarious business numbers about thirty persons, of various castes. The leaders are Kāpus and the rest mainly

CHAP. XIII. CRIMINAL JUSTICE.

talaiyāris. The gang has quite recently been notified under the Criminal Tribes Act of 1911. Its members appear to have launched into their career of crime about twelve years ago, but only came into prominent notice after the commission of a very atrocious murder in 1909. They operate chiefly in the taluks of Jammalamadugu, Proddatūr and Pulivendla, which constitute the black cotton tract of this district. The bitter factions among the Kāpus of this region, already alluded to, are pursued with such unrelenting animosity that the forcible and final removal of one of the leaders often becomes the supreme object of existence to the other party, who are only restrained from its accomplishment by the certainty that the commission of any such crime would entail suspicion on themselves. The remedy for this difficulty is found in the professional murderer, for whose services there has been an ever-increasing demand proportionate to the immunity of his employers. The atrocious murder referred to above was committed as follows. On the evening of September 8, 1909, one Gudetti Rāmi Reddi of Kottapēta, while returning to his village in a cart from Proddatūr where he had gone in the morning to register a document was waylaid and murdered, his head being cut off and the body thrown on the road about a mile or so outside Proddatūr. The head was never found. In this case the police investigation disclosed that the chief of the gang of professional assassins had, in consideration of a sum of a thousand rupees which he received from two of the deceased's enemies, employed several of his subordinates to commit the murder. Long before his murder the deceased had information that the leader of the gang had been hired by his enemies to murder him, and the assassins, knowing this, took no action for about a year so as to allay all suspicion and then committed the murder. This case being typical of the methods employed, it is unnecessary to recount others, of which some dozen are on record, all of which bear evidence of the handiwork of these hired assassins.

Police.

Police administration in the district is controlled by the District Superintendent. Under him is an Assistant Superintendent at Jammalamadugu, whose charge is conterminous with the revenue division administered from the same headquarters. A personal assistant is also occasionally given to the Superintendent. The force is organized on the usual lines. Some three hundred and fifty talaiyāris are in addition posted along the high roads and in jungly places which offer facilities for the commission of robbery and dacoity. Wherever possible land is assigned to these talaiyāris in the neighbourhood of their several *tānāhs*, and a recent order prescribes that as much as an acre of wet land and two acres of dry should be given in each case, but it is seldom that so large an extent is available.

It is said that investigation is rendered unduly difficult in Cuddapah owing to the hostile attitude of the people, which is not infrequently encouraged by the village magistrates, especially in the lawless black cotton taluks. Numerous cases of violent crime in this region are also rendered incapable of conviction owing to the universal spirit of faction by which nearly all evidence is tainted.

Jails.

There is no district jail at Cuddapah. Persons sentenced to terms of imprisonment exceeding one month are incarcerated in the central jail at Vellore. There is a sub-jail at each of the taluk headquarters.

Some sensational crimes.

The most remarkable crime occurring in the district subsequent to its reduction to order by Munro at the beginning of the last century was the murder of Mr. Macdonald, Additional Sub-Collector, at Cuddapah, in 1832. This crime, quite devoid of any political significance, was the outcome of a riot engendered by the fanaticism of a section of Musalmāns. Early in the morning of June 15, it was said that a small pig had been killed and thrown bleeding into the Jumma Masjid. It turned out afterwards that this pig was merely a bandicoot and had been purposely placed there by a Musalmān aided by two Hindus. But the populace speedily became excited and gave no thought to the possible origin of the incident or the perpetrator of the supposed offence. Meeting in the market place and the principal bazaars of the town the Pathans gathered in large numbers and fanned the passions of one and all. By 10 o'clock the crowd had assumed alarming proportions and exhibited so uncompromising an attitude that Mr. Macdonald sent a message to the Collector who resided at some distance from the town, reporting that he would endeavour to quiet the mob, but, if necessary, would send for the military from the cantonment. Mr. Macdonald then got into his palanquin and went to the cutcherry where he found the native subordinates assembled and in a great state of alarm. An order was at once sent for a detachment, but Macdonald was not destined to see its arrival. A letter was brought to him from a missionary, Mr. Howel, who lived in the middle of the town and who said that he feared an instant attack upon his house. Macdonald, in spite of the protestation of the cutcherry officials, at once determined to do his best to help the missionary. He went into the bazaar accompanied

CHAP. XIII. CRIMINAL JUSTICE.

only by a few peons. A naick and some of the treasury guard sepoys followed him, but it is probable that their presence only served still more to excite the crowd. Macdonald had scarcely reached the bazaar before he was attacked and cut down. His revenue peons ran away, but the guard tried to defend him and shared his fate. The last blow is said to have been given by a Pathan butcher; but after this had been dealt, the mob was taken aback. It dissolved as rapidly as it had gathered, and in a few minutes the streets were deserted. Five of the ring-leaders of this riot were publicly hanged near the present town police station. Macdonald was only twenty-four years of age at the time of his death, the tragedy of which is enhanced by the fact that his young wife only survived him twenty-one days, dying, it is said, of a broken heart.[1]

The episode of Narasimha Reddi's uprising in 1846 has been briefly referred to elsewhere.[2] Legends of the most fearful atrocities have grown up round his name and that of two others, Gaddam Bāligādu and Thīti Mallugādu. Of these two latter nothing whatever seems to be on record. The apocryphal crimes of all three figure in the songs and stories recited by a wandering class of beggars who are known as Thāndava Pātagāndlu.

Two crimes of later years, a murder and a dacoity, though not of very recent occurrence, are still well remembered, probably from having occurred in Cuddapah town. In 1885 on Telugu New Year's day about 9 o'clock at night a Kōmati widow by name T. Subbamma, who possessed much property secured in an iron safe in her house, was killed by being suffocated. She lived by herself in a house in the middle of the chief bazaar street of Cuddapah town. On going outside the house previous to retiring for the night, some thieves who were hidden in the backyard seized her, carried her inside, stuffed a cloth into her mouth to prevent her crying out, and

[1] There is a tomb to the memory of Macdonald and his wife in the cemetery near the Sidhout road. An inscription records that it was erected by the civil officers of the station "as a tribute of affection and esteem to the joint memory of Charles Edward Macdonald Esquire of the Madras Civil Service, aged 24 years, a civilian of the fairest promise who, while attempting in the fearless and conscientious discharge of his duty to appease by prompt and persuasive measures the fury of a fanatic rabble of Moormen assembled on the 15th June 1832 in the town of Cuddapah, was, though completely unarmed, attacked, deserted by all his peons and barbarously murdered, and of Agnes his wife, who only survived him 21 days, having died on the 7th July 1832, broken-hearted, in the 20th year of her age."

[2] Chapter II, end.

tried to find out where the key of the iron safe was. This key could not be found, and the thieves were unable to open the safe, and so failed to obtain the Rs. 30,000 worth of property for which they had come. The woman, however, was killed by suffocation, and the robbers took all the jewels she had on her body valued at Rs. 280. This case was most patiently worked out and detected by the Police. At first a bad character of Cuddapah town, tempted by the reward of Rs. 500 offered by the District Magistrate for the detection of the case, came forward and voluntarily, but falsely, confessed that he and five others had committed the crime. His confession, a most deliberate one, led to the arrest of himself and of the five persons whom he incriminated. Luckily, however, the Police hit upon the right clue in a village near Muddanūr of Jammalamadugu taluk, as a consequence of which five persons were arrested, one was made an approver, two were convicted and sentenced to transportation for life, and the two others were released. About Rs. 50 worth of the property lost was recovered.

The dacoity referred to took place in 1889. A well-organized gang of twenty or thirty dacoits with torches and weapons suddenly appeared at the outskirts of Cuddapah town and attacked the house of one Mākam Chenchayya. Some of the party armed with stones and slings prevented any assistance from reaching the unfortunate victim, while the rest broke into his house and carried off property valued at more than Rs. 5,500. They inflicted brutal wounds on Mākam Chenchayya, from which he subsequently died, and ran off leaving no clue whatever to their identity. The whole incident was reported to have occurred in less than half an hour.

CHAPTER XIV.

LOCAL SELF-GOVERNMENT.

THE LOCAL BOARDS—Their constitution—The unions—Receipts of the boards—Their expenditure. MUNICIPAL GOVERNMENT.

CHAP. XIV. THE LOCAL BOARDS.

EXCEPT in Cuddapah, the only municipality the district contains, local self-government is in the hands of the district board and the four Taluk Boards of Cuddapah, Jammalamadugu, Rāyachōti and Sidhout, the control of the district board over the taluk boards being the same as elsewhere. The jurisdiction of the taluk boards is in each case conterminous with that of the revenue divisional charge of the same name. The taluk board of Jammalamadugu exercises control over the taluks of Jammalamadugu, Proddatūr and Kamalāpuram, that of Rāyachōti is concerned with the two taluks of Rāyachōti and Pulivendla, the Sidhout Board has the three eastern taluks to manage, while that of Cuddapah is exclusively devoted to the taluk of that name.

Their constitution.

Excluding the ex-officio President, who is the District Collector, the district board consists of thirty-two members, half of whom are nominated and half elected, the election being by the taluk boards. Prior to July 1909 all members were nominated. The taluk boards are now similarly constituted, half the members being elected. As in other districts the revenue divisional officer is ex-officio president of the taluk board in his division. While the vice-president of the district board is nominated, a taluk board has the right of electing its vice-president, if it needs one. At present there are vice-presidents in only two of the taluk boards, namely, Cuddapah and Jammalamadugu.

The unions.

The larger towns have been constituted unions, of which there are fourteen in the district. They have the usual powers of raising taxation within their respective limits, the amounts thus realized being expended on works of public utility such as sanitation and the improvement of communications. There are two unions, Pātha Cuddapah and Chennūr, controlled by the Cuddapah Taluk Board, and six, namely, Sidhout, Badvēl, Pōrumāmilla, Chitvēl, Nandalūr and Rājampet by

CHAP. XIV. THE LOCAL BOARDS.

that of Sidhout. Rāyachōti, Pulivendla and Vēmpalle are the unions attached to the Rāyachōti Taluk Board, and there are also three, namely Proddatūr, Jammalamadugu and Kamalāpuram under the Jammalamadugu board. The income of these bodies is chiefly derived from the house-tax, which is levied at the maximum permissible rates in eight unions, at two-thirds thereof in four, and at half the maximum rates in two. The average incidence of the tax amounts to twelve annas per house taxed, the rate being lowest in Chitvēl and highest in Rāyachōti. The receipts in each union average about Rs. 2,800 annually, of which nearly one-half is spent on sanitation.

Receipts of the boards.

The incidence of local fund taxation throughout the district amounts to three annas and one pie per head of the population. As elsewhere, the chief item among the receipts is the land-cess, which is levied at the rate of one anna in every rupee of the land assessment and is collected in the ordinary manner. Next follows the income derived from the sale of the right to collect fees at the various weekly markets. There are fourteen of these in the district, of which those at Rājampet and Pulivendla are probably the most important.

The income derived from tolls and ferries constitutes another important source of revenue to the boards. The right to collect fees at markets is sold annually by the taluk boards, and the right to collect tolls by the district board. There are seventeen toll-gates and five ferries in the district. Tolls are levied at half the maximum rates allowed by law.

Their expenditure.

The income[1] thus realized is principally devoted to the improvement of communications and to the upkeep of medical and educational institutions. Particulars[2] of these have already been given.

MUNICIPAL GOVERNMENT.

Of the early history of the Cuddapah Municipality but little information is available owing to the destruction of its records by fire in the year 1885. The town was constituted a municipality in 1866, the councillors being appointed by nomination until the introduction of the Municipal Act of 1885, from which date the council has consisted of sixteen members, twelve of whom are elected by the rate-payers. The chairman of the municipality is elected, and holds office for three or two years according as he is or is not a member of the council. In point of population Cuddapah ranks but forty-ninth among the sixty-one municipalities of the Presidency. According to

[1] For statistics of local funds, receipts and expenditure, see Appendix, Vol. II.

[2] See Chapters VII, IX and X.

CHAP. XIV. MUNCIPAL GOVERNMENT.

the census of 1911 its inhabitants number 17,807 which is less than five hundred in excess of the figure recorded in 1891 and only exceeds the population of 1871 by about fifteen hundred.

Excluding the variable item of grants and contributions from Government, the annual revenue realized by the municipality amounts on the average to about fifty thousand rupees. From the accounts[1] of its receipts and expenditure in recent years the annual income of the municipality seems to fall short of its requirements by about Rs. 4,000, and when exceptional expenditure is to be met, owing, for example, to the outbreak of an epidemic of plague or cholera, a much larger subsidy is needed.

The town is provided with excellent water-works, which were completed in 1890 at a total cost of rather more than one lakh and six thousand rupees. The wells of the town seem to be a fruitful source of disease, and the introduction of pipe water had a very beneficent effect on the general health. In 1902 restrictions were placed on the cultivation of paddy within municipal limits with the result that malaria was rendered less prevalent. In 1912 a medical officer specially deputed to enquire into the best means of combating malaria visited the municipality, and the closing of all wells was a feature of the proposals made by him for still further improving the water-supply. The public health is also being consulted in the question of providing proper subsoil drainage, which has recently engaged the attention of the Public Works Department. The hospital at Cuddapah, which was built in 1872, is under the control of the municipality, but a sum of Rs. 3,000 is annually contributed from local funds towards its upkeep.

On the whole the town seems to be in a flourishing condition. It is said that the population has recently begun to show a marked upward tendency, and new buildings are rising rapidly. A town survey of the municipality has never been made, and is stated to be greatly needed. The medical and educational institutions in charge of the municipality have already been referred to.[2]

[1] See Appendix, Vol. II.

[2] See Chapters IX and X.

CHAPTER XV
GAZETTEER

CUDDAPAH TALUK—Cuddapah—Chennūr — Vallūr — Pushpagiri — Pendlimarri—Chinnadāsaripalle — Chintakommadinne— Khājipetasunkēsula — Nandimandalam. JAMMALAMADUGU TALUK—Jammalamadugu — Peddamudiyam — Kōdūr — Gandikōta — Gandlūr — Tāllaproddatūr — Yētūr—Muddanūr. PRODDATUR TALUK—Proddatūr—Duvvūr—Vanipenta—Kāmanūr — Rāmēswaram — Korrapād — Settivāripalle — Mudireddipalle—Maidukūru and Nandyālampet. KAMALAPURAM TALUK — Kamalāpuram—Pālagiri—Uppalūr—Animela—Nidujuvvi—Yerraguntla. PULIVENDLA TALUK—Vēmpalle — Pulivendla — Pārnapalle—Vēmula—Chilakampalle—Balapanūr — Yerraballa — Simhādripuram — Peddakūdāla—Mārellamadaka. RAYACHOTI TALUK—Rāyachōti — Tsundupalle — Lakkireddipalle — Gālivēdu — Nūlivēdu—Sānipāya—Vīraballe—Vangimalla—Gadikōta—Matli—Chinnamandem. BADVEL TALUK — Badvēl—Pōrumāmilla—Sankhavaram—Kalasapād—Kottakōta — Munelli—Palugurāllapalle. SIDHOUT TALUK—Siddhavattam—Vontimitta—Mādhavaram — Kuruguntapalle — Kōtapād — Ōbulām — Kondūr — Yāppirāla — Gangapērūr. PULLAMPET TALUK — Rājampet — Pullampet—Chitvēl—Pottapi—Kōdūr—Settigunta—Nandalūr—Pedda Ōrampād—Chinna Ōrampād—Penagalūr—Tangatūr.

CUDDAPAH TALUK.

CHAP. XV. CUDDAPAH TALUK.

THE taluk of Cuddapah is situated in the valley of the Pennēr, mainly to the south of that river and east of the Pāpaghni. The course of the latter from Vēmpalle to its junction with the Pennēr near Kamalāpuram forms a natural boundary between the Cuddapah and Kamalāpuram taluks. North of the Pennēr the Cuddapah taluk embraces the south-easternmost corner of the Kundēr valley and is separated from the Proddatūr taluk by an irregular boundary which, starting from the Kundēr a few miles north of its confluence with the Pennēr, crosses the Kurnool-Cuddapah Canal and the Kurnool road a little south of Maidukūru, and extends eastwards to the foot of the Lankāmalais. This range and that of the Pālkondas constitute well defined and natural boundaries on the east and south of the taluk. By the recent creation of the Kamalāpuram taluk that of Cuddapah was

CHAP. XV. CUDDAPAH TALUK.

considerably reduced in area. It formerly extended westwards as far as a point on the Muddanūr-Pulivendla road some six miles south of Muddanūr railway station. Its area now is 509 square miles and it contains a little over a hundred thousand inhabitants. It lies beyond the limits of the black cotton tract which overspreads the western taluks, and the prevailing soil is alluvial in origin, loamy and generally fertile. The country round Cuddapah and, roughly speaking, extending north-westwards through Chennūr to the Kundēr valley is rich land and repays high farming, while the area commanded by the Kurnool-Cuddapah Canal in this taluk is admirably suited to wet cultivation. The channels from the canal and the tanks which it feeds provide the best irrigation in the district. The taluk also contains some fair-sized tanks unconnected with this system such as those at Utukūr and Ambavaram; but these do not afford so sure a supply as the river channels from the Pāpaghni. The Pennēr though a larger river provides less facilities for irrigation in this part of its course owing to the steepness of its banks. The taluk is well provided with roads which radiate from the headquarters of the district, and contains within its limits three railway stations, namely, Cuddapah, Kristnāpuram and Ganganapalle. The following is an account of the few places of interest or importance in the taluk.

Cuddapah.

Cuddapah, the headquarters of the district, lies in the angle formed by the two branches of the Pālkonda hills, one of which proceeds northwards and merges into the Lankāmalais while the other passes due westwards a few miles south of the town. It contains a population of 17,807 inhabitants, of whom nearly half are Musalmāns. All the offices usual to a district headquarters are located at Cuddapah except those of the Executive Engineer and the Circle Inspector of the Salt and Abkāri Department. The former officer is stationed at Madanapalle and the latter at Sidhout. The town was constituted a municipality in the year 1866.[1]

The origin of the name Cuddapah cannot be determined with any certainty. It is generally considered to be so called on account of its position on the threshold (Gadapa) of the pass that leads through the Vontimitta valley to the sacred hill of Tirupati. Others derive the word from 'Kripa' signifying in Sanskrit 'mercy.' In old records, until the 18th century, the name of the place was written as Kurpa or Kurpah. It is possible that Pāta Cuddapah, the original village, is identical with Karige or Karipē which occurs in the

[1] See Chapter XIV.

geographical treatise of Ptolemy of Alexandria compiled in the 2nd century A.D.[1] The present town of Cuddapah is believed to have been founded in the latter part of the 16th century. After the battle of Talikōta in A.D. 1565 which marked the disruption of the Vijayanagar Empire, the country was overrun by bands of Musalmān adventurers in search of new settlements. A Pathan officer in the army of Golconda, by name Neiknam Khan, penetrated with a few followers into this region and whether on account of its apparent fertility or—which is more probable—its strategic possibilities he decided to remain. His proposal to found a Musalmān settlement here was approved by the Sultan of Golconda and he was permitted to name it Neiknamabād. The first Nawab of Neiknamabād was a relative of the Sultan, and Neiknam Khan himself was appointed the Nawab's chief minister. But the new settlement showed little signs of thriving. The original followers of Neiknam Khan had been few, and others who subsequently braved the long journey eastwards brought no wealth with them but had rather left their homes with the object of repairing their shattered fortunes. For some years the new Musalmān village remained isolated and resourceless, regarded with suspicion and distrust by the neighbouring Hindu population. Neiknamabād had been founded about a mile and a half south of the ancient Kurpah or Cuddapah which at this time was only known on account of its fine temple, the gift of a Vijayanagar Emperor. With the Hindus of this village the Nawab determined to make friends. In this he was successful and, by conceding them full liberty to follow their own religious and social customs, he persuaded them to settle in Neiknamabād, which from that time forward began to grow and prosper. In proof of his good faith the Nawab allowed the Hindus to erect a temple to Ānjanēyaswāmi near his own palace and mosque. Though Neiknamabād grew populous partly at the expense of Cuddapah, the latter village still continued to attract numbers of Hindu devotees on account of its well-known temple to Sri Vēnkatēswara. From the proximity of Neiknamabād and probably also the fact that many families had migrated thither from Cuddapah, the name of Cuddapah came to be applied by Hindus to the Musalmān town also, which—except for its one attraction—overshadowed the Hindu village in every particular. To the latter in course of time was given the distinguishing name of Pāta Cuddapah, which still survives.

[1] It is so identified in the Madras Manual of the Administration, 1885, Volume I. Geography, page 9.

CHAP. XV. CUDDAPAH TALUK.

The Musalmān rulers themselves gradually accepted the new appellation and Neiknamabād became Cuddapah.

No doubt this is approximately a true account of the early history of Cuddapah. It contains no Hindu temple of any antiquity except the Ānjanēya temple already alluded to, while the Musalmān predominance is proved not only by the existence of many old mosques and cemeteries but by the very names of the different quarters of the town, among which may be mentioned Sāyipet, Almospet, Meccapet, Muchimianpet or Muchampet and Nabikōt. The Siva temple in Muchampet was constructed subsequent to the British occupation.

The early history of the Nawabs of Cuddapah is wrapped in obscurity. Their very names are unknown though tradition assigns the first Abdul Nabi Khan to some period in the 17th century and regards the great Abdul Nabi Khan[1] of the early 18th century as the second of that name. The latter, though he never brought the poligars to order, wielded a more or less effective authority over the districts of Sidhout, Cumbum, Gandikōta and Gurramkonda. The two latter were strongly fortified places and served as effective outposts of his territory. Abdul Nabi was an enlightened ruler as well as a good soldier. To him is attributed the construction of the Pāta Cuddapah tank, for the supply of which he constructed an anicut across the Bugga vanka. This anicut was destroyed by dynamite after the floods of 1903,[2] and the tank is now supplied by a channel from the Kurnool-Cuddapah Canal. The Nawab is supposed to have died about the year 1730. An outlying suburb of the town on the other side of the vanka opposite his old palace is called Nabikōt, and testifies to the honour in which he was held by the people.

The following story lends colour to the tradition that Abdul Nabi was a patron of letters. A young Moulvi of great erudition, having heard of the prowess of the Nawab and his regard for learning, started out from Golconda to go to Cuddapah to ask the Nawab's daughter in marriage. But by the time he came to the end of his long journey it was only to find that the Nawab's daughter was already married. The Nawab himself was much disappointed and condoled with the young man in his misfortune. The latter settled down to a life of renunciation and devoted himself to good works. He remained a bachelor all his life and by his sanctity attained to the dignity of a kabīr, dying at Cuddapah in his old age. The old Nawab had long since passed away, but his tender-hearted daughter on hearing of the death of the Moulvi, who

[1] See Chapter II. [2] See Chapter VIII.

CHAP. XV. CUDDAPAH TALUK.

had sacrificed all for her, resolved to perpetuate his memory. In the centre of the town is a splendid mausoleum which she built as a remembrance of the holy man. The building is included in the List of Ancient Monuments and conserved by Government. The dome, which is very handsome, was recently repaired.

The old fort of the Nawabs with its gateway flanked by two towers is still in a good state of preservation. Within it are now located the jail, the District Forest offices and, temporarily, the Kamalāpuram taluk office.

After the departure of Munro and the bifurcation of the Ceded Districts into two Collectorates, Sidhout was for eight years the headquarters of the district. It was abandoned in favour of Cuddapah in the year 1817. Four years afterwards Cuddapah became a cantonment and continued as such till 1868. The murder of Mr. Macdonald in 1832 has already been referred to.[1]

The municipal water-works were opened in 1890. They are situated about four miles to the south of the town. The water, which is derived from a number of springs in the Bugga vanka, is collected into a deep well from which it is pumped by motive power into a large reservoir and conducted by pipes to the town. In the hot weather the supply has not proved quite adequate to the needs of the municipality, and a new and deeper well has consequently been recently constructed. It is recognized as highly important in the interests of health that the people of Cuddapah should not be compelled to resort to the old wells in the town which are mostly contaminated and a fruitful source of disease. The pipe water is extremely good and much appreciated by the people.

As a trade centre Cuddapah stands second only to Proddatūr. In a sense it is more important, as it taps a larger area within the district. Most of the trade of Badvēl, Sidhout, Pulivendla and Rāyachōti taluks passes through Cuddapah, and its situation on the main line to Bombay facilitates the export of its more peculiar products, such as melons and turmeric, to all parts of India.

Chennūr.

Chennūr contains, with its five hamlets, a population of 5,254 and is the largest union in the taluk. It is situated on the right bank of the Pennēr seven miles north-west of Cuddapah. It is the headquarters of a firka revenue inspector and contains two Board elementary schools, one of which is reserved for Musalmāns, besides a Hindu girls' school up to the third standard. The wet lands of the village are

[1] See Chapter XIII.

mainly irrigated by channels from the Kurnool-Cuddapah Canal and are very valuable. The melons grown in the bed of the Pennēr are also a source of much gain to their cultivators.

The antiquity of Chennūr is proved by an inscription on a stone in the oldest part of the village, from which we learn that in the early part of the 16th century when the Emperor Krishnadēva was ruling at Vijayanagar it was the headquarters of an administrative unit consisting of several villages and extending as far as Potladurti. This old division of Chennūr was included in the Gandikōta district of the Udayagiri province.

The village contains two choultries, one in the middle of the village and the other, of more recent construction, on the road from Cuddapah about two hundred yards north of the Yellammadēvata temple. It has about half a dozen Hindu temples, a masjid of some importance and a darga, none of which calls for particular notice.

Vallūr.

Vallūr, population 3,113, is situated on the Bellary road about ten miles north-west of Cuddapah. It contains large areas of channel-irrigated wet land and specializes in the cultivation of the variety of paddy called *pishāna* which is a favourite in some parts of the country. The export of this product is said to be the main business of a group of wealthy merchants residing in this village.

Many hundreds of years ago Vallūr was a place of considerable political importance. It was the headquarters of a province of the Chōla kingdom in the 12th century, the governor of which rebelled against the Chōla king Kulōttunga III and boasted to have levied tribute from him. His success was shortlived, as this Chōla king subsequently reduced all his enemies and became very powerful. In the following century Vallūr was also chosen by the Kākatīya kings of Warangal as their administrative headquarters for the government of a large tract of country embracing most of the present Cuddapah district. It continued as such till the downfall of the Kākatīyas in A.D. 1309, after which it ceased to be of any importance. Under the Vijayanagar Empire it was presumably included in the Chennūr *sima*. It is said that the Emperor Aurangzebe established a Nawab at Vallūr after the downfall of the King of Golconda in 1687. The ruined Musalmān stronghold in the village renders this possible; but as we find no such rival to the Nawab of Cuddapah in the early years of the following century Vallūr could not have been thus held for many years

Pushpagiri.

Pushpagiri is a hamlet of Kotlūr, a village situated on the Pennēr about ten miles north-west of Cuddapah. The hamlet takes its name from the sacred hill of Pushpagiri, the most important religious centre in the district. Vaishnavaites sometimes call it Tirumala Madhya Ahōbilam from its position midway between Ahōbilam in Kurnool and the famous Tirupati hill, both places of great sanctity, while Sivaites speak of it as Madhya Kailāsam as it is situated between Vārānasi and Chidambaram which are known to devout Sivaites respectively as Uttara and Dakshina Kailāsam. Two fantastic stories are told to account for the name Pushpagiri or Hill of Flowers. Some say that a Brahman, desirous of mingling the bones of his father in holy Ganges, passed this way and, setting down his burden, went to bathe in the Pennēr. On his return from the river he found the bones had been converted into jasmine flowers. Content with this miracle and assured that his father's soul had gone to heaven he resolved to go no further, and cast the flowers upon the waters of the Pennēr. The place where the miraculous conversion of the bones took place gradually assumed the form of a hill, to which the name of Pushpagiri was given to mark its wonderful origin. The second story, which my informant declares to be more credible, is as follows: An old man of the Kāpu caste, much worried by his troublesome sons who neglected the estate and passed their time in quarrelling, found himself obliged to labour in the fields himself and accordingly went forth to plough with a pair of old bulls. Having worked for some hours he drove the cattle to a large and deep *madugu* or pool near by, to give them water. To his astonishment the bulls, as soon as they had quenched their thirst, were transformed and became young and strong. The old farmer wondering at this phenomenon stepped into the pool himself and on emerging found himself changed in feelings and appearance to a youth of sixteen. His wife meanwhile, after upbraiding her sons for sending such an old man to work in the fields had taken food in a basket and gone out to search for him. She found no signs of him and passing near the pool asked the young man if he had seen her husband. The youth, recognizing the old woman as his wife, revealed his identity and told her the story of the transformation of himself and the bulls by the virtue of the wonderful pool. The woman would not believe, but scolded the young man for deceiving her. He, after bearing with her for some time, lost patience and dragged her to the pool and made her bathe. In a moment she too was transformed and

CHAP. XV. CUDDAPAH TALUK.

became youthful like her husband, whom she forthwith recognized. They then partook of the food she had brought and returned home in the evening with the young bulls. Their sons naturally failed to recognize them, but the truth was gradually forced upon them and also became known to others, who in their turn bathed in the wonderful pool, renewed their youth and became immortal. This state of things was discovered by Nārada, the wanderer in the three worlds, who went and reported to Brahma in Satyalōka that his mandates of destiny had become null and void by reason of a pool in the world which contained amruta or nectar and rendered men immortal. Brahma marvelled how a pool in the world could contain nectar which had been hidden even from the Rākshasas; but on enquiry he learned from Nārada that it was indeed a fact, as Garuda when taking nectar from Dēvalōka to relieve the sufferings of his mother had been attacked by the god Indra with his diamond sword and let fall a drop into this very pool. Being at a loss how to remedy the matter Brahma invoked the aid of Mahāvishnu. The latter forthwith ordered Ānjanēya to drop a hill into the pool and cover it up. This mandate was obeyed but the hill instead of sinking into the water floated on the surface like a flower. Then the gods all joined together and weighed it down while Vishnu and Rudra clamped it firmly by the imprint of their feet at each end, which are now represented by two temples. That the two temples are on the same side of the hill and not at either end is explained by the fact that one of them must have been subsequently removed from its original place.

Of the several temples on the Pushpagiri hill overlooking the river the greatest is the temple of Chennakēswaraswāmi with its lofty five-storied *gōpuram*. The front entrance is approached by a flight of steps from the Pennēr corresponding to a similar flight on the opposite or right bank of the river which leads from the village. At the time of the more important festivals the local authorities and the police make suitable arrangements for their satisfactory celebration and the control of the crowds that assemble. The great *brahmōtsavam* takes place about the middle of April, with a grand elephant procession and car festival, and attracts about 50,000 people.

At Adinimmayapalle, about a mile above Pushpagiri, the Kurnool-Cuddapah Canal crosses the Pennēr by an aqueduct near which is a travellers' bungalow belonging to the Public Works Department.

Pendlimarri.

Pendlimarri is a thriving village, about fourteen miles south-west of Cuddapah, on the road to Vēmpalle. It has a population of 1,419 and contains a police station and a travellers' bungalow. The latter is pleasantly situated in a tope by the roadside a little east of the village. Pendlimarri is the headquarters of a firka revenue inspector. The name is a composition of the Telugu words pendli, marriage, and marri, a banyan tree, and a story has been invented to account for its origin, but there is no large banyan tree near the village at the present day. Some houses on the western side of the village are enclosed in a ruined fort, the date of the construction of which is not ascertainable. The proximity of the village to Cuddapah renders it unlikely that it was ever the seat of a poligār, as even the weakest of the Nawabs of Cuddapah were probably able to maintain their authority unquestioned within a radius of twenty miles of their headquarters. The fort is also within the village, while poligārs' forts were generally built at a little distance from the village-sites. That Pendlimarri is of great antiquity is proved by an inscription in a temple of a neighbouring village from which we find that a certain Kathāri Mangayya was ruling "Pendlimarri and Tummalūr" in the year S.S. 1292 (A.D. 1370) during the reign of the Vijayanagar Emperor Bukka I.

The village contains a temple of Vīrabhadraswāmi, in which religious service is conducted once a week. The *pūjāri* is a goldsmith.

Chinnadāsaripalle.

Chinnadāsaripalle is situated about two miles south-west of Pendlimarri. It is quite a small village, but contains a fine temple of Lakshmi Narasimhaswāmi picturesquely situated in "the valley of a thousand wells," *Ōnūtula* (a corruption of *veyyinūtula*) *kōna*. Like other beauty spots in the Pālkonda hills, blessed with perennial springs of water in a thirsty land, this *kōna* is regarded as a place of great sanctity, and the annual festival in May attracts large crowds to the temple. This is about a mile and a half south of the village and formerly the only way to it lay along the bed of the hill stream which rises at the "thousand wells." Subsequently a cobble-stone cart-track was constructed by a devotee of the temple, so that carts can now be taken as far as its very entrance. About a hundred yards from the temple, towards the hills, are three stones bearing inscriptions, one of which is undecipherable. Of the others one is that already referred to above which refers to the ruler of Pendlimarri and Tummalūr in the reign of Bukka I. The other records the remission of taxes on weavers' looms in the reign of the Emperor Achyuta. The date is illegible, but from the mention of the Emperor's name it must fall between A.D. 1530 and 1544.

Chinta-kommadinne.

Chintakommadinne is situated some six miles south of Cuddapah and about a mile west of the road from Cuddapah to Rāyachōti. Inclusive of its seven hamlets, it has a population of 3,017 inhabitants and thus deserves notice on account of its size though possessing no feature of peculiar interest. It contains a tank with a waterspread of more than three hundred acres which, for Cuddapah taluk, is fairly large. An inscription near the bund of the tank records the grant of some lands to Reddis, Karnams, Kāpus and Kammas for having repaired and strengthened the bund in S.S. 1669, i.e., A.D. 1747.

It may be mentioned here that in this village as in others in the neighbourhood of Cuddapah (where the practice also prevails) white butter is used instead of ghee and is retailed by weight instead of by measure, being sold at so much per seer of twenty-four tolas.

An inscription in the temple of Janārdanaswāmi records that in S.S. 1478 or A.D. 1556 in the time of the Vijayanagar Emperor Sadāsiva two fields, one wet and the other dry, were gifted to the temple by one Yellappa Nāyaningādu for the performance of religious services.

Khājipēta-sunkēsula.

Khājipētasunkēsula, population 2,228, is a village about four miles due north of Pushpagiri and some twelve miles north-west of Cuddapah. It contains a police station, two Board elementary schools—one for Musalmāns—and a branch post office. Sunkēsula is a common name of villages in this part of the country and the prefix Khājipet is employed to distinguish this village from other Sunkēsulas. The village of Khājipet is said to have been built by one Meera Khan, a captain in the army of one of the Nawabs of Cuddapah.

No account of Khājipētasunkēsula, however brief, would be complete without some mention of Duggi Reddi Venkata Reddi, headman of the village from 1870 to 1904. His term of office was marked by exceptional efficiency and the utmost devotion to duty. In the early years of his life, before the great famine, he already gave such proof of his ability that a Tahsildar of Cuddapah wanted him to be made a revenue inspector. For having superintended the construction of a road from Khājipet to Kamalāpuram during the great famine he was rewarded with a gold bangle on which is an inscription to the effect that it was presented to him by Government "as a reward for conspicuous energy and devotion to duty in connection with the execution of relief works during the famine of 1877." His whole-hearted co-operation with Mr. MacCartie in his successful introduction of prickly-pear as cattle fodder in 1877 was also commended by Government. Later on he was given a silver ring as a reward for promoting vaccination. Throughout his term of office he was frequently employed in assisting less efficient village officers to collect outstanding balances. He was a taluk board member from 1886 to 1903 and in the latter year was elected a member of the District Board. As remarkable as his long and faithful service to Government was his devotion to public charities, in recognition of which he was in 1903 granted a certificate by the Viceroy in the name of His Majesty the King-Emperor.

CHAP. XV. CUDDAPAH TALUK.

Nandi-mandalam.

Nandimandalam is a large village situated on the right bank of the Pāpaghni about six miles north-east of Vēmpalle, at the trijunction of the three taluks of Pulivendla, Kamalāpuram and Cuddapah. The village is said to have been an important place many years ago and inhabited chiefly by Chandravamsa Rāzus. People of the Rāzu caste calling themselves Nandimandalam Rāzulu are found in various parts of this and the adjoining districts, but the circumstances of their dispersal are not known. It is said that they suffered a crushing defeat at the hands of Musalmāns who took their territory, and that their womenfolk, whom they had left in the village when they went out to battle, hearing of their defeat, joined together and made a pit of fire into which they threw themselves to escape the consequences of capture by the Musalmāns.

An enclave in the Pālkonda hills to the south of the village, approached by a narrow winding gorge, contains some perennial springs, which as usual are regarded as sacred, and a temple to Chennakēsavaswāmi. The god is also called Kōna Chennarāyaswāmi on account of the locality.

JAMMALAMADUGU TALUK.

JAMMALA-MADUGU TALUK.

This taluk occupies the north-western corner of the district. On three sides its boundaries are artificial, while on the south it is separated from Pulivendla taluk by the Bhānukōta and Mallyāla hills which mark the first uprising of the Erramala range from the western boundary of Kamalāpuram taluk to where it abuts on the Chitrāvati river. Proddatūr and Kamalāpuram taluks adjoin it on the east, while on the north and west are respectively the Kōilkuntla taluk of Kurnool and the Tādpatri taluk of Anantapur district. The Cuddapah, Anantapur and Kurnool districts meet on the Gandikōta hills which start

[1] See Chapter VIII.

CHAP. XV. JAMMALAMADUGU TALUK.

a few miles west of Proddatūr and traverse Jammalamadugu taluk in a north-westerly direction to the Kurnool frontier. The Pennēr river enters the taluk near Kōdūr in the west and skirts the southern flank of the Gandikōta hills as far as Gandlūr where the Chitrāvati joins it from the south. Thence the stream turns slightly north and forces its way by a winding narrow gorge through the Gandikōta hills. A few miles further down it takes a sharp curve near Jammalamadugu and proceeds south-eastwards across the black cotton plain into Proddatūr táluk.

The entire taluk lies within the black cotton tract. The purest stretch of this soil lies north of the Pennēr and attains its highest development north and east of Jammalamadugu towards the adjacent taluk of Proddatūr, where it attains a depth of twenty feet or more. The cotton soils in the south-west of the taluk adjoining the Tādpatri plain are not much inferior to those north of the Pennēr, but show a fair general average of fertility rather than any marked superiority. Owing to the nature of this tract there is less irrigation in Jammalamadugu than in any other taluk of the district, but such as it has is mainly afforded by excellent river channels from the Chitrāvati and Pennēr. There are but few tanks.

The area of the taluk is 609 square miles and its population 106,350. It contains but one town.

Jammalamadugu.

Jammalamadugu, the second largest in the district, with a population of 16,099. This, the headquarters of the taluk and of the Divisional Officer, is situated in a central position on the north bank of the Pennēr, twelve miles from Muddanūr railway station. The town is compactly built round the fort which commands the river. Since the redistribution of districts in 1911 it has been the headquarters of the Assistant Superintendent of Police. An Inspector of the Salt and Abkāri Department is also to be stationed here shortly, in charge of the recently sanctioned circle. The town was constituted a union in 1886 and contains, besides the Union office, a Sub-Registrar's office, a police station, a combined post and telegraph office, travellers' bungalow and local fund market. It is the headquarters of the London Mission Society in this district, whose substantial stone bungalows in their extensive compounds to the north of the town have added much to its appearance. The Local Fund dispensary was closed some years ago, as the London Mission hospital supplies all the medical needs of the neighbourhood. The principal trade of the town is in cotton. Weaving of a more ambitious character than usual is carried on by families of Mahratta extraction. In addition to turbans which are chiefly exported to the Bombay Presidency there is also a considerable manufacture of coloured table-cloths, curtains and similar articles, which are dyed by Rangarāzus and block-stamped with patterns of animals and birds. The largest temple in the place, dedicated to Vēnkatēswaraswāmi, lies about half a mile to the south-west of the town literally in a sand heap on the banks of the Pennēr. In the Musalmān cemetery—also on the bank of the river—is the grave of the first and last Nawab of Jammalamadugu, Abdul Syed Khan, to whom the town and the surrounding territory were granted as a jaghir by Tipu. Legend relates that the Nawab declined to allow his last resting place to be covered even with the slab of stone which is shown close by, and the simple earthen mound is in striking contrast to the large and ornate tomb of his wife not far distant. A descendant of the Nawab still receives an allowance from Government for the upkeep of the mosque.

Peddamudiyam.

Peddamudiyam, a village on the left bank of the Kundēr about 12 miles north of Jammalamadugu. To the west of the village there is an extensive *pādu* or old village-site on which is situated a group of ancient temples. The central one is dedicated to Mukkantīsvara or the three-eyed Siva. To the left of this is a temple of Narasimhaswāmi in whose honour a new image has been set up by the piety of a Reddi of the village. A small shrine at the north-west corner of the site shelters the village goddess Mādemma, while in the north-west corner there is an old Vishnu temple falling into ruins. The chief interest attaching to the place lies in the fact that it seems to have been the birth-place of Vishnuvardhana who founded the Chālukyan Empire. The arguments in favour of this view are ably set forth by Mr. J. Ramayya Pantulu in a note, printed in the Report of the Archæological Survey for 1904-05, which is unfortunately too long to give *in extenso*. The story of Vishnuvardhana's birth may be given in Mr. Ramayya's own words: "According to the Chellūr plates of Vīrachōda among others (South Indian Inscriptions, Vol. I, 49), Vijayāditya, a prince of the lunar race and the 67th in the direct line of descent from Arjuna, left his ancestral home at Ayōdhya and went to the southern country (Dakshinapatha) in quest of territory. He fought with the Pallava king Mukkanti *alias* Trilōchana and was killed. His queen who was pregnant escaped with the purōhits and ministers and took shelter under a pious Brahman named Vishnubatta Sōmayājin in the Agrahāra of Mudivēmu. The

Brahman treated the queen as his own daughter and when she gave birth to a son, he named him Vishnuvardhana. When the prince grew up he learnt from his mother the history of his family and, resolving to accomplish what his father had failed in, he proceeded to the Chālukya hill and made penance to the satisfaction of the gods, by whose grace he collected a large army and conquered the Kadambas, the Gangas, etc., and ruled the country from the Narbuda to the bridge of Rama." Mr. Ramayya's argument is based on the fact that an old Canarese inscription of the Mukkantīsvara temple gives the name of the village as Mudivēmu and describes it as an agraharam of pious Brahmans who are referred to as "a lotus tank to the birth of the sun that was king Vishnuvardhana." That the Pallavas ruled over this part of the country can scarcely be doubted as their inscriptions have been found as far as Bellary.

Whatever truth lies concealed in the story of Vishnuvardhana's birth, of the immense antiquity of the place there can be no doubt. Over the whole of the village-site is a thick deposit of débris wherein a large number of interesting finds were made. Earliest of all come celts and implements of monolithic times to connect the place with the aboriginal inhabitants of South India, while Buddhist coins of the Āndhra dynasty, archaic sculptures, ancient implements and ornaments show that so far back as South Indian history can be traced Peddamudiyam was a centre of civilized life. Its inscriptions give the connecting lines through Pallavas, Chālukyans and Chōlas down to the Vijayanagar kings, and further discoveries in this region may help to lift yet higher the curtain that still shrouds so much of the period between the fables of the Rāmāyana and the foundation of Vijayanagar.

Kōdūr.

Kōdūr, population 2,020, is situated in the extreme west of the taluk, about a mile north of the Pennēr. The limits of the village extend about seven miles northwards into the Erramalas and up to the Kurnool frontier. Half-way across the hills about five miles north-east of Kōdūr is a hamlet called Dabbudapalle situated on a plateau which at an altitude of about a hundred and fifty feet above the plain extends along the centre of the range from the vicinity of the Gandikōta gorge north-westwards to the trijunction of the Cuddapah, Anantapur and Kurnool districts. Near this hamlet is a strongly built stone fort, which appears to have been an outpost of the Gandikōta stronghold during the time of the Cuddapah Nawabs.

As in other "dry" villages of this taluk the principal crops grown are cholam, groundnut and cotton. The ryots themselves convey their cotton to Tādpatri, which is only seven miles distant, and sell it in the mills.

In the temple of Chennakēsavaswāmi to the north of the village there are three stone inscriptions recording grants to the temple during the reign of the Vijayanagar Emperor Sadāsiva. One of them mentions a certain Yēnugula Pāpā Nāyudu as a minister of Rāmarāju, the great Hēmrāj of Muhammadan historians, who was defeated at the battle of Talikōta in A.D. 1565. It is interesting to note that there is still a family of this name—Yēnugula—residing in Dabbudapalle, the hamlet above referred to.

Gandikōta.

Gandikōta is a village of less than a thousand inhabitants, situated on a hill about five miles west of Jammalamadugu. The name is comprised of two Telugu words, *gandi*, a gorge, and *kōta*, a fort; and in these lie all the interest and importance that the place possesses. It is perhaps the most striking spot in the district. The gorge where the Pennēr has cut its way through sheer rugged cliffs of bedded sandstone some two or three hundred feet high is four miles long, and the height overlooking the river on the south bank is crowned by extensive fortifications, which, even apart from their historical associations, are well worthy of a visit.

The following is the purport, omitting irrelevancies, of the *sthala purāna* relating to the foundation of the village and its fortification, as well as the building of the temple of Mādhavaswāmi. In the 1213th year of the era of Sālivāhana there lived a certain king called Kāka Mahārāju in Bommanapalle, a village close by Yerrakonda, about two miles to the east of the Pennēr. The site of Gandikōta was discovered by this king during a hunting expedition and, being struck with the place, he made enquiries and, finding it was sacred, took counsel with learned men who advised him to found a village which would flourish. He accordingly founded the village and fortified the hill which afterwards came to be known as Gandikōta. In the 1297th year of the Sālivāhana era, continues the record, Harihara Bukkarāyalu reigned in Vijayanagar. His reign was very prosperous. He visited Benares and brought water from the holy Ganges, and on his way back he found the images of four gods buried in the sand of the Gōdāvari river. These he was miraculously instructed to instal in newly-built temples. On his return to his capital the king built two temples for two of the gods at Gooty and Sashagrundipuram (Pamidi). Then he came to Gandikōta

CHAP. XV. JAMMALAMADUGU TALUK.

and saw the fort. While he was out hunting, the god Mādhavaswāmi appeared and told him that as the place was sacred and contained many holy streams he ought to build a temple there. The king accordingly did so.

The point of most interest in the above account is the name of the king, Kāka Mahārāju, who is said to have built the fort, and the date of its construction, which corresponds to A.D. 1290. We know from recently discovered inscriptions that in the latter part of the 13th century the Kākatīya kings of Warangal held sway over the greater part of Cuddapah district, ruling the province from Vallūr.[1] It seems to be a legitimate conclusion that the Kāka Mahārāju of the *sthala purāna* was either the Kākatīya king himself, that is, Ambadēva the usurper or his successor Pratāparudra, or possibly his viceroy ruling at Vallūr. That the account should omit all reference to the eventful period between the building of the fort by Kāka Mahārāju and the building of the temple by "Harihara Bukkarāyalu" is in no way remarkable, for it was a time of great political disturbance. In A.D. 1309 the Deccan was invaded by the Muhammadans, the Kākatīya dynasty was overthrown, and it was not till A.D. 1344 that the Hindu confederation drove back the invaders and established the kingdom of Vijayanagar. The *sthala purāna* regards "Harihara Bukkarāyalu" as the name of one man. Harihara and Bukka were in reality the two brothers,[2] refugees from Warangal, who engineered the Hindu confederation and subsequently founded the Vijayanagar Empire. Bukka I reigned from A.D. 1352 to 1376, and S.S. 1297, mentioned in the *sthala purāna*, corresponds to the year A.D. 1375. During the Vijayanagar ascendancy Gandikōta *sima* was a district embracing the present taluks of Pulivendla, Proddatūr, Kamalāpuram and Cuddapah, and possibly a part of Kurnool district. It was subordinate to the Udayagiri province, the Governor of which was generally a near relative of the reigning emperor.

The *sthala purāna* contains two other dates. It is related that Harihara Bukkarāju who succeeded Kāka Mahārāju was himself succeeded by Krishnarāyalu in S.S. 1421. Krishnarāya was the most famous emperor after Bukka I, but more than a century elapsed between their reigns. The date of his accession was really S.S. 1431, corresponding to A.D. 1509 or ten years later than the date given in the *sthala purāna*, which may be due to a clerical error. The last date given in

[1] See Chapter II.

[2] According to Sewell, "A forgotten Empire."

the record is S.S. 1523 or A.D. 1601, when it is said Krishnarāya was followed by one Thimma Nāyudu. In the latter's time the fort fell into the hands of the Muhammadans. By Thimma Nāyudu may be meant Timmala, the brother and successor of Rāmarāja, who conserved part of the empire after the battle of Talikōta and ruled from Penukonda. But if the date is correct Thimma Nāyudu cannot be the Emperor Timmala, nor is it likely on general grounds that the emperor would be styled Nāyudu without the usual royal titles. It seems more probable that a local officer of the Vijayanagar empire made himself master of Gandikōta after the downfall of the Emperor at Talikōta and maintained his independence for several years till the forces of Golconda turned their attention to this part of the country after dislodging the Hindus from Penukonda towards the end of the 16th century.

The king of Golconda was not slow to recognize the strategical importance of Gandikōta, and it became the headquarters of a Nawab. The name of the first Nawab is said to have been Meer Jumla. His name is held in the utmost abhorrence on account of his intolerance of the Hindu religion and his desecration of the temples, the materials of which he used for the construction of the Jumma Masjid. He is said to have killed the hundred cows belonging to the Mādhavaswāmi temple. He greatly strengthened the fortifications and is supposed to have been recalled by the king of Golconda on account of having boasted when rebuilding a part of the dilapidated fort that the king would never enter it without his permission. The State granary within the fortifications—now used as a travellers' bungalow—was built by Meer Jumla or one of his successors, the names of six of whom are on record, though nothing is known of them.

Early in the 18th century Abdul Nabi Khan, the greatest of the Cuddapah Nawabs, extended his authority over this part of the district, and Gandikōta became an important outpost of his territories. It was here that his grandson,[1] whose name was also Abdul Nabi, sent his family for security after his defeat by the Mahrattas in 1740. The fort presumably fell into the hands of Haidar Ali or Tipu Sultan after the defeat and deportation of the last Nawab of Cuddapah in 1780. The fortifications were, it is said, still mounted with cannon and contained ammunition at the time of the cession to the East India Company. Some cannon balls are preserved in the Jammalamadugu taluk office to this day.

[1] The relationship is doubtful, see Chapter II.

CHAP. XV. JAMMALAMADUGU TALUK.

Within the fort are several wells, strongly revetted and provided with stone steps, and a *kōnēru* known as Rāyalcheruvu the springs of which are perennial. These provide irrigation for the numerous lime and plantain gardens which are a feature of the place.

Gandlūr.

Gandlūr, population 1,075, is situated on the Madras-Bellary road about half a mile south of the confluence of the Pennēr and Chitrāvati. The nearest railway station is Kondāpuram, two miles to the south-west. There was formerly a police station here, but it was recently removed to Tāllaproddatūr. In the great storm of May 1851 the floods caused much damage to Gandlūr, but it is said no lives were lost. Such was not the case with Chautapalle on the other bank of the river, which was completely washed away, nearly all its inhabitants being drowned. Evidence of previous floods is afforded by the existence of a ruined temple between Gandlūr and the river, which is almost completely buried in sand.

Close to the confluence, on the north bank of the river, are the ruins of a temple of Sangamēswaraswāmi. It is said to have been destroyed by the Muhammadans who built near its site the village of Nēkunāmpet which was granted, and is still held, for the upkeep of the masjid at Gandikōta.

About three miles south of Gandlūr there is a wooded hollow in the Erramalas containing a picturesque waterfall and perennial springs. The place is called Guriginjakōna. The inhabitants of the adjacent hamlet of Kottālapalle have taken advantage of the excellent soil and water-supply to plant gardens of lime trees, plantains, mangoes and turmeric, the produce of which finds a ready market at Jammalamadugu and the weekly fairs at Yētūr and Simhādripuram. Like similar spots, Guriginjakōna is sacred and contains an ancient temple of Vēnkatēswaraswāmi, opposite to which is an exceptionally large banyan tree. Near Gandlūr is a forest tope of about thirty-eight acres in extent, containing mango and tamarind trees. The produce is annually sold by auction. The Forest Department maintains a watcher to look after this tope and the one at Ōbannapet near Kondāpuram railway station.

Tāllaproddatūr.

Tāllaproddatūr is a thriving village situated on the south bank of the Pennēr about eighteen miles west of Jammalamadugu. It lies close to the Bellary road and about two miles north of Rēgadipalle, the nearest railway station. In the last twenty years its population, which is now 1,675, has increased by 30 per cent. The village contains a police station and a local fund choultry. A mango tope on the river bank provides a good camping ground.

Tāllaproddatūr contains about a hundred handlooms, and is a weaving centre of some importance. The workers, who are mostly Padma Sāles, Thogatas and a few Musalmāns are, like the weavers of many other villages in the west of this taluk, employed by Tādpatri merchants who supply them with yarn and pay them piece-work wages. The better kinds of cloths woven in this and neighbouring villages are said to be exported to Hubli, Dhārwar, Gulburga and other distant places.

Near the village to the west are two Musalmān tombs concerning which a queer story is told. One of these tombs is dedicated to a certain Caliph and the other to his rat. It is said that the Caliph used to pass all his time in a masjid near his house saying prayers. The rat used to supply him with provisions every day. It happened once that the Caliph's rat went to a Musalmān's house and devoured some food that had been prepared for him. The Musalmān in a rage struck at the rat with a stick and killed it. Alarmed at what he had done and fearing the wrath of the Caliph, he went to the Caliph and told him what had happened, showing him the corpse of his beloved rat. The Caliph was so horrified at the sight that he immediately expired. The heinousness of his sin so weighed on the Musalmān's mind that he erected two tombs side by side, one to the Caliph and the other to his rat. The tombs are still maintained by the Musalmān's descendants who live close by.

Yētūr.

Yētūr, population 1,379, is situated in the south-west of the taluk, on the left bank of the Chitrāvati, about twenty miles from Jammalamadugu. The railway stations of Rēgadipalle and Kondāpuram lie two miles north and three miles east of the village respectively. Yētūr was the seat of one of the older poligārs who date from the time of the Vijayanagar Empire. An inscription on a stone step in front of the Chennakēsavaswāmi temple records that the poligār Kondayya granted some lands to the temple and dug a channel from the Chitrāvati for their irrigation. The poligār's full name was Padigala Kondā Reddi, of a family of Kodide Kāpus. The date of the grant is not given, but from the mention of Gandikōta Rājas it must be assigned to a period prior to the Musalmān conquest. In the 18th century the poligārs paid peshkash to the Nawabs of Cuddapah. When the country was ceded to the British, the poligār of Yētūr, though not very powerful, was one of the most recalcitrant.

CHAP. XV. JAMMALAMADUGU TALUK.

His poliem was accordingly forcibly resumed by Munro, and he was not even granted a pension. The ruined fort of the poligārs lies to the south of the village on the brink of the river. The village contains no irrigation sources except the river channel mentioned above. The cotton grown here is taken by the ryots themselves to Tādpatri and sold in the mills. It is done up in bags weighing fifteen maunds each. This weight of cotton is locally called a *kantlam*.

The worship of the god Narasimhaswāmi by Musalmāns, a curious feature of this village, has been referred to elsewhere.[1]

Muddanūr.

Muddanūr, population 1,586, lies about twelve miles south of Jammalamadugu and twenty-three miles north of Pulivendla. It contains a police station and a branch post office. The metalled road from Kadiri and Pulivendla to Jammalamadugu crosses the railway line near Muddanūr railway station. The village has therefore attained some importance on account of the trade that passes through it from the taluks of Jammalamadugu and Pulivendla. Most of the groundnut crop of these taluks is exported by way of Muddanūr to Madras and Pondicherry, and to meet the increased output two husking mills have recently been established here.

PRODDATŪR TALUK.

PRODDATUR TALUK.

The taluk of Proddatūr occupies a central position on the northern frontier of the district, abutting on the Sirvēl taluk of Kurnool. On the west it is separated from Jammalamadugu taluk by an artificial line terminating at the Pennēr, whence the river in its course south-eastwards marks it off from the Kamalāpuram taluk till within a few miles of its confluence with the Kundēr. In the latter stream the three taluks of Proddatūr, Kamalāpuram and Cuddapah meet at a point about four miles north of the confluence, whence the boundary between Proddatūr and Cuddapah follows an arbitrary line eastwards to the Nallamalais. This range of hills constitutes the eastern boundary of Proddatūr taluk, separating it from that of Badvēl.

The taluk contains a rich tract of pure black cotton soil which overlaps from Jammalamadugu taluk eastwards as far as the road from Proddatūr to the Kurnool frontier. To the east and south of this the soils become lighter in texture owing to the action of the rivers; but the transition is gradual, and several villages in the north of the taluk commanded by the Kurnool-Cuddapah Canal contain heavy soils which do not respond well to irrigation. Southwards the soils are more

[1] See Chapter III.

friable and better suited to the cultivation of wet crops. At the foot of the Nallamalai hills they are red and often sandy.

The canal system, including the Chāpād and Maidukūru projects, supplies this taluk with the best irrigation in the district, both by channels and channel-fed tanks. There are also some river channels from the Pennēr.

The area of Proddatūr taluk is 430 square miles. It has a population of 96,359 and contains seventy-nine villages and one town. The latter is—

Proddatūr.

Proddatūr, population 15,756. This, the taluk headquarters, is situated on the north bank of the Pennēr eight miles from Yerraguntla railway station. It contains the usual offices and is also the headquarters of a District Munsif and a Sub-Registrar. It possesses a combined post and telegraph office, a police station and a local fund dispensary. There is a Board lower secondary school as well as the national High school which was recently acquired by the Theosophical Society.

Proddatūr is certainly the wealthiest town in the Cuddapah district and possibly in the Ceded Districts. In its pressing and ginning factories large quantities of raw cotton are prepared for the market by power-driven machinery. The trade of the town, the bulk of which is concerned with cotton, indigo and food-grains, is chiefly in the hands of the rich Kōmati community which is here very largely represented. Evidence of their prosperity is seen in their substantial stone-built houses and the jewellers' shops with which the place abounds. The town has a very busy bazaar and a local fund market where country produce is brought in and sold every day. The Government offices lie to the north of the town, and the cluster of houses near them, which are inhabited chiefly by officials and vakils is known as Holmespet after a former Sub-Collector of that name. This again is divided from the main bazaar by the reservoir from which the town gets its water-supply. This is fed by a channel from the Pennēr. On two sides of it the Union authorities have rows of lifts working by pulleys to ensure the water-supply against contamination; but these are not generally used, as the people prefer to risk disease and fill their vessels by descending into the water by the steps on the other sides. Adjoining the reservoir is a small park opened in 1903 in honour of the coronation of the King-Emperor Edward VII.

Of the four large temples in the town the only one possessing any special interest is that of the goddess Kanyakamma in the main bazaar, which was recently erected by

CHAP. XV. PRODDATUR TALUK.

the Kōmati community at a cost of a lakh of rupees. The front is most elaborately carved and is an excellent specimen of modern work. The carving is very good of its kind and some of it is very spirited. The god Subramania riding a *yāli* in puttees and boots adds a touch of modernity. These carvings are the work of the famous sculptors of Gumpramānudinne.[1]

In the decade ending with the year 1901 the population of Proddatūr more than doubled itself. Since then the increase has been steady, though not remarkable. The town was constituted a union in 1886. Its importance and increasing wealth have led to proposals in recent years to convert it into a municipality. The Kōmatis have made it a very important centre of trade and, though Cuddapah may attract more of the raw products of this district on account of its railway station, Proddatūr is the market for much of the Kurnool and Anantapur districts, while the wealth of the leading traders renders possible transactions of a magnitude unequalled in this part of the Deccan.

Some years ago a scheme was formulated to connect Proddatūr with the railway system by means of a branch line from Yerragudipād, and it is believed that this will shortly materialize.

Duvvūr.

Duvvūr, population 2,555, lies ten miles north-east of Proddatūr on the high road from Cuddapah to Kurnool, a little to the west of the Kurnool-Cuddapah Canal. It contains a branch post office, a police station and a good travellers' bungalow on the bank of the canal, once the residence of an Assistant Engineer. In former days it was a place of considerable importance. A gap in the low ridge of hills due east of the town afforded facilities for the construction of a fine tank, and the existence of several natural springs gave that combination of pure water and cool shade which formed a suitable retreat for Hindu priests and saints and the favourite site of their temples. Some of these temples are now in ruins and those that are still maintained are small and of no architectural merit, but they are evidently of ancient origin. An inscription in the temple of Kōthandarāmaswāmi recording a private gift to the temple is dated S.S. 1531 (A.D. 1609).

In the 17th century Duvvūr acquired political importance and became the headquarters of one of the districts subject to the Cuddapah Nawabs, when a large fort was built, surrounded by a fine moat the bed of which is now dry and converted into paddy fields. It was against this position

[1] Referred to above, see Chapter VI.

that Haidar Ali advanced in 1779 when he attacked the Cuddapah Nawab. The Nawab's Pāthan cavalry were defeated in an engagement on the banks of the Kundēr a few miles to the west and driven into the town which they surrendered at discretion. A couple of old cannon of the period may still be seen lying at the south-west corner of the moat.

Even after the country was ceded to the British Duvvūr continued to be the headquarters of a "district" as taluks were then called. On the left side of the road as one passes through the old town there is an interesting memorial of Munro's great survey. Two slabs of stone are set upright at a distance of 11 yards from each other and on the larger is a Telugu inscription stating that they represent the standard chain of the paimash. Literally translated it runs as follows: "The Company Sircar's paimash, fasli 1211, the year Durmati, a standard chain; one chain equals 22 cubits, one kunta equals 4 square chains."

The District Munsif's Court at Duvvūr was abolished in 1860, and the taluk office had probably been transferred to Proddatūr prior to that date. In 1874 the population of the village still exceeded 4,000, but it suffered greatly in the famine of 1877, and about fifteen years ago the old village-site in the vicinity of the fort became so unhealthy that it was abandoned and a new village has grown up near the canal. It is now in a thriving condition and cultivation under the canal has extended rapidly in recent years.

Vanipenta.

Vanipenta, population 4,360, is, after Proddatūr, the largest village in the taluk. Its importance is of comparatively recent origin, being mainly due to the development of the metal-working industry, to which reference has already been made.[1] The workers are principally Musalmāns, but the industry is financed by Kōmatis, through whose enterprise the village has also become a trading centre of some local importance. It is situated at the foot of the Nallamalais about fifteen miles east of Proddatūr on the road to Pōrumāmilla. It is the headquarters of a Sub-Inspector of Police, a Sub-Inspector of the Salt Department, and a Deputy Forest Ranger. It contains two elementary Board schools, one of which is reserved for Musalmāns, and a mission school belonging to the London Mission. Though a large and important place Vanipenta has not yet been constituted a union. It is a straggling, insanitary village with a stony soil and badly laid streets in which water stagnates during the rainy season.

[1] See Chapter VI.

CHAP. XV. PRODDATUR TALUK.

The fort at Vanipenta is believed to have been built in the first half of the 16th century when, as we learn from an inscription on the wall of the Chennakēsavaswāmi temple, the village was granted for an annual rental to one Nārapanāyani Pina Avubala Nāyudu during the reign of the Vijayanagar Emperor Krishnarāya. This inscription is dated S.S. 1447, i.e. A.D. 1525, and another in the same place records that the tank in front of the temple was built in the same year. Part of the temple and its outer wall are said to have been washed away by floods many years ago when the tank breached. The bed of the tank is now held on patta, and only a portion of the bund remains.

In the main street in the centre of the village is a large temple of Kanyakamma erected by the Kōmati community who specially worship this goddess. It is of modern construction and built of Cuddapah slabs. The only temple to this deity in the taluk exceeding this in size and importance is the one at Proddatūr.

Kāmanūr.

Kāmanūr, population 1,742, is situated about half way between Proddatūr and Duvvūr, on the left bank of the Kundēr. The village has benefited in recent years by the Chāpād channel which feeds its tanks, and there has consequently been a large increase in the cultivation of wet crops, notably turmeric. The principal dry crops are cholam, groundnut and cotton, including the cambodia variety. Besides the agricultural population there is a small colony of Sāle weavers who dispose of their products at Proddatūr.

The passage of the Kundēr at this village is attended with some risk when in flood. The stream is not broad, but the banks are high, the water rises very suddenly and the current is exceptionally strong. There being no raft or ferry the crossing is made with the aid of swimmers who are generally carried two or three hundred yards downstream before they reach the other bank, and the bed of the stream is so churned up by the violence of the torrent that it is dangerous to seek a foothold till it is safely crossed.

The temples of the village afford evidence of its antiquity. The most important is the Vēnugōpālaswāmi temple, to which is attached a garden of nearly four acres for supplying flowers for the daily worship of the god. The annual festival in May is attended by considerable numbers from surrounding villages.

Rāmēswaram.

Rāmēswaram, population 3,764, lies on the north bank of the Pennēr about a mile west of Proddatūr and forms part of the Proddatūr union. It has long been a place of great sanctity and the story of its origin is as follows: On his return from Ceylon Rāma received divine intimation that he would be relieved of the sin of beheading Rāvana if he constructed two Siva temples. He accordingly erected one at the famous Rāmēswaram in the south and another here. When this temple was in course of construction Rāma sent Hanumān to Benāres to get a lingam, but as Hanumān did not return within the time fixed for the *prathishta* Rāma made a lingam of sand and planted it. This lingam was afterwards miraculously converted into stone but it still bears the marks of Rāma's fingers. This temple of Rāmalingēswara is situated on the bank of the Pennēr. The village is called Rāmēswaram because the lingam was planted by Rāma. The temple is often visited by pilgrims from the north on their way to Tirupati. The *brahmōtsavam* which is held in the month of April attracts a concourse of about ten thousand people. The temple contains about half a dozen stone inscriptions the earliest of which records a gift of land and assignment of revenue to the temple in the time of the Rāshtrakūta king Krishna III who reigned from A.D. 940 to 956. The others belong to the time of the Vijayanagar Empire.

The white cloths and turbans woven by the Sāles and Thogatas of Rāmēśwaram are of superior quality and are exported by the sowcars of Proddatūr to various parts of the country.

Korrapād.

Korrapād, population 2,107, is situated five miles north of Proddatūr on the road that passes due north to Chāgalamarri in Kurnool district. It thus has full opportunities for such trade as its resources allow, and is in a flourishing condition. It is the first village benefited by the Chāpād channel, the water of which is carried across the Nalla vāgu, a tributary of the Kundēr, by an aqueduct close by. This was constructed in 1901. Besides affording irrigation to some low-lying lands in the village the channel provides a constant supply of good drinking water and is much appreciated on that account. The village contains a Board elementary school and a London Mission school. There is a good choultry near the main road.

The fort at Korrapād was built during the 17th century in the following circumstances. Early in the 16th century one of the sirdars of the Vijayanagar Emperor Krishnarāya had been rewarded with a jagir comprising some villages of the present Kurnool district in recognition of the aid he had rendered in the recovery of the province of Udayagiri.

CHAP. XV. PRODDATŪR TALUK.

Subsequently, after the country had come into the possession of the king of Golconda a descendant of the grantee applied for an exchange and offered to pay a peshkash of ten thousand kantarāya pagodas for an estate of equal value in the Gandikōta *sima.* This was eventually done when one Kumāra Sunki Reddi received from the Nawab of Cuddapah an estate comprising Korrapād and five other villages of the Duvvūr district at the peshkash agreed upon. It was Kumāra Sunki Reddi who built the fort. It is now in ruins, with but one bastion and two gateways remaining, though it is still possible to distinguish the court-room and other apartments within the structure. This jagir was resumed by Munro in 1801 and the jagirdar granted a pension which is still enjoyed by his descendants.

Evidence of the antiquity of the temple of Chennakēsavaswāmi at Korrapād is afforded by a stone inscription recording the grant of lands to the temple in S.S. 1449 (A.D. 1527) during the reign of the Vijayanagar Emperor Krishnarāya.

Settivāripalle.

Settivāripalle is situated three miles south of Vanipenta and about the same distance north of the road from Proddatūr to Badvēl. It is one of the large villages of the taluk, with a population of 2,673, and contains two elementary schools, one of which belongs to the London Mission. Tradition says that this was once the site of a large town called Parnapād, traces of which are to be seen in the fragments of wrought stone and pottery scattered in the neighbourhood and the foundations of houses long ago demolished. A little to the west are the ruins of a large fort, the origin of which is not known. It contains a deserted temple of Bukka Chennarāyadu which may indicate that it was founded by a dependant of one of the earlier Vijayanagar Emperors.

About two miles east of the village is an outlying spur of the Nallamalais called Mukkonda, on the summit of which is a small temple of Mallikārjunaswāmi. Opposite Mukkonda, on the south-west, is the hillock called Gaggula Tippa, and the valley between them has been dammed to form the Elampalle tank. The temple of Tirumalanāthaswāmi occupies an imposing situation on a rock overlooking the tank and is approached by a flight of about seventy stone steps. The entrance is flanked by figures of elephants skilfully carved in stone.

An inscription on a stone lying near the Gaggula Tippa bears the date S.S. 1350 (A.D. 1428), but its contents are unfortunately undecipherable.

Mudireddipalle.

Mudireddipalle is a small village situated in the Nallamalais near the road leading to Pōrumāmilla. It was formerly of some importance, but it is said that owing to the prevalence of malaria the rich Kōmatis who once lived here migrated to Vanipenta about eighty years ago. It deserves mention for having been one of the fortresses held by Vannūramma, the only woman poligār known to the district. From the stories which are still told of her she was evidently a most vigorous and capable woman, and a terror to the neighbourhood. It appears that she was the wife of one Kumāra Narasimha Nāyudu who held the village of Tippireddipalle, about a mile west of Mudireddipalle. At his death she established herself in the heart of the Nallamalais some fifteen miles north of Tippireddipalle and built a fort and village called Chākarlapād. In this fort which, but for two narrow approaches on the north and south, is completely surrounded by the hills, Vannūramma generally entrenched herself when not engaged in raiding the country. The rest of her time seems to have been spent in robbing defenceless villages to replenish her granaries. The forts at Mudireddipalle and Tippireddipalle at the entrance to the pass leading to Chākarlapād are said to have been built by her. She was finally reduced by Haidar Ali, as she murdered one of his Amildārs who is said to have been her paramour. Haidar attacked her at Chākarlapād, reduced the fort and took her captive. She was put to death by his order at Ganjikunta. After her death the poliem was divided between two brothers of the family, Kumāra Narasimha Nāyudu and Venkatādri, of whom the former continued to live at Tippireddipalle and the latter at Dāsaripalle where he built a fort. At Neelāpuram a few miles south of Dāsaripalle is an old widow lady of the family. She is called 'Dorasāni Venkatamma' by the inhabitants of the village who are mostly *Pātravāndlu*, i.e., descendants of the poligār's retinue.

Formerly iron smelting was the principal industry of Mudireddipalle and other villages in the east of the taluk under the Nallamalais. It ceased to be remunerative about forty years ago. Abandoned workings, locally called *inupakolumulu*, are to be seen here and there along the foot of the hills.

Maidukūru and Nandyālampet.

Other villages of this taluk which deserve mention on account of their size, though otherwise little worthy of remark, are **Maidūkūru** (3,883) and **Nandyālampet** (3,608). The Kurnool-Cuddapah road crosses the Proddatūr-Badvēl road at Maidukūru; and Nandyālampet lies at the foot of the Nallamalais on the road to Badvēl.

KAMALĀPURAM TALUK.

KAMALĀ-PURAM TALUK.

The taluk of Kamalāpuram was constituted in 1911 and consists of sixty-one villages formerly belonging to the taluks of Cuddapah, Proddatūr and Jammalamadugu. It is the smallest taluk in the district with an area of 303 square miles, but in density of population is second only to Proddatūr. It contains 64,353 inhabitants, a population practically identical with that of Sidhout taluk which is just twice as large. It occupies a fairly fertile tract enclosed on the north-east and south-east by the Pennēr and Pāpaghni rivers respectively, which unite near Kamalāpuram. About a mile north of Vēmpalle the boundary at its southernmost corner turns to the north-west and continues in an irregular line to the junction of the Pulivendla and Jammalamadugu taluks on the road to Muddanūr, whence it takes a north-easterly direction crossing the railway just east of Muddanūr and terminating at the Pennēr.

The soils of Kamalāpuram taluk mark the transition from the black cotton tract to the free loams that mostly characterize the Cuddapah taluk. The depth of the black cotton soil in the west of the taluk is less than in the tract north of the Pennēr, but its fertility is scarcely inferior. East of Yerraguntla the soils are alluvial and generally lighter in texture. The best of these are in the valley of the Pennēr; on the other hand in the lower reaches of the Pāpaghni, where its banks are shallow, the deposits are often sandy and consequently less fertile. The channels from these rivers provide the best irrigation in the taluk. There are also some good tanks of which that at Kamalāpuram is one of the largest in this part of the district.

Four railway stations lie within the limits of this taluk, the chief of which are Kamalāpuram and Yerraguntla. The latter is the station for Proddatūr and is connected therewith by a metalled road. There are also two roads to Yerraguntla from the south of the taluk, one from Vēmpalle and another further west from Rāmireddipalle on the Pulivendla frontier.

Kamalā-puram.

Kamalāpuram population 4,825, is the headquarters of the taluk. It was formerly the station of a Deputy Tahsildar in charge of a division of the Cuddapah taluk. The new taluk office is still under construction. Kamalāpuram was constituted a union in 1885. It is the headquarters of a Sub-Assistant Inspector of Schools and contains a Local Fund travellers' bungalow, a police station and a branch post office. A branch hospital was opened here by the London Mission in 1909.

The town is situated about a mile north of the railway station and the same distance west of the Pāpaghni. The railway bridge over the river consists of twenty openings of 70 feet span each, with wrought iron plate girders over screw pile tressles. A pier is formed of two tressles, each consisting of five wrought-iron piles traced together and surmounted with strong casting for the reception of the girders.

The Kamalāpuram tank lies north of the railway line about a mile west of the station. It is the largest in the taluk and the valuable lands which it irrigates have mainly contributed to the prosperity of the town. Rice is exported on a large scale to the principal towns in the black cotton tract as far as Bellary, besides being purchased by merchants from Madras and Salem. Jasmine flowers are grown in some abundance and find a market in Proddatūr and Cuddapah.

When the country was ceded to the British Kamalāpuram was made the headquarters of the troops which Munro had to assist him to reduce disorderly poligārs. In 1821 the cantonment was removed to Cuddapah.

Pālagiri, population 4,767, is situated on the left bank of the Mogamēru, a tributary of the Pāpaghni, and about two miles west of the road from Vēmpalle to Yerraguntla. It contains a post office and a Board elementary school. The village lies at a slight elevation above the surrounding plain and possesses no source of irrigation. It grows the usual dry crops of the country including groundnut, and the ryots dispose of their surplus produce without difficulty at the weekly market at Vēmpalle, about five miles to the south. Some of the inhabitants are Dēvāngas and Thogatas who live by weaving. A few families of the latter caste weave silk *ravikas* and upper cloths, getting the thread ready coloured from some Thogata merchants at Uppalūr.

In the north of the village is a ruined fort, the history of which is not known. It may have been an outpost of one of the poligārs of Pulivendla taluk, possibly him of Vēmula. An inscription near the temple of Chennakēsavaswāmi records a grant to the temple in S.S. 1426 or A.D. 1504 in the time of the Vijayanagar Emperor Narasimha Dēva Rāya. A much older record of some historical value is the inscription near the Bhīmēswaraswāmi temple which tells of its restoration by a Vaidumba chief in the year A.D. 1056-57 and refers to a previous grant by the Rāshtrakūta king Krishna III who died in A.D. 956

Some twenty kistvaens are to be seen scattered about in the neighbourhood of this village.

CHAP. XV. KAMALĀPURAM TALUK.

Uppalūr.

Uppalūr is situated about seven miles south of Muddanūr and is enclosed on the south and west by the range of hills which continuing westwards form the boundary between the Pulivendla and Jammalamadugu taluks. It has a population of 1,861 and contains a Board elementary school. It is, after Mādhavaram in Sidhout taluk, the most important silk-weaving centre in the district. The weavers are Thogatas and for the most part work independently though some are employed by capitalists of the same caste. It is the latter who obtain the thread from Bangalore and after colouring it distribute it to their employees or sell it to independent workers in this and a few other villages. The thread is said to cost from Rs. 4 to Rs. 5 per seer of twenty-six tolas and after being coloured is sold at a price ranging from one and a half to two rupees per seer higher. Piece-work is paid for at the rate of Rs. 4 for every *chāpu* which consists of four cloths, each of two and a half yards length and weighs from 100 to 130 tolas. Silk and mixed silk and cotton cloths of all kinds are exported in large quantities to the Nizam's Dominions and parts of the Bombay Presidency as well as the principal places in the Ceded Districts.

This village was once the seat of a powerful poligār who proved one of the most recalcitrant when the country came into the possession of the British. Our earliest information about the village is obtained from an inscription on a stone near the Rāmalingaswāmi temple which records the grant of some irrigated lands for the benefit of the temples of the village in the year S.S. 1534 or A.D. 1612 and further relates that in S.S. 1415 or A.D. 1493 the village had been granted as an agrahāram to certain Brahmans by the Vijayanagar Emperor Narasimha Dēvarāyalu, and that it was this Brahman community who had built the temples, constructed the tanks and finally set apart some lands for the above purpose. The latter history of the village is gleaned from an old document in possession of a relative of the last poligār as well as Munro's brief account of the poliem. The prosperity of the village is said to have declined in the first half of the 17th century. In A.D. 1670 one Patte Khan settled in the village at the bidding of the Musalmān authorities, built a residence on the hill to the west of the village and constructed a masjid. After the downfall of the Golconda kingdom one Gōpāla Reddi of Nossam (in Kurnool district) obtained Uppalūr and some other villages from the Musalmān governor of Gandikōta about the year 1690, on condition of paying 350 kantarāya pagodas as peshkash and maintaining a hundred peons. In 1712 the Nawab of Cuddapah remitted the service and fixed the peshkash at seven hundred pagodas. In 1748 the poligār was expelled and his poliem resumed, but he was restored in 1766. He was again driven out by Haidar Ali in 1779, but he returned during the war in 1791 and obtained under the Nizam's weak administration two additional villages to which he had no title, and the peshkash was again revised. Whether the poligār paid peshkash to the British in the year 1800 is doubtful. His family document states that he did. However in February of the following year Munro directed the Amildār to resume the two villages which the poligār had illegally appropriated. As the poligār refused he was deprived of the villages by military force, and as he still declined to pay his peshkash for the remainder of the poliem which he was allowed to retain this was also resumed and he was seized by a detachment of cavalry and immured in the fort at Gooty.

Animela.

Animela is situated in the hills of the same name which are little more than an isolated spur of the Pālkonda range extending about ten miles north of Vēmpalle between the Pāpaghni and the road to Yerraguntla. The village lies a mile and a half west of the confluence of the Mogamēru and Pāpaghni and about the same distance east of the road. It has a population of 3,029 and contains a Board elementary school. It is a weaving centre of some local importance.

The village is chiefly of interest on account of its temples, the principal of which is the temple of Sangamēswara. This is situated near the confluence of the rivers upon the heights overlooking the Pāpaghni and its *gōpurams* are visible for many miles. It has some remarkable stone-carving, the finest work being on the porches of the northern and southern gates and the walls of the inner shrine. The latter are ornamented throughout with small sculptured figures representing various scenes from Hindu mythology and surmounted with floral decorations. The work is said to possess a finish of delicacy and character such as the best artificers of these parts are unable to produce at the present day.

There are numerous inscriptions in the village, mostly belonging to the Vijayanagar period. From an earlier record we learn that Animela was included in the territories of the Vaidumbas, feudatories of the Rāshtrakūtas, at the end of the tenth century. A later inscription records a grant to the Chennakēsavaswāmi temple in S.S. 1566 or A.D. 1644 by Matli Kumāra Ananta Rāja, though this part of the district could scarcely have fallen within the sphere of his political influence unless the earlier Nawabs of Cuddapah were even weaker than has been supposed.

CHAP. XV. KAMALĀPURAM TALUK — Nidujuvvi.

Nidujuvvi, population 2,122, is situated on the Bellary road thirteen miles west of Kamalāpuram. It is one of the principal places for the quarrying of Cuddapah slabs, which provides occupation to a large number of labourers and cart-men. In recent years a Reddi of the village had a remarkable stroke of luck with a cow. The animal had eighteen calves and was thus a continual source of wealth to its owner who grew quite rich. He regarded his cow with such affection and respect that on its death he buried it and constructed a tomb of Cuddapah slabs, erected a lingam thereon and enclosed the burial ground with a compound wall. Members of his family do pūja at the cow's tomb every Monday and on Sivarātri day distribute jaggery water and *pānsupāri* in its honour. He subsequently buried both his parents in the same compound and covered them with Cuddapah slabs like the cow. Last of all the man died also, but whether his bones lie in the same resting place is not recorded.

Yerraguntla.

Yerraguntla, population 1,742, lies ten miles to the west of Kamalāpuram. It contains a police station, branch post office, Board elementary school and a London Mission school for Panchamas. Its railway station has a double importance being the station for Proddatūr as well as the depot for the export of Cuddapah slabs. Proddatūr lies about eight miles to the north across the Pennēr. Double-bullock carts are to be hired at the station at all times and there are three choultries close by with two large wells of good water. Cuddapah slabs are sent to Yerraguntla mainly from the large quarries at Nidujuvvi some three miles distant and from here they are exported to all parts of India.

PULIVENDLA TALUK.

PULIVENDLA TALUK.

Of the three western taluks which abut on the district of Anantapur, Pulivendla occupies the central position, and forms roughly a parallelogram running from north-west to south-east between two ranges of hills. On the north the Bhānukōta and Mallyāla hills divide it from the Jammalamadugu taluk, a depression near the centre of the range giving access to the railway by the ghat road leading to Muddanūr. On the west a purely artificial line divides it from the Anantapur district, and the eastern boundary adjoining the Kamalāpuram and Cuddapah taluks has similarly been determined purely by administrative convenience. On the south, however, separating Pulivendla from the upland taluk of Rāyachōti the Pālkonda hills form an abrupt and natural barrier extending from the Anantapur boundary on the west to Vēmpalle on the east where the Pāpaghni enters the low country through the well-known gorge which has been described elsewhere. Here a small enclave known as the Surabhu valley extends to the south of this natural boundary, access thereto being obtainable only through the river-bed. Down the western flank of the valley flows the Pāpaghni, its level margins lined with green paddy flats, while outlying spurs of the Pālkondas penetrate it from the east and south. Such attractiveness of scenery as the taluk may be said to possess entirely disappears to the north of the Pālkondas which slope rapidly to a level plain of black cotton soil extending, with scarcely a tree to break the monotony, in an unbroken stretch to the bare and unlovely hills on the north. Nearly the whole taluk is drained by the Pāpaghni and its only tributary of any importance, the Mogamēru.

In point of population Pulivendla stands third of the taluks of the district, both in actual numbers and in the percentage of increase recorded for the decade ending with the census of 1911. It contains one hundred and three villages of which about half fall within the black cotton tract extending over the west and north of the taluk into Anantapur district and Jammalamadugu taluk. Generally speaking the soil deteriorates rapidly towards the south and east, and is least fertile in that part of the Surabhu valley which borders on Rāyachōti taluk. More than 47 per cent. of the dry land of the taluk is assessed at eight annas an acre and less. It contains no very good tanks, but the river channels from the Pāpaghni provide excellent irrigation to the villages along its banks. The principal of these is—

Vēmpalle.

Vēmpalle, with a population of 10,291. This is the only town in the taluk. It was constituted a union in 1886, and contains a police station, a local fund dispensary and a Board school. The town is situated eighteen miles east of Pulivendla village, the headquarters of the taluk, and about thirty miles south-west of Cuddapah which is the station on the railway line most easily accessible. The wet lands of Vēmpalle, which are unusually extensive, enjoy the best irrigation that the taluk affords and are the source of its prosperity. It exports large quantities of rice to the less favoured villages of the taluk as well as to Rāyachōti and Kadiri, with which places a pretty brisk trade is maintained by means of weekly markets. It is said that merchandise of the average value of six thousand rupees changes hands at the Vēmpalle market which is held every Friday The village of Alireddipalle which is situated on the right bank

CHAP. XV PULIVENDLA TALUK.

of the Pāpaghni opposite to Vēmpalle once formed part of it. In this village there is a temple to Vrishabhāchalēswaraswāmi, conspicuously situated on a hill, visible from some distance on the Vēmpalle side of the river. The curious name of the god is accounted for by a myth which relates that a Rākshasa named Vrishabhāsurudu once inhabited the neighbourhood and caused general unpleasantness until he was vanquished by Vishnu after a seven days' contest. The scene of the Rākshasa's defeat is the hillock and the temple was built thereon in honour of Vishnu's victory. The *brahmōtsavam* takes place in the month of Vaisākham and lasts for nine days. It used to be conducted with great splendour, but, owing, it is said, to dissensions between the Kōmatis and Kāpus, such is not now the case. The Kāpus claim to be garlanded at the time of the festival, and the Kōmatis have in recent years objected,—a point of some interest in that it affords evidence of the increasing importance of the trading community and its claim to equal consideration with the cultivating class.

There are several other temples of less importance, and two mosques. The Musalmān element in Vēmpalle constitutes nearly twenty per cent. of its population, which is a higher proportion than is found anywhere else in Pulivendla or Jammalamadugu taluk.

Pulivendla.

Pulivendla, the headquarters of the taluk, is situated on the road from Kadiri to Muddanūr, being twenty-seven miles north of Kadiri and twenty-three miles south of Muddanūr railway station. It is a union and contains, besides the taluk office, a police station, a Sub-Registrar's office and a local fund dispensary. There is no telegraph office. A travellers' bungalow has been recently constructed. The name Pulivendla is said to denote the 'the haunt or abode of tigers,' and may have been appropriate to the place some hundreds of years ago; but it is certain that there are no tigers nowadays in the Pālkonda hills to the south of the village nor indeed in any portion of the taluk. The Pulivendla vanka, a tributary of the Mogamēru, flows through the village, and a number of spring channels rising in its vicinity provide good irrigation to the low-lying fields bordering the village on the north and east, where betel-vines, plantains and other fruits, as well as flowers, are grown in some profusion. The Local Fund market at Pulivendla is the largest of its kind in the district. It is held every Thursday in an extensive and commodious walled compound and attracts a great deal of business. Traders from Anantapur and Bellary districts frequent it, and it forms a convenient link between the plateau taluks and the main line of railway at Muddanūr or Kondāpuram. More than ten thousand rupees worth of merchandise is said to be brought to the market every week, mostly in the shape of various grains and country cotton goods.

It is a peculiarity of this village that its principal temple is situated a mile away to the west in the midst of the fields. In spite of this, daily worship is conducted, and some thousands of people attend its two principal festivals, at one of which, the Pavithrōtsavam, which lasts three days, a colonnade of bamboos decorated with flowers is erected from the *mūla vigraham* to the gateway of the temple.

There is a ruined fort on a small hill above the village, a reminiscence of the political ascendancy of the poligārs, which is specially characteristic of this part of the district. Pulivendla was subject to the poligārs of Vēmula.

Pārnapalle.

Pārnapalle is situated on the right bank of the Chitrāvati where a narrow strip of the Pulivendla taluk juts out like a wedge into the Anantapur district near the junction of the three taluks of Kadiri, Dharmavaram and Tādpatri. About a mile south of the village the Pālkonda range of hills which stretch from the boundary of Sidhout taluk westwards across the middle of the district terminates and throws out irregular spurs as far as the river bank, which lend a wild and picturesque appearance to the village. A metalled road provides direct communication with Pulivendla about twenty miles to the south-east. The nearest railway station is Chinnayakuntapalle at a distance of seven miles, on the Dharmavaram-Pākāla branch line of the Madras and Southern Mahratta Railway. The village has a population of 1,614 and contains a Board school and a branch post office.

The position of the village is rather precarious owing to the possible occurrence of floods in the Chitrāvati. A faded inscription on a rock near the river bank about half a mile south of the village, the date of which appears to be S.S. 1318 (A.D. 1396) records—if its contents have been correctly deciphered—that a village called Chīkatipalle was washed away by floods and an irrigation channel destroyed. Pārnapalle itself was partially destroyed by the floods in 1851, and many lives were lost owing to the rapidity with which the river rose and burst its banks.

About two hundred acres of land are irrigated by river channels from the Chitrāvati. Rice is exported principally to Pulivendla, Simhādripuram and Dharmavaram. The hills adjoining the road about half a mile from the village have

CHAP. XV. PULIVENDLA TALUK.

recently been quarried for steatite by the Indian Steatite Company, London. The enterprise was presumably found unremunerative, as operations were discontinued towards the end of 1912. Other metals in the neighbourhood which have a saleable value are *gandhapu rāllu* of a superior sort, and *palugu rāllu.* The former stone is used in the manufacture of sandalwood paste and is exported to various parts of the Ceded Districts as well as to Mysore and Nellore. *Palugu rāllu* are ground into powder and mixed with salt earth in the manufacture of common black bangles. These are chiefly made by Musalmāns in Pārnapalle who work for cooly for Gājula Balijas. They are paid between one and two annas for every thousand bangles.

The ruined fort west of the village is still inhabited by the descendants of the poligār—Kōnēti Nāyudu—who is said to have built it; but they are unable to give any account of their ancestors. Close to the fort is a temple of Chennakēsavaswāmi, long deserted but not yet fallen into ruin. It appears that the image of the god was removed from the temple and lost many years ago. The story runs that the god appeared in a dream to the Tahsildar of Tādpatri about thirty years ago and ordered him to recover the image and convey it to Anantapur. The image was accordingly found in the bed of the river, cast there presumably by Musalmāns in earlier times, and the Tahsildar took it away to Anantapur where he established it and built a temple over it in honour of the god.

The village appears to have been visited by Tipu Sultan on more than one occasion. The construction of the Jumma Masjid and another mosque on the site of a ruined Hindu temple is attributed to him. Near the latter is a tomb in honour of one Miskin Vali, a saint, who, having returned from Mecca, halted a night at the mosque on his way from Tadmarri and died there. Tipu established a weekly fair on the hill where the mosque is, and had pukka buildings constructed for the use of the merchants, devoting the market fees to the upkeep of the *vali's* tomb. With the fall of Tipu the enterprise languished; but the market buildings still exist, though roofless, to lend colour to the story.

About a mile from the village are some perennial springs and a natural cave, the depth of which has never been explored. It is of course the abode of rishis who may not be disturbed. The Kōnēru fed by the springs is of special sanctity and attracts pilgrims in the month of Kārtigai for ceremonial bathing. Like other places situated amidst wild and picturesque scenery, Pārnapalle abounds in legends of a semi-sacred character.

Vēmula.

Vēmula, population 1,744, is situated about nine miles south-east of Pulivendla on the road to Vēmpalle. It contains a police station, a Board school and a branch post office. It is invested with some historical interest as having been the seat of a powerful family of poligars who called themselves Ekili Rājas and were, in Munro's words, "the most remarkable for their turbulence and depredations of any in the Ceded Districts." The earliest of the family of whom anything is known is Basavappa Nāyudu who maintained a force of six hundred men for military service under the Vijayanagar Emperor, and received for their payment the village of Vēmula and twenty-five others, the subsequent *kamil* assessment of which amounted to 9,796 kāntarāya pagodas. The peshkash varied under the Muhammadan governments and the force was reduced to five hundred men, till in 1712 the Nawab of Cuddapah remitted the service and fixed the peshkash at 3,500 pagodas. Forty years afterwards the poligār rebelled and was made prisoner by the Nawab who blew him from the mouth of a gun, circumcised his son and resumed the poliem. In 1756 Vēmula fell into the hands of the Mahrattas who restored the late poligār's son for an increased peshkash. The Mahrattas were not long in possession of the country, and as the poligar failed to pay regularly he was expelled by Mir Sahib, the Governor of Gurramkonda, in 1766, and subsequently died in exile. In 1791 when the district fell into the hands of the Nizam, Basavappa Nāyudu, a distant relative of the late poligār, got possession of the poliem but was driven out the following year. He returned in 1794 and took forcible possession of Vēmula, defying the central authority. He was succeeded by his son Kumāra Nāyudu in 1796 who died without issue. A distant relative of the family, a blind and imbecile old man, was set up as a puppet by subordinate officials. When Munro summoned him with the intention of giving him a pension and resuming the poliem he was prevented from appearing. After four months' waiting without result, Munro requisitioned the military authority. The fort of Mīdipentla, a few miles south of Vēmula, where the poligār was lodged, was surprised and captured. The poligār was made prisoner, and died at Gooty.

The ruins of the Vēmula fort are still visible. Its position is strategically good, backed by the Pālkondas and flanked by isolated hills. The village is of no particular importance nowadays, though, judging from its population, which has increased by thirty per cent. in the last thirty years, it is in a thriving condition.

CHAP. XV. PULIVENDLA TALUK.

Chilekāmpalle.

Chilekāmpalle is a village in the east of the Surabhu valley, situated about a mile south of the Pālkonda hill range. It is about ten miles from Vēmpalle, and Cuddapah, at a distance of thirty miles, is the nearest railway station. Like other villages in the east and south of this enclave it partakes more of the characteristics of Rāyachōti taluk than of that to which it belongs. It consists of a very small " casba " and numerous hamlets, the population of which amounts in the aggregate to 2,095. The dry lands of the village are extensive but poor in quality, mostly grown with castors, dhall, red-gram and horse-gram which the ryots exchange in the Vēmpalle market for such requisites as salt, kerosene-oil, chillies and tobacco. There is one fairly large tank in the village, the name of which, Chekrayya cheruvu, suggests some connection with the neighbouring village of Chekrāyapet. On the tank-bund is a ruined temple with a broken inscription. The temple is dedicated to Chekrayya, who is supposed to have constructed the tank.

Every five or six years a big *āvula parupu*[1] takes place in this village, which is attended by several thousands of people from the adjoining taluks. About a dozen cows and three bulls are devoted to the purposes of this worship and are maintained by the pūjāri who holds inam lands to the extent of more than twenty-five acres for the support of the cattle and the regular performance of the festival. This begins on the Sunday preceding the full moon of Vaisākham. The date is intimated by the villagers a week in advance by sending to every supporter of the festival a four-anna piece tied in a saffron cloth. They make the fact known and on the following Sunday they attend with their cattle and little silver umbrellas, bringing a large concourse of people. In the afternoon the worshippers with their cattle and silver umbrellas make a procession three times round the stand where the sacred cattle are placed, and then depart. The villagers give a meal to every one who produces the four-anna piece in a saffron cloth which was sent by way of invitation. The festival costs about Rs. 400 or Rs. 500 which is contributed by the ryots of this and adjoining villages.

Balapanūr.

Balapanūr is a large village of over four thousand inhabitants, situated on the road to Kondāpuram about eight miles north-west of Pulivendla. It marks the southern extremity of the great black cotton plain which stretches north and west from here towards Jammalamadugu and Tādpatri. It is the headquarters of a Police Inspector and of

[1] Cow-worship.

a firka revenue inspector. In the Board elementary school of this village more than a hundred boys are under instruction. The London Mission also has an institution here for the primary education of Māla converts. It is said that this village was a Brahman *agrahāram* in the time of the Vijayanagar Emperors but was resumed by the Cuddapah Nawabs who set apart certain inam lands for the Brahmans. In the early part of the 18th century it was included in the poliem of Tondūr and protected by the poligār with the usual fort and watchtower. The latter as well as the gateway of the fort are still standing.

In a taluk practically devoid of good tanks, the Vūra kunta of Balapanūr deserves mention. It provides irrigation to its ayacut for over six months in a good year and furnishes the principal drinking water-supply of the village. The water is said to be unusually palatable and the situation of the tank by the road side is a boon to thirsty travellers.

An appreciable proportion of the population of the village is employed otherwise than in agriculture. Weaving provides occupation to considerable numbers. Some Voddes and Yerukulas have also settled in the village. The former are masons and the latter make bamboo tatties and baskets which they sell principally at Pulivendla market.

Yerraballa.

Yerraballa, population 2,396, is situated about five miles south-west of Pulivendla. The Pālkonda hills form its southern boundary. The big tank of Yerraballa affords an example of the disappointing nature of tank irrigation in Pulivendla taluk. In the scheme report for the resettlement of the taluk it is referred to as follows: "The Yerraballa tank occupies a fine natural position in the hills to the south of Pulivendla and when it receives a good supply all the spring channels lower down have a copious flow. Its history of late years is, however, one of short supplies and large remissions . . . Another feature of the tanks of this taluk is the great percolation through and beneath the bunds owing to the porousness of the soil and the lie of the stratas underneath. So marked is this that for several tanks such as Yerraballa and Vēmula no sluice is provided at all, the water escaping by percolation into the main supply channel."

The waterfall near Yerraballa, called *Panchalingālakōna*, is worth a visit. It is situated in that part of the Pālkonda hills known as the Dorigallu reserve from the village of that name in the adjacent taluk of Kadiri. The water descends the face of a rock in a depression between two hills and falls into a *gundam* or reservoir whence it is carried away by the hill stream known as Lingāla vanka. The waterfall is named

CHAP. XV. PULIVENDLA TALUK.

Panchalingāla from the sacred cave near by which contains five lingams. The cave is approached by a winding passage the entrance to which is marked by a temple gateway. The passage is little more than a fissure in the rock, overhung by beetling crags, and at one place is so contracted that a man must crawl to get through it. On Mondays in the month of Kārtigai the place is visited by numerous devotees. The temple of Gundāla Mallikārjunaswāmi in this neighbourhood is also situated opposite a picturesque waterfall and attracts visitors at the same time of the year. The forest abounds in panthers and wild pig.

Simhādripuram.

Simhādripuram is a small village with a population of less than a thousand situated about sixteen miles north-west of Pulivendla. Though so small it contains about a hundred hand-looms. The weavers are mostly Thogatas. The village deserves notice on account of its sheep-market. Some four or five thousand sheep and goats are driven in to the weekly fair every Sunday, which is well patronized by farmers from all parts of the black cotton taluks.

A branch hospital was opened in this village by the London Mission in 1910.

Peddakūdāla.

Peddakūdāla, population 2,313, lies about six miles north-west of Pulivendla on the road to Pārnapalle. It occupies a depression surrounded by hillocks with channels on two sides which unite in the vanka passing on the east. The water is so near the surface in this depression that the channels never dry up except for a few weeks in the hot weather. This prevailing dampness and the practice of heaping the refuse of the village near the channels render the place very insanitary. The wells of the village are impregnated with guinea-worm, and it is one of the most feverish places in the taluk. The Kodide Kāpus of this village are bitterly quarrelsome and have earned the unenviable reputation of being addicted to all manner of crime. In the 18th century when nearly all the villages in the south of Pulivendla taluk were in the hands of poligārs Peddakūdāla seems to have retained its independence. In place of the usual exterior fort and watchtower it contains a circular stronghold in the middle of the village. It is said that the villagers assigned some land to the *kāvaligār* [1]

[1] Munro in a letter to the Board, dated 20th March 1802, says: "Had the poligārs been always confined to the charge of their own districts, their existence would not have proved so ruinous as it has been to the country; but it was the constituting them as *Kāvaligārs* or protectors of the property of the inhabitants and of travellers, not only in their own, but in the adjacent districts, that rendered them rebels during war, and robbers and murderers during peace."

of Lōpatanūtla in consideration of his sending men to their assistance in times of danger.

Mārellamadaka. **Mārellamadaka** is a little village situated at the entrance of the gorge through which the Pāpaghni pierces the Pālkonda hills. On the face of the rocky hill overlooking the river on the right bank is a temple to Ānjanēya, to the antiquity of which the following legend gives colour. Vāyu, the father of Ānjanēya, dwelt here in religious contemplation at the time of Rama's expedition to Ceylon. Rama himself had also sojourned here during his exile and, on his triumphant return from Ceylon with his wife Sītā after having defeated and slain Rāvana, Vāyu prepared to welcome him and flung a wreath of golden flowers across the ravine through which the conqueror should pass on his way northwards to Ayōdhya. At the earnest request of Vāyu, Rama halted here for a day with his troops and before leaving he impressed the mark of his bow on a rock, whereon the figure of Ānjanēya was subsequently fashioned by the sage Vyāsa. On this spot the temple was erected. There is some beauty in the popular superstition that a vision of the golden flowers is still vouchsafed at the approach of death to such as have found favour with the gods. It is said that Sir Thomas Munro saw the wreath as he passed through the gorge on his last journey and drew attention to it; whereat his followers were grieved, for they knew he would shortly die.

RĀYACHŌTI TALUK.

RĀYACHŌTI TALUK. Rāyachōti, the most extensive taluk in the district, occupies the north-eastern extremity of the broad upland generally known as the Mysore plateau. It lies at a considerably higher elevation than the rest of the district and rises gradually towards the south to an altitude of some 1,900 feet above sea level. It is separated from the low-lying taluks on the north and east by the great hill ranges of the Pālkondas and Sēshāchalams. Its other boundaries are irregular and correspond to no natural features. Westwards it faces the Kadiri taluk of Anantapur district while the taluks of Madanapalle and Vāyalpād of Chittoor district enclose it on the south. It has an area of 997 square miles and a population of 113,982, the density being 114 to the square mile as against the district average of 153. Only one taluk, Sidhout, is more sparsely populated. The rivers of the taluk are the Pincha, Bāhudā, Māndavya and Pāpaghni. The two first-named enter the taluk from that of Vāyalpād in the south-east and unite at

CHAP. XV. RĀYACHŌTI TALUK.

Rāyavaram below the Sēshāchalams whence, under the name of the Cheyyēr, the river flows through a winding gorge in the hills till it emerges into the low country in the north of Pullampet taluk. The Māndavya river, fed by numerous hill streams in the south-west of the taluk, first attains importance as it approaches Rāyachōti whence it takes a north-easterly course and after entering an enclave in the Sēshāchalams, turns south some three miles below Gadikōta and finally joins the Cheyyēr in the heart of the hills about three miles north of the road to Rājampet. The Pāpaghni in the extreme west flows in a rocky bed through hilly country northwards to the Surabhu valley and is of no value to the taluk as a factor in irrigation.

There is no railway in the taluk, and the country is so rocky and uneven as to make travelling by cart very uncomfortable except along the main roads. The chief of these are the Chittoor-Kurnool road and the Kadiri-Rājampet road which meet at Rāyachōti and cross at right angles. The former is joined a mile south of Rāyachōti by the road from Madānapalle through Gurramkonda, and a little north of the town by the road from Vēmpalle. Of other roads, which are little better than cart-tracks, may be mentioned those connecting Rāyachōti with Vīraballi and Tsundupalle on the east, and in the west of the taluk the road from Gālivādu northwards through Nūlivēdu joining the Vēmpalle road at Kōnampet, and the road passing south through Āravēdu into the Madanapalle taluk.

There are numerous tanks in the taluk, but they are mostly too small to afford sufficient irrigation for wet crops; hence the number of wells in wet ayacuts is unusually large. Some half a dozen villages in the south-east of the taluk have the advantage of good channel irrigation from the Bāhudā river. Except in this corner of the taluk soils are poor and irrigation is generally precarious.

The following is an account of some of the places of interest or importance in the taluk:—

Rāyachōti.

Rāyachōti is the headquarters of the taluk. From old inscriptions it is clear that the original name was Rāja-vīdu or the "king's dwelling-place;" but the early history of the village is obscure and it is impossible to say to what dynasty the king or chief who settled here belonged. Rāyachōti has a population of 8,012, is a union and contains, besides a travellers' bungalow, all the offices usual to a taluk headquarters. There is no telegraph. The nearest railway station is Kalikiri on the Pākāla-Dharmavaram line twenty-eight miles to the south. The distance to Cuddapah on the north is thirty-three miles, and Rājampet and Kadiri lie some thirty-five miles east and west respectively. Rāyachōti is thus situated in the very centre of the taluk. Eight roads converge on the town and most of the surplus produce of the taluk finds its way to the weekly market which is held here every Sunday. Trade, which is largely in the hands of Balijas, is chiefly carried on with Cuddapah, Rājampet and Vēmpalle. Superior cloths are woven and embroidered by weavers of the Sāle caste and sold locally. The town has no other industry of any importance.

There are a large number of Lingāyats at Rāyachōti and an important temple of Vīrabhadraswāmi. It contains some old inscriptions recording grants to the temple by local chiefs at various periods. Some curious practices are observed in connection with the worship of this god. Early in the morning of the day of the car festival a big ruby of the size of a nutmeg is placed between the two eyebrows of the god to represent the third eye of Siva. In front of the idol is placed a large heap of boiled rice so as to catch the first glance of the ruby eye at the rising of the sun. Till this is done the doors are shut and the people are prevented from entering lest they should be instantly killed by the fierce rays from the eye of Siva. The person who conducts the ceremony stands behind the idol, out of the range of the eye, and remains there till the rite is over. At another time of the year the god is taken out hunting. He is carried to a small *mantapam* half a mile from the town, and there placed on the ground. The place is said to be full of scorpions, but while the god takes his rest there his attendants can catch the scorpions and hold them without being stung though at other times they are as venomous as the rest of their tribe.

In old Rāyachōti near the river to the west of the town is a stone very conspicuously set up, with a Tamil inscription dated S.S. 1155 which corresponds to A.D. 1233. It records a grant to a temple by a certain king, but none of the names given can be identified with any place in the vicinity. The king is called Nissankapratāpa Rāya, lord of Karkatapura. Another inscription of the same date at Abbavaram, a village included in the Rāyachōti Union, mentions the name of another king, Thomba, who was 'first ruling from Kalukatāyapuram and then Marujavaduyandapuram his capital.' It is probable that Karkatapura and Kalukatāyapuram refer to the same place and it is possible that Thomba who 'was first ruling' there was expelled therefrom by Nissankapratāpa

CHAP. XV. RĀYACHŌTI TALUK.

who calls himself 'lord of Karkatapura.' It is not known to what dynasties these kings or chiefs belonged.

Tsundupalle.

Tsundupalle, population 3,538, is situated on the left bank of the Bāhudā river, twelve miles south-east of Rāyachōti. It contains a police station, a branch post office and a Board elementary school. The arable lands of the village extend some miles to the west of the river and some are watered by fairly good tanks, but the most valuable irrigated lands are those under the river channels, the ayacuts of which are very extensive.

There is a weekly market every Monday, which is held in a compound specially constructed by the Local Board. It is the most important fair in this part of the taluk and is also attended by merchants from Kalakada and other places in the Vāyalpād taluk.

In the temple of Ghatturāyaru there is a copper plate with an inscription dated S.S. 1463 (A.D. 1541) which tells of a caste-dispute between the Padma Sāles and Jāndras. The point of dispute appears to have been which of the two castes could really trace their origin to the goddess Lakshmi. The Padma Sāles approached their *guru* whose name was Tālla-pāka Tiruvēngalanādhayya and requested him to discover the truth of the matter. He prayed the goddess Lakshmi at Tiruchānūr to settle the point. The goddess gave her decision in favour of the Padma Sāles and they in their gratitude had the temple constructed with stone from Allaghattu east of Chandragiri. Half the merit of this deed belonged to the guru, a quarter to the Padma Sāles who built the temple and the other quarter remained to the caste as a whole. The community further promised to pay their guru annually one gold coin for every weaver's loom and a silver piece for every marriage.

Lakkireddi-palle.

Lakkireddipalle is situated nine miles north-west of Rāyachōti on the road to Vēmpalle near the low ghat leading into the Surabhu valley. It has a population of 1,207, is the headquarters of a Deputy Tahsildar and a Sub-Inspector of Police, and contains a Board elementary school. The Deputy Tahsildar's division is of recent creation, following the redistribution of districts which took place in 1911. There is a big watch-tower or bastion near the village which is said to have been erected as a means of defence against the powerful poligārs of these parts. The whole of the west of the taluk as well as the Surabhu valley appears at one time to have been more or less dominated by some local chiefs called Ekili[1]

[1] See under Vēmula, Pulivendla taluk.

rajas or poligārs and many stories are told of their depredations. Several villages about here contain people who still call themselves Ekilivāndlu.

There is a community at Lakkireddipalle known as Jinkala Musalmāns who follow the trade of masons and builders. They were recently employed on the construction of the new Deputy Tahsildar's office.

It was at the ghat near Lakkireddipalle that the Nizam Muzaffar Jung was assassinated in the year 1751 as the result of a conspiracy engineered by the Nawab of Cuddapah.[1]

Gālivādu.

Gālivādu, population 3,500, is situated about eighteen miles west of Rāyachōti on the road to Kadiri. It contains a police station and a branch post office. There is a travellers' bungalow, about three miles west of the village, at Veligallu. A market is held every Wednesday and, as a business centre, it is to the west of the taluk much what Tsundupalle is to the south-east. The village-site lies on the right bank of the Chinna ēru which enters the taluk from the south and flows into the Pāpaghni near the north-west corner of the village boundary. Some channels taking off from this stream irrigate small areas on both its banks. There is one large tank and several small ones, but the entire irrigated area is small in comparison with the extent of arable land in the village which mostly consists of the coarse red soil so characteristic of this taluk and will often grow nothing but horse-gram, one of the principal exports of the village.

There is a ruined fort close to the "casba," the history of which is not known. It was probably an outpost of the Ekili poligārs, as some of their descendants or retainers, called Ekilivāndlu or Ekili Nāyanivārlu, still reside in the village.

There is a curious old *sakti* stone just outside the village, inscribed with unintelligible symbols, to which pūja is done in times of trouble.

Nūlivēdu.

Nūlivēdu is an extensive village situated among low hills on the by-road which leads from Gālivādu to Kōnampet. It has more than forty hamlets with a total population of 2,608 and is the headquarters of a firka revenue inspector. The fort to the south-east of the village is said to have been built by Kaluva Nāyanivāru of the family of Ekili poligārs. The interior is now overgrown with scrub-jungle and nothing remains of the fort but its broken walls and southern gateway. Such irrigation facilities as the village possesses have been provided by damming the narrow valley which runs between the hills from the south-east boundary some three miles

[1] See Chapter II.

CHAP. XV. RĀYACHŌTI TALUK.

northwards. A chain of tanks and kuntas has thus been formed, the principal of which is the Merugulacheruvu.

There are about forty hand-looms in the village, and the weavers, after supplying purely local requirements, sell their surplus products at Gālivādu and Rāyachōti. Some Musalmāns find employment in tanning. Date mats are manufactured by Voddes and sold in the surrounding villages. There is a community of the Yānādi[1] tribe permanently settled in this village.

Sānipāya.

Sānipāya is situated on the Rāyachōti-Rājampet road close to the ghat by which the road passes over the Sēshāchalams into Pullampet taluk. It has a population, including its hamlets, of 1,922 and contains a travellers' bungalow and a police station. Its distance from Rāyachōti is fifteen miles. The villagers generally purchase their requirements at Rājampet which is twenty miles distant as it has a better market than Rāyachōti. Contractors for minor forest produce export honey, bees' wax and nuts such as the *sārapappu* to Cuddapah as well as to Rājampet. Merchants of Rāyachōti on their return from the weekly market at Rājampet halt at Sānipāya on Thursdays and sell a few necessaries to the villagers before proceeding on their journey.

Sānipāya was once the seat of a poligar whose family obtained this and some other villages from the king of Golconda early in the 17th century soon after the *kamil* survey. These villages formed several poliems held by different branches of the same family. Chintakuntabanda and Sānipāya belonged to one branch, while others held respectively the poliems of Mōtakatla and Yerramnēnipālem. The *kamil* of the Chintakuntabanda and Sānipāya poliem was 217 kantarāya pagodas and the peshkash was fixed at 168. This was raised by the Cuddapah Nawabs to 224 and again by the Mahrattas in 1756 to 253 kantarāya pagodas. The poligār was expelled by Mir Sahib, the Governor of Gurramkonda, under Haidar Ali in 1775, but he recovered his villages temporarily during the war in 1791, losing them again the following year. He returned finally in 1799 and the poliem was assessed by Kamar-ud-din at 1,776 kantarāya pagodas. Such is the account given by Munro. The family papers, however, state that three brothers of the family served under the Vijayanagar Emperor Narasimha Dēva Rāya at the end of the 15th century and obtained from him the village of Malinēnipatnam in Sidhout taluk as a jagir free of rent. In the following reign the two sons of one of these brothers served under the Emperor

[1] See Chapter III.

Krishnarāya and followed him to Gurramkonda. While the Emperor was there he received complaints of the turbulence of the country and ordered the two brothers to bring the disturbers to book. This they did and received as a reward the villages of Mōtakatla, Yerramnēnipālem, Guriginjakunta, Chintakuntabanda and Sānipāya as free jagirs and the right to collect fees, known as *kāvali rusums*,[1] for the protection of twenty-four other villages.

Vīraballi.

Vīraballi lies under the Sēshāchalam hills on the right bank of the Māndavya river. It has a large number of hamlets, with an inclusive population of 3,332. It is the headquarters of a revenue inspector and contains a travellers' bungalow, police station, branch post office and Board elementary school. There is a direct road to Rāyachōti which is distant about ten miles south-west. Two miles south of the village-site is one of the largest tanks in the taluk. It is formed by the erection of a dam a mile and a half long across the vanka which is fed by hill streams from the Sēshāchalams close by and also receives the drainage of the uplands of Polimērapalle north of the Bāhudā valley. In the heavy floods of 1903 when numerous smaller tanks in the taluk were destroyed this one sustained an enormous breach in the middle of the bund near the principal sluice. The flood in its course three miles northwards to the Māndavya swept away every vestige of arable land depositing sand and exposing here and there the underlying rock. The tank, which has an ayacut of four hundred acres, was taken up for repairs by the Public Works Department about two years ago.

A stone with an inscription in archaic characters, formerly set up on the bank of the Māndavya, has now fallen into the river. The inscription, which has not yet been satisfactorily deciphered owing to a defect in the impression obtained, would probably repay examination. A weekly market is held in this village every Saturday.

Vangimalla.

Vangimalla, as its name seems to imply, is situated where the hill range of the Pālkondas bends to the west. It lies close under the hills on the left bank of the Gangana, a small stream which joins the Māndavya half a mile before it enters the winding gorge leading to Gadikōta. The distance to Rāyachōti by the road through Vīraballi is eleven miles. There is a co-operative credit society in this village.

The village contains several temples, the largest of which is that of Mallēswaraswāmi under the Pālkonda hills half a mile north of the village. The eight pillars of the front

[1] See footnote regarding *kāvaligārs* under Peddakūdāla, Pulivendla taluk.

CHAP. XV. RĀYACHŌTI TALUK.

chamber are tastefully carved with figures bearing reference to Vishnu, though the temple is dedicated to Siva. Opposite the temple is a stone with an inscription of the Vijayanagar period dated S.S. 1466 or A.D. 1544. Near the hamlet of Rāchapalle is a temple of the tutelary goddess known as Arinamma. Hers is a terrible figure, nine feet high, and eight feet broad, with eyes as large as oranges and four arms, while round her feet are snakes and the heads of men. An inscription records that she was established here in S.S. 1367 during the reign of the Emperor Dēva Rāya.

Some Yerukulas have settled in this village and obtain their livelihood by the manufacture of baskets and tatties.

Gadikōta.

Gadikōta lies on the left bank of the Māndavya river in an enclave in the Pālkonda hills. It can only be reached by way of the sandy river-bed, but it is worth a visit for the sake of the scenery which is very fine, the cliffs rising in many places precipitously on both sides of the river. There is a large fort near the village which is said to have been built by one of the Matli family.

The river provides good irrigation to the lands on its banks, which are for the most part grown with tobacco. The soil is a very good quality of red loam and this crop appears to do exceedingly well as the profit on an acre is said sometimes to exceed Rs. 200. Tobacco from here is sent in large quantities to Rājampet and Cuddapah whence it is exported to more distant markets.

Matli.

Matli is situated on the Māndavya river about five miles north-east of Rāyachōti. It contains a small fort, now in ruins. It was the original home of the Matli rajas who attained to considerable political importance in the eastern division of the district during the Vijayanagar period and maintained their ascendancy till the end of the 18th century. The village is of no particular importance at the present day.

Chinnamandem.

Chinnamandem, population 2,870, is situated some ten miles south-west of Rāyachōti, on the right bank of the Māndavya river and a little west of the road to Gurramkonda. It contains a police station and a branch post office. A weekly market is held every Friday. About three miles further south, on the other side of the road, there is a travellers' bungalow near the hamlet of Kēsāpuram. In this hamlet also is a village goddess, Pālēti Gangamma, who is regarded with more than usual importance. Her annual festival in March attracts a concourse of about two thousand people, many of whom come from the Vāyalpād and Madanapalle taluks.

There are two ruined forts in the village, the history of which is not known. CHAP. XV. RÂYACHÔTI TALUK.

There is a sacred pool of unknown depth in the hills which separate the village of Paramatakōna, once a part of Chinnamandem, from Tsākibanda. The hill in which it is situated is locally known as *Akkadēvatala konda* or "hill of the holy sisters." The pool has the appearance of a well sunk in the solid rock and is about fifteen feet in diameter. In the hot weather the water sinks to a depth of twenty or twenty-five feet below the brim and in the rainy season rises nearly to the top. It used formerly to overflow—as is evident from the appearance of the face of the rock on the Paramatakōna side—but never does so now because, as the people say, a shepherd boy once committed the sacrilege of drinking from it; hence however heavy be the rains the water does not rise higher than about three feet from the top. A few hundred yards west of the pool is a natural cave which is called the temple of the Akkadēvatalu. Six or seven stones within the cavern represent the goddesses and their foot-prints are clearly visible on the flatstone in front of the temple entrance. People desirous of some blessing, especially the childless who wish for a family, perform their vows at the temple and feed an assembly on the hill. The place is generally visited in the month of November when the water in the sacred pool will have reached its highest level. Once in two or three years a festival will take place at the expense of any person who desires to show his gratitude to the goddesses for blessings received. A cardinal feature of the ceremonies performed is the offering of food to the goddesses beneath the water. The offerings are let down into the water by the pūjāri and sink at once, a few fragments subsequently rising to the surface to show that they have been accepted. The pūjāri also offers saffron and *kunkumam* on a betel-leaf in the same way, and if, when the leaf rises again to the surface, it shows the impression of finger nails it is confidently believed that the wishes of those who then perform vows will be fulfilled. There are inam fields set apart for the performance of worship to these goddesses, and the pūjāri is a Brahman.

BADVĒL TALUK.

Badvēl is the northernmost of the three taluks forming the eastern division of the district. On the west it is separated from Proddatūr and Cuddapah by the Nallamalai and Lankāmalai hills, while the Veligondas along the Nellore frontier BADVĒL TALUK

CHAP. XV. BADVĒL TALUK.

constitute its eastern boundary. Irregular and artificial boundaries divide it on the south from the Sidhout taluk and on the north from the Cumbum taluk of Kurnool district. It contains an area of 755 square miles and a population of 95,896.

The Sagilēr is the only river in the taluk. It rises in the Nallamalai hills within the Kurnool district and flowing eastwards for the first few miles of its course along the northern boundary of the taluk turns southwards and proceeds through the centre of the taluk to its southern boundary, finally joining the Pennēr in Sidhout taluk. As a factor in irrigation some value has been imparted to the Sagilēr by the project which bears its name and was designed to improve the supply to the great tank at Pōrumāmilla and others higher up. The steepness of the banks through most of its course, while affording opportunity for irrigation by doruvu wells, is generally unfavourable to the construction of river channels. The prosperity of the taluk depends rather upon the irrigation afforded by its tanks, of which those at Badvēl and Pōrumāmilla are the largest in the district.

In the quality of its soils Badvēl taluk is less favoured than the other taluks of the eastern division. It contains no such alluvial deposits as are found in the valleys of the Pennēr and Cheyyēr, while such regar soils as it possesses are generally poor and often highly impregnated with deleterious salts. Red soils predominate and vary greatly in texture and value. The best tract is a light clay in the neighbourhood of Kottakōta in the north-east. The taluk is also unfortunate in its rainfall. The annual average no doubt exceeds that of the western taluks, but the porous soils of Badvēl require a much heavier drenching than the black cotton soils of Jammalamadugu and Proddatūr. The other taluks of the eastern division are much better off in this respect, the rainfall of Sidhout and Pullampet exceeding that of Badvēl by over five and eight inches respectively.

In communications the taluk is no less at a disadvantage. It is further removed from the railway than any other part of the district, and its metalled roads are few. Of these the most important is the Cuddapah-Cumbum road through Sidhout, which passes northwards through Badvēl and Pōrumāmilla to Giddalūr and Cumbum in the Kurnool district. At Badvēl this road meets the main road from Nellore which is continued westwards over a low ghat in the Nallamalais to Proddatūr. From the latter town there is also a direct road to Pōrumāmilla. The largest and most important place in the taluk is its headquarters.

Badvēl.

Badvēl, with a population of 11,590. This is the fifth largest town in the district. Its nearest railway station is Vontimitta at a distance of nearly thirty miles to the south. Except that there is no stationary sub-magistrate at Badvēl, it contains all the offices usual to a taluk headquarters. It has also a local fund dispensary. Near the junction of the Sidhout and Proddatūr roads is a travellers' bungalow maintained by the Public Works Department. Formerly there was a District Munsif's Court at Badvēl, but it was transferred to Proddatūr in 1884.

The great tank at Badvēl is its principal source of wealth. It affords irrigation to seven villages, of which Badvēl receives the greatest share. It has an area of about a thousand acres under the tank, of which more than half consists of inam lands. Surplus rice is chiefly exported to Udayagiri in Nellore district. Turmeric and indigo find a market in Cuddapah. Its position on the main roads connecting Cuddapah with Cumbum and Nellore renders Badvēl a trade centre for the eastern taluks only second in importance to Rājampet. In the making of shoes and sandals it has developed a considerable industry affording occupation to a large proportion of the Musalmān population. Badvēl was constituted a union in 1886. It has an income of rather more than two thousand rupees, principally made up of house-tax receipts, minor items being cart-stand and market fees. There is a school for Musalmāns and a girls' school as well as an ordinary primary school, all maintained by Local funds.

The Hindu temples present no feature of particular interest. There are two dargas in the town. That in the name of Saiyid Khaja Ghouse Muhi-ud-din is the more important, whereat vows are performed by Hindus as well as Musalmāns.

Pōrumāmilla.

Pōrumāmilla, with a population of 5,634, is a Union town on the Cuddapah-Cumbum road situated some twenty miles north of Badvēl. It contains a travellers' bungalow belonging to the Public Works Department. Like Badvēl it derives its importance from its great tank. On the bund opposite to the ruined temple of Bairavaswāmi are two large stones bearing an inscription of considerable historical interest, recording that the tank was constructed by Prince Bhāskara, Viceroy of the Udayagiri province, in the reign of his father the Emperor Bukka I. The following is an abstract of its contents.[1]

[1] Kindly furnished to me by Mr. H. Krishna Sāstri, Assistant Archæological Superintendent for Epigraphy, Southern Circle.

CHAP. XV.
BADVĒL
TALUK.

[The first three verses are devoted to an academic discussion of how the sanskrit verses in a *sāsana* (document) are to be composed.]

(v. 4) An intelligent man of kind words issues a deed.

(v. 5) Invocation to Hēramba—the elephant-faced god.

(v. 6) Invocation to the boar incarnation of Vishnu.

(v. 7) Invocation to Siva of Srīgiri (*i.e.*, Srīsailam).

(v. 8) Praise to the earth-goddess.

(v. 9) The *Sapta-santānas* (*i.e.*, seven permanent issues of a man) mentioned, one of which is the construction of a tank.

(v. 10) King Bhāskara Bhavadura performed these *santānas* (charities). His genealogy is thus described:—

(v. 11) Moon from the milk ocean :
| in his race. . .
Guru son of Brahman :
| in this family
Purūravas and Nahusha,
His son Yayāti :
| in this family
Nīlāmbara and Sri-Hari :
| in this race in Kali age was born
(1) Samgama.

(v. 12) His son was Harihara.

(v. 13) All kings between the eastern and western oceans became his subordinates.

(v. 14) His brother was Kampana and the latter's brother Bukka.

(v. 15) Bukka's brothers were Mārapa and Muddapa. They were thus five brothers in all.

(vv. 16 and 17) As Vishnu was the servant of the Pāndavas in olden times so was Anantarāja minister of Bukka.

(v. 18) Bukka's capital was Vijayanagara on the bank of the Tungabhadra and in presence of god Virūpāksha.

(v. 19) Bukka had many sons.

(v. 20) Of them Prince Bhāskara was appointed by Bukka to rule over the eastern province.

(v. 21) Bhāskara was ruling from his capital on the top of the Udayagiri mountain.

(v. 22) Of all charities, he was informed that the charity of water was the most meritorious.

(vv. 23 to 27) The importance of water in creation described.

(v. 28) Prince Bhavadura wanted to construct a tank.

(vv. 29 to 31) To the south of Srīparvata, 2 *yōjanas* east of Ahōbila, at the same (?) distance from Siddhavatanātha, in the Sākali-country, 2 *yōjanas* from Udayagiri hills, to the east of town Pōrumāmilla (the tank was founded). The exact date was :—

(vv. 32 to 35) Saka 1291, Saumya (A.D. 1369–70), Kārthika, Sukla 14, Thursday, Pushya, Karkatakalagna.

(v. 36) For the benefit of future kings the twelve (favourable) conditions for tank construction as specified in the *sāstras* are enumerated here :—

(vv. 37 and 38) (1) The king (who undertakes the work) must be charitable, wealthy, healthy, famous and not fond of money ; (2) he must also be well acquainted with hydrology or the science of water (*pathassastra*) ; (3) the ground (selected) must be of hard soil ; (4) (there must be) a fresh water river at a distance of 3 *yōjanas* and (5) a mountain close by (?) ; (6) the bund which should not be too long must be strongly constructed of huge blocks of stone ; (7) and (8) at the two ends (of the bund ?) there must not be land yielding fruit (*i.e.*, cultivable land) ; (9) the bed (?) (*udāra*) must be deep and extensive ; (10) must have long and broad stone mines (imbedded within it ?) ; (11) the fields near (*i.e.*, the irrigated lands) must be fertile and of even surface ; and (12) the passage of water (out of the tank ?) must steadily flow on hilly slopes. Thus, O ! men, an excellent tank on earth is easily brought into existence by observing these twelve conditions of work.

(v. 39) These are the six defects :—(1) holes in the bund ; (2) sterile soil ; (3) rising ground in the middle and the two ends (?) ; (4) scanty supply of water ; (5) too much or too little of ground (catchment area ?) and (6) excessive supply of water.

(v. 40) Without any defects, but with all good points in it, the tank Anantasāgara was founded by King Bhāskara.

[The details of labour.]

(v. 41) One thousand men worked each day in the construction of the bund and the stone work in the revetment of waste-weir ; also (were employed) one hundred carts.

(v. 42) It was completed in two years. The money and grain spent were unlimited.

CHAP. XV. BADVEL TALUK.

(v. 43) The height, breadth and length of the bund extending as far as the mountains (on either side) is given in terms of the *Rēkha-danda*.

(v. 44) 5,000 *rēkha-dandas* long; 7 (*rēkha-dandas*) high; the outlet of water is by 4 *bhramas* (or sluices) and breadth is 8 (*rēkha-dandas*); gods Vighnesa, Īsvara, Vishnu, Bhairava, Mahā-Durga protect it (*i.e.*, the shrines for these gods are found on the bund). Many Brahmans too received presents of land below the tank. Then follow imprecations.

There is a ruined fort in the town, reputed to be of great antiquity. Nothing is known of its history.

Sankavaram. **Sankavaram** is a prosperous village lying about three miles north of Pōrumāmilla near the road to Kalasapād. It has a population of 3,737 and contains two Board schools and three Mission schools belonging to the Kalasapād branch of the S.P.G. Mission. It has a large area of irrigated land under the Mudireddipalle, Chintalapalle and Pōrumāmilla tanks, of which the two latter are fed by the Sagilēr project channel. The ryots sell their surplus produce at Pōrumāmilla, notably turmeric and jaggery. The large number of date trees in the vicinity supply toddy to various shops in the north and centre of the taluk. The health of the village formerly suffered owing to the prevalence of guinea-worm, but this has largely decreased since the construction of the Sagilēr channel, the water of which is said to have percolated into the wells and purified them.

To the west of the village is a small fort with a circular tower said to have been built by "the Kondavāndlu family" of Kāpus who were very famous and powerful in old times.[1] At a subsequent period it was occupied by a certain Desay Marka Reddi, who seems to have been a powerful poligar during the 18th century. His descendants own some shrotriem villages in the neighbourhood which are said to have been granted to the family by Sir Thomas Munro.

About a hundred yards north of the fort are the remains of an old temple which tradition says was built by a Vijayanagar king. On a stone close by is a faded inscription wherein are only legible a date, S.S. 1517 (A.D. 1595), and the name of Venkatapathi Rāja of Vijayanagar. This illustrates how the Vijayanagar suzerainty was acknowledged at least in name, many years after the battle of Talikōta. During the whole of

1 Possibly the Reddis of Kondavidu who continually menaced the northern frontier of the Udayagiri province, and occupied a portion of it about the end of the 15th century, from which they were ousted and defeated by the Emperor Krishnaraya A.D. in 1514.

his reign Venkatapathi Rāja resided at Chandragiri in the present Chittoor district.

Another inscription records that the temple of Iswara which is built on the slope of a hill about five miles north of the village was constructed in the year S.S. 1205 or A.D. 1282 in the time of Thrighavari Dēva Mahārāja of the Kāyastha family. The Kāyasthas were powerful feudatories of the Kākatīya kings of Warangal who extended their authority over most of the Cuddapah district in the last quarter of the 13th century. Ambadēva who usurped the sovereignty about A.D. 1287 belonged to the Kāyastha family.

Kalasapād.

Kalasapād is one of the more important villages in the north of the taluk. It is situated on the left bank of the Sagilēr eight miles north of Pōrumāmilla and twenty miles south of Giddalūr in Kurnool district, the nearest railway station. Its population, according to the recent census, was 1,783. It contains a police station, a branch post office, five private choultries, a church and a mission school. It is the headquarters of a branch of the S.P.G. Mission.

The Kalasapād tank is the first of the series of tanks served by the Sagilēr project, and has an ayacut of about two hundred acres in Kalasapād and three smaller villages. Some three miles north of the village a hill stream flows through a narrow valley between two ridges of hills across which a dam has been thrown at the southern outlet to form a large tank known as Rācheruvu. This is one of the most picturesque spots in the taluk. The tank has an ayacut of over a thousand acres and irrigates lands in eight villages including Kalasapād. The Rācheruvu and the village of Rājupālem, about a mile to the south of it, are said to have been built by Prince Bhāskara at the same time as the Pōrumāmilla tank.

Attached to the temple of Chennakēsavaswāmi is the mutt of Indūri Appayya, a latter day saint held in great repute by Brahmans. His native place was Rangasamudram in Madanapalle taluk, but he lived at Kalasapād. The following is an example of the stories that are told of him. On the day of the *Garudōtsavam* of Sri Vēnkatēswaraswāmi at Tirupati his mother expressed the wish that they were there. He directed his mother to lie on a mat and close her eyes. She did so, and shortly afterwards both she and her son were seen wandering in the streets of Tirupati by people of their village who had gone to the festival. On their enquiring with amazement how he and his mother came there, he replied that the god Vēnkatēswarulu has brought them. Then he conducted them to the temple and showed them round the town till the evening. On going to a choultry to retire for the night his mother expressed a regret that she had bought no presents in the bazaar for her grandchildren. In the morning she awoke and found herself in her own house at Kalasapād, and on opening the door of a room in the house she found all the presents she had regretted not buying the previous day. This holy man died at Kalasapād and was buried there about forty-five years ago. It is said that he tried to have himself buried alive at Rangasamudram, but the police forbade him. So he went back to Kalasapād and expired after eight days' fasting and religious contemplation. Even now puja is performed at his tomb by one of his relatives.

Kottakōta.

Kottakōta is situated between the Sagilēr and the Nallamalais about five miles north-west of Kalasapād. For account purposes the village and its hamlets still go by the name of Kottakōta though the casba is no longer inhabited. It is said to have been abandoned after the destruction of the fort, of which nothing now remains but crumbling walls and a half-filled moat. It must have been a place of considerable importance at one time, as the ruined fort is nearly as extensive as the one at Sidhout. Its history, however, is a matter of conjecture. Tradition says it was built by a poligār named Krishnā Reddi who also built the forts at Kalasapād, Narasapuram and another in the Nallamalai hills some ten miles west of Kottakōta. Within the fort on the hills is a large square tank, stone revetted, with steps on every side, sunk to a great depth and supplied by perennial springs. It seems more probable that these forts were constructed in the time of the Vijayanagar Empire to protect its north-east frontier which was continually exposed to hostile raids. Of the traditional poligār Krishnā Reddi nothing is known.

The principal hamlet of the village is Eguva Rāmāpuram, whose inhabitants, chiefly wealthy Kammas and Peddakanti Kāpus, number 1,081 according to the census of 1911. Furniture-making provides employment to some skilful carpenters in this village who obtain excellent timber from the Nallamalai forests. They make chairs of various kinds, stools, cots and tables, besides doing a large business in agricultural implements and country carts which they export to Kōilkuntla and Proddatūr taluks. Poorer people of the village trade in minor forest produce.

Munnelli.

Munnelli, population 2,750, is situated on the left bank of the Sagilēr about fifteen miles north-west of Badvēl. Though the village itself is not large, the area attached to it for administrative purposes extends from the Sagilēr on the west to the ridge of hills on the east which marks off the valley containing the Pōrumāmilla and Badvēl tanks. The distance between its northern and southern boundaries is nearly as great, so that it covers, together with its numerous hamlets, an area of about ten square miles. The village contains five fairly large tanks irrigating in the aggregate several hundreds of acres.

Two inscriptions in this village as well as others in the Sagilēr valley show that in the middle of the 16th century this part of the district was included in the Gandikōta *sīma*. At an earlier period of the Vijayanagar ascendancy Badvēl taluk appears to have fallen within the Siddhavattam *sima*; but it is possible that the latter was a sub-division of Gandikōta and not a separate district.

Every four or five years a big *jātra* takes place at Munnelli in honour of the village deity Dēvagiri Ankālamma. It lasts seven days and attracts an assembly of about four thousand people from various parts of the taluk. Animal sacrifices are, as usual, the principal feature of this festival. Hundreds of sheep and goats are thus immolated, the sacrifice being inaugurated on the fifth day by the slaughter of a buffalo. At Rājupālem, a hamlet of Munnelli, another great festival is occasionally held in honour of the goddess Pālnāti Ankālamma. Several villages in the Sagilēr valley worship this goddess. Her cult is said to have been introduced by a Māla from Pālnād in Guntūr district. No buffaloes at all are sacrificed at this festival, but only sheep and goats. People of the Bainēni caste are paid to come from Pālnād and recite the *pālnāti suddulu* during the festival.

Coarse country cloths are woven by people of the barber caste in this village.

Palugurāllapalle.

Palugurāllapalle. with a population of 2,703, is situated about twelve miles north-west of Badvēl on the right bank of the Sagilēr. It is the headquarters of a revenue inspector and contains a branch post office, a Board school and a mission school. It is an important outstation of the Kalasapād Mission. Its church, which is a stone building with a roof of Mangalore tiles, was dedicated by the Bishop of Madras in 1904.

The village has four tanks, of which the two larger have good catchment areas and irrigate fairly large ayacuts; but the soils are on the whole very poor, abounding in deleterious salts and *palugu rāllu*,[1] the prevalence of which presumably gave the village its name.

There is a mutt at this village in the name of one Gōvindaswāmi, a saintly Brahman who performed many

[1] See under Pārnapalle of Pulivendla taluk.

miracles during his lifetime. A curious story is told to the effect that the swami in one of his journeyings came to Maidukūru where the Collector was holding jamabandi. While there he was observed by the Collector to wring his hands vehemently. On the Collector asking him to explain this unaccountable action the saint replied that the screen of Varadarājaswāmi at Conjeeveram was being burned. The Collector thereupon wrote to the Collector of Chingleput and enquired if any such thing had happened, and received a reply to the effect that the event had actually occurred at the time the swāmi had spoken of it. The Collector of Cuddapah, it is said, appreciated the powers of the swāmi so highly that he gave him an inam of three acres in Dorasānipalle, a hamlet of Rāmēswaram in Proddatūr taluk.

SIDHOUT TALUK.

SIDHOUT TALUK.

Sidhout is the central taluk of the eastern division. Its northern and southern boundaries correspond to no natural feature, but the Veligondas separate it from the Nellore district on the east and the Pālkondas from Cuddapah taluk and the north-east corner of Rāyachōti taluk on the west. The area of the taluk is 606 square miles. It contains seventy-nine villages with a total population of 64,333. The Pennēr in its course through the taluk from west to east receives the waters of the Sagilēr on the north and the Cheyyēr, a more important tributary, on the south. Further east the Tummala vanka which drains the Ōbulām valley joins it from the north. The valley of the Sagilēr is separated from the Ōbulām valley by a ridge of hills which starts from the neighbourhood of Kalasapād in the north of Badvēl taluk and extends southwards as far as the confluence of the Cheyyēr and Pennēr, where it turns eastwards and merges with the Veligondas on the borders of Pullampet taluk, thus terminating the Ōbulām valley. A few miles west of this ridge and separated therefrom by a narrow strip of low country along the right bank of the Pennēr is an offshoot of the Pālkonda range which encloses the Vontimitta valley. The railway line enters this valley about three miles north of Nandalūr station and takes a north-westerly direction following the Madras-Bombay trunk road through the gap in the hills to Cuddapah.

Like Badvēl, the Sidhout taluk depends for its irrigation mainly upon rainfed tanks of which the largest are those at Vontimitta, Rāmāpuram and Mādapūr. River channels are scarce as the banks of the Pennēr and Sagilēr are steep and more suited to the construction of doruvu wells. The best soils in the taluk, alluvial in origin, are found in the valley of the Pennēr, west of Sidhout, and the lower reaches of the Sagilēr. Elsewhere red soils largely predominate, and their quality is good in parts of the Vontimitta valley. North of the Pennēr there are stretches of saline soil which make for a low average of fertility.

On the left bank of the Pennēr about ten miles east of Cuddapah is—

Siddhavattam.

Siddhavattam or Sidhout, the headquarters of the taluk. It is a union, with a population of 3,636. A metalled road connects Sidhout with the Vontimitta railway station at a distance of eight miles. The Sidhout railway station, though much nearer, is situated in the jungle and comparatively inaccessible. After the departure of Munro and the bifurcation of the Ceded Districts, Sidhout was for some years the residence of the Collector, but was abandoned in favour of Cuddapah in the year 1817. It was till recently the headquarters of the Revenue Divisional Officer. The office is still located there, while the Sub-Collector resides at Cuddapah pending the completion of a bungalow and office premises at Rājampet. An Inspector of the Salt and Abkāri Department is stationed at Sidhout, which also contains, besides the taluk office, a Sub-Registrar's office, Forest Range office, Local Fund dispensary and a post office. There is no telegraph office. The Public Works Department maintains a travellers' bungalow. The historical interest of Sidhout centres in its fort. Within it are to be seen traces of Hindu temples of which, prior to the Musalmān ascendancy, there were three, named the Siddhēswaraswāmi, Siddhavatēswaraswāmi and Ranganāthaswāmi temples. Early in the 17th century Anantarāmarāju, a powerful prince of the Matli family, whose authority over this part of the country was practically unchecked, was invited by the Brahmans of Sidhout to visit the temples on his return from Badvēl to his headquarters in Pullampet taluk. During his halt there he gave orders that the temples should be surrounded with a strong compound wall. On the south-east side of the wall an inscription records its construction by Matli Anantarāmarāju in the year S.S. 1527 (A.D. 1604). This wall became the nucleus of the fort which was built by Abdul Alam Khan, Nawab of Cuddapah, about A.D. 1755. A moat was dug and water let into it from the Pennēr. Upon the southern wall of the fort, where it rises sheer above the river bank, the Nawab constructed a mosque, with a residence for himself close by. The mosque being still in use is kept in good repair. When the river comes down in full flood and washes the foot of the wall the view from the top of it across half a mile of swirling torrent to the hills on the south is sufficiently striking to repay the trouble of a visit. After the Musalmān occupation the Hindu temples within the fort were dismantled and the idols removed and installed in fresh temples. It was in the Sidhout fort that the Nawab Alam Khan was finally captured by Haidar Ali in 1779 and sent a prisoner to Seringapatam. He is reputed to have been but a poor soldier and addicted to a life of pleasure. About a mile west of Sidhout in a little village called Rājampet which forms part of the union of Sidhout is a well called "Bhōgandāni bhāvi," curiously built, with pillared verandahs on every side. It is only possible to discern the well—square-shaped, with stone steps—after passing within the verandah. It is said to have been constructed by Alam Khan at the request of his favourite dancing-girl, who lived in a two-storied house close by, and hence its name. The Bhōgandāni well is included in the List of Ancient Monuments conserved by the Archæological Department.

Three miles west of Rājampet is another little village on the same side of the river, named Jōti. It contains a temple of Siddhēswaram which is almost completely buried in the sand. It is an ancient structure and is supposed to contain very valuable inscriptions at present concealed. There are also two Vishnu temples of archæological interest about a mile west of the village.

Owing to some resemblance, real or imagined, in its situation on the Pennēr and the relative position of neighbouring villages Sidhout is sometimes known as Dakshana Kāsi or Southern Benāreṣ. That the Pennēr was thus associated with the Ganges from very early times is also indicated by the existence of two villages called Pēnnapērūr and Gangapērūr on the south bank of the river, a few miles north of Vontimitta. Again, in such matters as ceremonial bathing and cremation, the Pennēr is held to be endowed with the greatest religious efficacy.

The cultivation of "Cuddapah melons" in the river-bed is carried out more extensively at Sidhout than anywhere else in the district. They are raised between December and March, that is to say, as soon as the freshes run dry after the cessation of the cold weather rains. The growers mark out their plots in the sandy bed of the river and raise the fruit either by transplanting seedlings or sowing the seeds in pits. The plants require heavy manuring thrice in the season. Some fifteen hundred plants creep over an acre of sand and produce on an average from ten to twelve melons each. No assessment is charged, and the only expense involved in their cultivation is the cost of manure. To the necessity of procuring this in large quantities is due the fact that Cuddapah melons are only grown in the neighbourhood of big villages or towns. CHAP XV. SIDHOUT TALUK.

Vontimitta, the largest village in the taluk, is situated about eight miles south-east of Sidhout on the main road to Cuddapah. The railway station is three-quarters of a mile to the east of the village. Its population, inclusive of outlying hamlets, is 4,309. It contains a travellers' bungalow in charge of the Forest Department, two local fund choultries, a post office and a police station. The Vontimitta tank, which is the largest in the taluk, lies between the railway line and the road, the latter passing over the bund. It has an excellent catchment area and a large ayacut of over a thousand acres. Vontimitta.

The village is remarkable for its temple of Kōthandarāmaswāmi, one of the largest in these parts. It has three *gōpurams*, of which the central and loftiest is adorned with carved figures, the others being plain. Within the courtyard are two stone *mantapams*, a large one with thirty-two pillars and a smaller with fourteen. The former is the place where the *utsava vigrahams* are decorated during festivals, and the latter is the *kalyāna mantapam* where on the day preceding the car-festival the ceremony of the god's marriage with Sītā is performed. The great annual festival is conducted with much splendour for nine days during April and attracts some thousands of people. The temple was quite recently declared a protected monument under the Monuments Preservation Act of 1904.[1] Two inscriptions within the temple record grants made for its benefit in the reign of the Emperor Sadasiva of the Vijayanagar dynasty, of which one, dated S.S. 1477 (A.D. 1554-55), consisted of three villages of the Pottapi *sīma* and fifty *kuntas* of land under the Vontimitta tank, the donor being the Emperor himself.

Mādhavaram, population 1,915, is situated on the Pottapi-Vontimitta road on the right bank of the Pennēr, about two miles west of its confluence with the Cheyyēr. About a mile beyond Mādhavaram the road turns sharply to the west and passes over an outlying spur of the Pālkondas into the Vontimitta valley. The distance to Vontimitta railway station is about ten miles. The village contains a travellers' bungalow and four choultries; one of the latter, situated in the hamlet of Bōyanapalle, is maintained by the Local Fund Department. The village contains numerous tiled houses, with upper stories. Mādhavaram.

[1] See *Fort St. George Gazette* of May 26, 1914, page 769.

Its prosperity is principally due to the silk-weaving industry. About three-quarters of the inhabitants belong to the weaving caste of the Pādma Sāles and are the most skilful silk-weavers in the district.[1] But they are said to be thriftless and addicted to drink, and the capitalists who employ them were, on this account, recently agitating for the removal of the liquor shops.

A temple of Bhāvanarāyanaswāmi, or "Bhāvana Rushi," the caste god of the Padma Sāles, is in course of construction. It is designed on a grand scale and will be a feature of the place when completed.

Kuruguntapalle.

Kuruguntapalle lies two and a half miles south-east of Mādhavaram and the same distance south-west of the confluence of the Pennēr and the Cheyyēr. Its nearest railway station is Vontimitta, twelve miles to the west. In point of size the village ranks third in the taluk, containing a population of 3,395. Being near the road connecting Vontimitta with the principal villages of the Cheyyēr valley in Pullampet taluk it is favourably situated for local trade. The village contains a large number of Setti Balijas who are skilful weavers as well as agriculturists.

Kōtapād.

Kōtapād, population 1,390, lies about two miles north of Mādhavaram and half a mile west of the Pennēr. Its nearest railway station is Vontimitta, about nine miles to the south-west. The village contains a local fund choultry. Tradition says that the site of the present village was once occupied by a fort and a *pēta*, the name of the latter being Basannagadda, and that on their destruction many hundreds of years ago the place came to be known as Kōtapād or "ruined fort." No traces of any fort are to be seen at the present day.

About two miles from the village is a fenced enclosure with a wooden gateway, known as *Avula male*, where sacred cattle were kept. An *āvula parupu*[2] used to be performed periodically by a sub-sect of *kāpus* called Rāyas, who formerly lived in Kōtapād. Near the enclosure are four stones containing representations of cattle and *vigrahams* of Krishna and Siva. Against each bull and cow so portrayed is written its name, such as, Lempalapu Āvu, Pallabolli Eddu and so forth. Near the gate is a stone inscription recording that in the year S.S. 1500, *i.e.*, A.D. 1578, in the time of Kōtapōti Bhakki Reddi, Karnam Veerappa and others, six *kuntas* of dry land and half a *kunta* of wet land were assigned by one Inge Bheema Reddi for the performance of the *āvula parupu*. The sacred cattle were under the special protection of the *Rāya Kāpus*. They

[1] See Chapter VI—"Silk-weaving."

[2] Cow-worship. See under Chilakampalle, Pulivendla taluk.

were never milked or used for agricultural purposes, and after death they were buried and not given to the Mādigas like other cattle for the sake of their skins. The sacred cattle became extinct many years ago, and the family who protected them no longer lives at Kōtapād. Some descendants of these Kāpus are said to reside at Upparapalle, a hamlet of Pattapurāyi in this taluk.

Ōbulām.

Ōbulām, with a population of 2,964, is situated about two miles north of the Pennēr, some five miles below its confluence with the Cheyyēr. It is the principal village in the valley which bears its name, and is the headquarters of a firka revenue inspector and a sub-inspector of police. It has eleven hamlets and its boundaries extend east and west to the hills which enclose the valley. The village itself is in the centre on the left bank of the Tummala vanka. Nothing is known of its history, but it is believed by its inhabitants to have been a place of great importance "when Bōyas ruled the country."

The Veligonda hills to the east of the village are locally known as the Mallemkondas and are held in great sanctity on account of their perennial springs and wooded hollows, which are still thought to be the abode of *rishis*. Chief among such picturesque spots is the Vēlpula *kōna* wherein is the temple of Mallemkondayyaswāmi. Within this hollow are seven pools of water, the most sacred of which is the Mōksha-gundam to which a flight of steps leads down from the temple. Every visitor to the temple first bathes in this pool before worshipping the god. The principal tank in the village is called Musalnāyani cheruvu and is said to have been constructed in the 17th century by a minister of the Matli rajas named Musalnāyadu.

The wells of the village are impregnated with guineaworm, and a very large proportion of the inhabitants suffer from the disease.

Kondūr.

Kondūr is situated in the Sagilēr valley about a mile east of the road to Badvēl and eleven miles north of Sidhout. It contains a police station, a local fund choultry and a travellers' bungalow. The latter, which belongs to the Forest Department, is on the roadside and makes a convenient half-way house between Sidhout and Badvēl. The boundary of the village extends westwards as far as the Lankāmālais, wherein is a temple of Vēnugōpālaswāmi. This is held in great sanctity and often visited from long distances for the purpose of fulfilling vows.

Yappirāla.

Yappirāla lies on the north bank of the Pennēr some four miles south-east of Ōbulām and twenty-five miles east

CHAP. XV. SIDHOUT TALUK.

of Sidhout. It has a population of 1,261 and is the only village of any importance in the Ōbulām valley south of Ōbulām. It is a recognized halting-place for travellers and merchants passing to and from Kaluvāya in the Nellore district. About sixteen miles of the journey from Vontimitta to Kaluvāya has to be performed along the sandy river-bed as there is no other road between Mādhavaram and Sōmasīla; consequently merchandise by this route is generally conveyed by pack-bullocks. The *panchalingālakōna* in the Veligondas to the east of the village is a place of some religious importance and attracts numerous devotees. Spotted deer are sometimes to be seen at the foot of the hills near this village.

Gangapērūr.

Gangapērur, population 1,074, is situated three miles north of Vontimitta near the road to Sidhout, and about a mile south of the Pennēr. In the name of the village some profess to trace the influence of the early Ganga dynasty in these parts; but it seems more probable that the names of Gangapērur and its neighbour Pēnnapērūr merely serve to mark the old association in the popular mind between the Pennēr and the Ganges. In connection with the temple of Narasimhaswāmi in this village a curious story of Munro is told by the people to this day. The Collector had come to the village for the purpose of examining the inam tenures. He confirmed the village service and artizan inams but declined to allow the inam granted for the worship of Narasimhaswāmi. At length in response to the earnest representations of the karnam, Munro declared that he would confirm the inam if he should see the god in person. The karnam, therefore, prayed the god to appear to the Collector, in order that the inam might not be resumed. In the evening Munro hearing the sound of a galloping horse came out of his tent, and saw the god ride past on a white horse. He was so pleased at the sight that he at once confirmed the inam.

A copper-plate inscription dated S.S. 1699 (A.D. 1777) records the grant of some land for the upkeep of a mosque in the hamlet of Mukundāpuram. Among other items the grant speaks of a contribution of grain for feeding the partridges in the mosque.

PULLAMPET TALUK.

PULLAMPET TALUK.

Pullampet is the southernmost of the three taluks forming the eastern division and, like Sidhout, is flanked on the east and west by the great hill ranges of the Veligondas and Pālkondas or Sēshāchalams. These two ranges coalesce in the southern extremity of the taluk and terminate a little to the west at the sacred hill of Tirupati. About fifteen miles north of Rēnigunta a narrow gap in the hills leads the railway line from the Chendragiri taluk into that of Pullampet, whence it proceeds in a north-westerly direction till it enters the Sidhout taluk a few miles north of Nandalūr. The taluk is drained by the Cheyyēr which forces its way through a winding gorge in the Sēshāchalams about sixteen miles south-west of Rājampet and turning northwards near Tangatūr enters the Sidhout taluk about three miles south of its junction with the Pennēr. Its only important tributaries in this taluk are the Pullangi and the Gunjāna which join it from the south.

The area of Pullampet taluk is 979 square miles and it contains a population of 145,230, which exceeds that of any other taluk in the district, though in point of density it ranks but sixth. It has a better rainfall than the rest of the district, and its irrigation facilities are excellent. The Cheyyēr river channels below Nandalūr are as good as any in the district, and there is no scarcity of large tanks though there is none to equal those at Pōrumāmilla or Badvēl. Of these may be mentioned the tanks at Pedda Ōrampād, Pōli, Cherlōpalle and Penagalūr each of which irrigates an ayacut of over a thousand acres. The soils of the taluk call for no particular notice; generally speaking, the nearer the rivers the better the soils. The red ferruginous series largely predominates, as in the rest of the division.

The taluk is well provided with communications. There are eight railway stations within its limits and the more important of these are connected by metalled roads with the principal villages of the interior, which lie to the east of the railway line.

The following places in the taluk deserve notice:—

Rājampet.

Rājampet, with a population of 14,649, is the fourth largest town in the district. About twenty-five years ago it was made the headquarters of the taluk in preference to Pullampet. The town, which is a mile from the railway station, contains a travellers' bungalow, a combined post and telegraph office and all the offices usual to a taluk headquarters except the Sub-Registrar's office which is still located at Pullampet. It is situated on the left bank of the Pullangi which flows into the Cheyyēr four miles further north. On the other bank of the stream, opposite the town, is a hill called Kondūr Tippa which bears traces of old fortifications. It is said to have been an outpost of some ruling chiefs, now spoken of as the Kondūr rājas, who founded the adjoining town and called it Rājampet.

Historically there is nothing to relate of Rājampet. Its importance is of modern origin and dates from the opening

CHAP. XV. PULLAMPET TALUK.

of the Madras Railway some fifty years ago, by which it received a great stimulus to trade and rapidly became the principal centre of distribution not only for Pullampet but for much of Sidhout and Rāyachōti taluks. The transfer of the taluk office to Rājampet increased its importance, and it was constituted a union in 1888. It will be made the headquarters of the division when the Sub-Collector's bungalow and office, now under construction, are completed.

A large weekly market is held every Wednesday. Weaving is the only industry that provides occupation to any considerable section of the population. Petty shopkeepers and traders, large and small, constitute the majority. The proportion of Musalmāns is lower in Rājampet than any other town in the district.

Pullampet.

Pullampet, formerly the taluk headquarters, is situated about seven miles south-east of Rājampet and three miles from Reddipalle railway station. It has a population of 2,274 and contains a local fund travellers' bungalow, a Sub-Registrar's office and a police station. There is also a choultry on the Madras road. A metalled road branches from the main road at Pullampet and passes over the low hills eastwards to Chitvēl in the Gunjāna valley. It is crossed by the Pullangi close to Pullampet, which probably derives its name from this river.

The weavers of Pullampet have a reputation for excellent workmanship. They belong to the Sāle caste, the most skilful weavers in the district. There are three subdivisions of this caste in these parts, namely, the Padma Sāles, Pattu Sāles and Kanna Sāles. Neither class will take food with the members of another and intermarriage is of course prohibited. The two first-named wear the sacred thread. They are all flesh-eaters and by no means teetotalers. Fine white turbans and white or coloured cloths for men's wear are woven by the Sāles of Pullampet, who specialize in the manufacture of gold and silver embroidery with which these are so often embellished. No better embroidery of the kind is made in the district.

The temple of Ānjanēyaswāmi at Pullampet was erected by a Tahsildar of the taluk about fifty years ago. There is also a Siva temple of more recent construction.

Chitvēl.

Chitvēl, a union and the headquarters of the Deputy Tahsildar's division, is situated on the Gunjāna about twelve miles east of Pullampet. Besides the direct road to Pullampet, a metalled road connects Chitvēl with Kōdūr on the south and joins the Rājampet-Tangatūr road on the north near Nārāyananellūr. Another road leads eastwards from Chitvēl over the Veligondas by the Rāpūr ghat to Nellore district.

Besides the office of the Deputy Tahsildar and Sub-Magistrate the village contains a Sub-Registrar's office and a police station. There was formerly a travellers' bungalow here, but it was demolished some years ago and it is proposed to construct a new one. The Lutheran Mission has an out-station at Chitvēl and a small church near which is a mango tope where tents can be pitched.

About the beginning of the 18th century Chitvēl became the headquarters of the powerful family of Matli or Matla princes whose authority once extended over the whole of the eastern division of the district. Though the Matli family are spoken of by Munro as "poligārs of Chitvēl" the term is really a misnomer. There were no poligārs in this part of the district, and the origin and nature of the political ascendancy of the Matli princes have nothing in common with the rise of the poligārs in Pulivendla and Rāyachōti taluks. They ruled the Pottapi-nādu under the Vijayanagar Emperors and were thus the political successors of the Telugu Chōdas who had held the same position under the suzerainty of the Chōlas till the latter part of the 13th century. The removal of their headquarters to Chitvēl in the reign of Abdul Nabi Khan, the most energetic of the Nawabs of Cuddapah, marks the beginning of their decline, and by the middle of the 18th century their authority certainly did not extend beyond the limits of the Pullampet taluk. Their political influence was further undermined by Tipu and finally extinguished by Munro. For many years after the British took possession of the country Chitvēl remained the headquarters of a 'district' (*i.e.* taluk), and the exact date of the transfer from Chitvēl to Pullampet is not now ascertainable.

Turmeric is a favourite garden crop in Chitvēl and other places in the Gunjāna valley. The raw product is sent to Cuddapah where the powder is extracted by motive power and exported to various parts of India.

Pottapi.

Pottapi, population 1,453, is situated on the left bank of the Cheyyēr, about fifteen miles north of Rājampet. It is a pleasant village and full of historical interest. The Telugu Chōdas established themselves here about A.D. 1000, and Pottapi remained the headquarters of this part of the country under various dynasties for about seven hundred years. There are several old inscriptions, some of which have not been deciphered, in the temples of Mūlastānēswaraswāmi and Gōpālaswāmi. Their systematic investigation would probably add to our knowledge of the early history of these parts. An inscription in the first-named temple appears to record its

CHAP. XV. PULLAMPET TALUK.

foundation in S.S. 1115 or A.D. 1193. In the other temple are two inscriptions one of which states that the temple was built in S.S. 1459 by a Matli prince named Anantarāmarāzu. The date indicates that this was Matla Ananta, the author of the Telugu poem Kākusthavijayamu.[1] The other inscription records that in S.S. 1643 or A.D. 1721 three kuntas of wet land were granted to the temple by Kumāra Ananta Rāja, another member of the same family.

Of the extensive fort the foundations are now alone visible, and the broad moat is under cultivation. The gardens between the village and the Cheyyēr, irrigated by river channels, lend the place a picturesque appearance.

There is a good camping ground in a tope near the river about half a mile north-east of the village.

Kōdūr.

Kōdūr, is a large village with numerous hamlets and an inclusive population of 6,592. It is situated on the Gunjāna river a mile north-east of the railway station of the same name and contains a travellers' bungalow belonging to the Forest Department. The making of bamboo cots, baskets, tatties and the like, material for which is obtainable from the adjoining forests, constitutes the only important industry in the place. A metalled road following the course of the Gunjāna river connects Kōdūr with the principal villages of the Chitvēl valley, exports from which are generally entrained at the Kōdūr railway station, while its comparative proximity to Madras gives it some advantage over Rājampet in the distribution over the same area of rail-borne goods from the south of the Presidency. Some years ago a Mārwāri from the Bombay Presidency established a power-driven factory for the cleaning of turmeric preparatory to its export to the north of India, but being found unremunerative it was closed about two years ago; possibly it was unable to compete with the saffron mill at Cuddapah.

There is a valuable red sanders plantation at Kōdūr dating from 1865, particulars of which have already been given.[2] The Forest Department also maintains a fuel depot which was established in 1871 as well as a large mango plantation.

A branch of the German Lutheran Mission was established at Kōdūr about thirty years ago. Some account of its activities will be found elsewhere.[3] The Mission Church at Kōdūr was built in 1887. The Leper Asylum maintained by the Mission at Krupapalle lies about a mile and a half south-east of Kōdūr.

A peculiar custom obtains in Kōdūr among *sūdra* castes. When a child falls ill the toe-ring is removed from the

[1] See Chapter II. [2] See Chapter V. [3] See Chapter III.

mother's left foot and tied round the child's neck with an indigo-coloured thread with the object of restoring it to health. It is also worthy of note that the pūjāri who conducts the worship of Ankālamma, the village goddess, is a woman; a peculiarity of which there appears to be no other example in the district.

Settigunta

Settigunta is the southernmost village of the taluk. Its limits extend northwards to within two or three miles of Kōdūr railway station, so that its length from north to south is about ten miles. Its eastern and western boundaries are the Veligondas and the Sēshāchalam hills. The "casba" is situated near the Settigunta railway station. The village, which contains many hamlets, has a total population of 5,431.

It is supposed to be named after the big tank on its western side, which, tradition says, was built by a Setti or Linga Balija. The tank occupies a fine natural position in the centre of the valley and receives the water of hill streams from both ranges, but its utility is somewhat impaired by the railway line which cuts off a portion of the bed on the east.

As at Kōdūr, the adjoining forests supply material for the making of cots, baskets, tatties and mats. This is particularly the occupation of a caste of people called Medaravāndlu. They claim to be Balijas, but the latter do not admit them to social equality. A special industry has arisen at Settigunta in the making of wooden figures out of the heartwood of the red sanders tree, for which there is a considerable demand among pilgrims to Tirupati.[1]

A few miles south of Settigunta are the Bālapalle fuel reserves. They are in a very flourishing condition and under the present system of working are expected to afford an unfailing supply of fuel.

Nandalūr.

Nandalūr is situated on the left bank of the Cheyyēr about six miles north of Rājampet. It is a mile south-east of the railway station which lies in Nāgireddipalle village. As the latter forms part of the Nandalūr union the two villages may be conveniently dealt with together. They contain in the aggregate a population of 4,322. The Union office, District Munsif's Court, travellers' bungalow, post office and office of the Sub-Assistant Inspector of Schools are all situated in Nāgireddipalle, as is also the railway dispensary. The railway line crosses the Cheyyēr about half a mile south of the station. The bridge, which was reconstructed after the disaster of 1870,[2] consists of forty-six openings of 64 feet span each, with wrought iron-plate girders over stone and cast-iron

[1] See Chapters V and VI. [2] See Chapter VII.

CHAP. XV. PULLAMPET TALUK.

cylinder piers. The latter are of immense girth and very deeply imbedded in the river. The bridge has successfully withstood some very heavy floods, notably those of 1874, and 1903.[1]

The wet lands of Nandalūr are irrigated by river channels from the Cheyyēr and by the Kannekala tank which is also river-fed. The tank is rather unfavourably affected by the railway but in good years it affords an excellent supply to its entire ayacut. "Kannekala cheruvu" means "the tank of the maidens," and tradition relates that seven virgins were sacrificed at the time of its construction to ensure that it would never breach. Nowadays when the tank surpluses Brahman matrons go to the bund of an evening and make offerings to the shades of the departed maidens.

The temple of Saumyanāthaswāmi at Nandalūr is of immense antiquity and was formerly held in great repute. It contains on its walls and elsewhere no less than fifty-four inscriptions dating from the 11th century to Vijayanagar times, from which much information of historical value has been gleaned. At the present day the temple is unfortunately somewhat neglected.

Nandalūr contains one of the only two Board lower secondary schools in the district, and a Government Muhammadan school.

Pedda Ōrampād, Chinna Ōrampād.

Pedda Ōrampād and **Chinna Ōrampād** are two villages situated on the north and south respectively of the great Pedda Ōrampād tank. Chinna Ōrampād lies on the Madras road about a mile north-east of the Ōrampād railway station, and despite its name, is the larger of the two villages, containing a population of 4,730, while Pedda Ōrampād has but 3,294 inhabitants. The local tradition runs that these villages were founded about two hundred years ago on the site of a town called Bukkapatnam which had been founded by the Vijayanagar Emperor Bukka and subsequently destroyed by the Musalmāns. The story is not supported by history, so far as is yet known.

The tank is one of the largest in the taluk and irrigates some half a dozen villages. It is fed by a hill stream from the Sēshāchalams called Pāmalēru and the surplus water flows into the Pullangi. Part of the bund is formed by the hillock known as Duddine Tippa. In the foreshore of the tank is a hamlet of fishermen called Bestapalle, all the inhabitants of which belong to the Besta caste of fishermen, and subsist solely on their hereditary occupation.

[1] See Chapter VIII.

Penagalūr.

Penagalūr, population 2,196, is situated near the right bank of the Cheyyēr about twelve miles north-east of Rājampet. It contains a large tank with an ayacut of over a thousand acres, which irrigates nearly all the land in the village. In the course of years the tank has silted up to a considerable extent, but its supply has recently been improved by the renewal of a feeder channel from the Cheyyēr. The tank is also known as Kannekala cheruvu, and the name is accounted for by a variant of the story already given in connection with the Nandalūr tank, according to which the Penagalūr tank actually breached in seven places the year after its construction and, in obedience to the god Gōpālaswāmi whose temple is near the bund, the seven daughters of the man who had built the tank sat one in each of the breaches, which were then filled up; since when the tank has never breached again.

Reference has already been made[1] to an ancient grant of some lands of Perungandura (Penagalūr) to Brahmans which was confirmed by the Telugu Chōda chief Manumasiddhi in the latter half of the 13th century. It is interesting to note that part of the village is still held by Brahman shrotriemdars with whom is a copper-plate showing that the grant was again renewed in S.S. 1493, *i.e.*, A.D. 1571 by Tirumalarāja, a chief of the Matli family. It is conjectured that the grantees obtained this confirmation for fear that their rights might be called in question subsequently to the downfall of the Vijayanagar Empire, which had occurred but six years before at the battle of Talikōta.

Tangatūr.

Tangatūr, population 1,665, is situated on the left bank of the Cheyyēr where the river turns north towards Sidhout taluk. It is a place of some historical interest. An inscription near the ruined temple of Siddhēswaraswāmi, dated S.S. 1237 (A.D. 1315) mentions the Kākatīya king Pratāparudra. This shows that his authority in these parts was still recognized in spite of the Musalmān invasion of the Deccan six years earlier. His deposition and removal to Delhi did not in fact take place till ten years later, in A.D. 1325.

Some time in the 17th century the Matli princes made Tangatūr the headquarters of one of their administrative divisions in place of Pottapi.

[1] See Chapter II.

INDEX

A

Abbavaram, 219.
Abdul Alam Khan, 44, 235.
Abdul Nabhi Khan, 40, 41, 42, 193.
Abdul Syed Khan, 189.
Abkāri, 163.
Accidents on railways, 123.
Achyuta, 36, 186.
Adina cordifolia, 99.
Adinimmayapalle, 184.
Aditya, 1, 30.
Administration of justice, 166.
Ādōni, 46, 148.
Agudūr, 22.
Agriculture, 108 ; and irrigation, 72.
Agriculturists, economic condition of, 87.
Agudur, 22.
Akkadēvatula Konda, 225.
Akkisettipalle tank, 87.
Albizzia amara, 99 ; odoratissima, 99.
Ali Khan, Dost, 41.
Alireddipalle, 209.
Allah-ud-din, 35.
Aluminium, 112.
Amada, 117.
Ambadēva, 34, 231.
Amelapalle, memorial stones at, 25.
Ammavāru or Lakshmi, 16.
Amruta, 184.
Amusements, 62.
Ānanda Ranga Pillai, the private diary of, 97.
Ananta Matla, 39, 244.
Anantarājupuram, 39.
Anantarāmarāju, 235, 244 ; constructs the Badvēl tank, 39.
Āndhra dominions, 28.
Animela, 29, 207.
Anjanēya, 184.
Ānjanēyaswāmi temple, 179.
Ankalamma, 245.
Anogeissus latifolia, 99, 100.
Anthrams, 65.
Arinamma, temple of, 224.
Arrack, 163.
Arts and industries, textile, 108.
Ashbeds, 11, 12.
Asoka, 26.
Asophs, 45.
Athirala, 34.
Atlantia monophylia, 99.
Aurangzebe, 38, 148.
Avenues, 120.
Āvula parupu or cow worship, 214, 238.
Ayōdhya or Oudh, 26.

B

Babool tree, 3, 20, 100.
Baday Miah, 42.
Badvēl, 30, 38 ; construction of its tank, 81 ; fuel working circle, 102 ; breach of its tank, 137 ; dispensary at, 142 ; district munsif's court at, 167 ; Sub-Registrar's office at, 168 ; descriptive note of, 227.
Badvēl taluk, 2, 4, 226.
Baggira, 16.
Bāhudānadi, 3, 80, 201.
Bainapalle fuel working circle, 102.
Balanadar, Monsignor, J., 56.
Bālapalle, 4, 121 ; fuel working circle, 102 : fuel reserve, 100, 101, 245.
Balapanūr, 214.
Balavanta Rao, 44.
Balijas, 66, 67 : stone carvers, 112.
Bamboos, 105.
Bānas, 27, 28
Bandāru, 94.
Banganapalle group of quarzites, 14.
Banyan tree, 21.
Bāpōji Nāyakkan, 42.
Baramahal, 41.
Bāredu, 116.

Basannagadda, 238.
Basavappa Nāyudu, 213.
Bāskara, son of Bukka I, constructor of the Porumamilla tank, 35.
Bastar State, 28.
Bears, 22.
Beddome, Colonel, 100, 101.
Beggars, 71.
Bellary, 38.
Bengal gram, 78.
Bentinck, Lord William, 152.
Bestapalle, 247.
Betel vines, 75.
Bezwāda-Guntakal railway line, 122.
Bhatrāzus, 71.
Bhāvanārāyanaswāmi temple, 238.
Bhīma Mahārāja king of the Vaidumbas, 30.
Bhōgandāni bhāvi, 236.
Bhūsakti, 64.
Bijāpur, 37.
Binga bendu, 16.
Blackbuck, 23.
Black cotton country, agricultural practices peculiar to, 77.
Black cotton soil, 6.
Blankets, 110.
Bommalātam, 63.
Bommanapalle, 191.
Bonnand, Bishop, 55.
Bonnet monkey, 23.
Boots, manufacture of, 111.
Bōyanapalle, 237.
Bōyas, 67.
Brahaswāmi, 66.
Brahma, 184.
Brahmans of Perungandura, 33.
Brecciated quartz, 10.
Buchanania latifolia, 99.
Buckingham canal, 132.
Buddayāpalle 139.
Budubudukulas, 71.
Buffaloes, 21, 105.
Bugga Vanka, 12, 138.
Building materials, 18.
Bukka Chennarāyudu, 202.
Bukka I, 185.
Bukka, founder of the Vijayanagar Empire, 35.
Bukkapatnam, 246.
Bulāki, 61.
Bullmen, 102, 106.
Bulls, 105.
Bungalows, travellers', 120.
Buruz, 60.
Bussy, M., 43.
Bustard, 23.
Butea frondosa, 99.

C

Cactus, 20.
Caliph and his rat, story of, 195.
Calotropis gigantea, 20.
Campbell, Dr. T. V., 142, 144.
Campbell, Major-General, 48, 50.
Canal, the Kurnool-Cuddapah, 83 to 85, 120.
Canthium didymum, 99.
Carissa carandas, 20, 94.
Carnatic, the, 35, 42.
Cart tracks and bridle paths, 107.
Cassia auriculata, 20.
Cassia fistula, 99.
Castes, 66.
Cattle bells, 112.
Cattle, food of, 79.
Cattle, manure from, 73.
Cattle, Mysore and Nellore breed of, 21.
Celltombs, 25.
Census, 53.
Chālukyan adventurer Vijayāditya, 26.
Chālukyans, western and eastern, 27.
Chandanam, 94.
Chandā Sahib, governor of Trichinopoly, 42.
Chandrāditya, 28.
Chandragiri, 37.
Chandragiri province, 35.
Chāpād and Mydukūr projects, 85.
Chaplin, Mr. W. W., 152.
Charcoal, 106.
Chautapalle, 138, 194.
Cheetah, 22.
Chekrāyapet, 214.
Chenchunātakam, 63.
Chenchus, 69.
Chennakēsavaswāmi temple, 187, 231.
Chennakēswaraswāmi temple, 184.
Chennamma, 39.
Chennampalle, 39.
Chennangi, 74.

Chennūr, 36, 181.
Chennūr taluk, 153.
Chēra or Kērala, 26.
Cheyyēr group, 11, 12.
Cheyyēr river, 3, 4, 30, 39, 120, 241.
Cheyyēr valley, 9.
Chīkatipalle, 211.
Chilakampalle, 214.
Chilamakūr, 36.
Chilla, 93.
Chindhu dance, 68.
Chinkara or Bennett's gazelle, 23.
Chinna althi, 115.
Chinnadāsaripalle, 185.
Chinnamandem, 224.
Chinna Orampād, 246.
Chinnayakuntapalle Railway station, 211.
Chintakommadinne, 113, 186.
Chintakunta, 9.
Chintakuntabanda, 222.
Chintakunta hills, 12.
Chintalapalle tank, 87.
Chitrāvati river, 2, 138.
Chitvēl, 3, 159, 168; valley of, 5, 6; Sub-Registrar's office at, 168; descriptive note of, 242.
Chloroxylon swietenia, 99.
Chōdas, the Telugu, 30.
Chōla, Kingdom and dynasty, 26; kings, 27 to 29.
Chōlam, 78, 114, 127, 155, 157; staple food grain of the black cotton country, 61.
Cholera, 139.
Choolya state, 27.
Choultries, 120.
Christians, 54.
Civil Justice, 166.
Clays, 11.
Clay slate, 11.
Climate, 6.
Cocoanut trees, not tapped for toddy, 164.
Coffee, 115.
Communication, means of, 118.
Conglomerates, 11.
Conjeeveram, 26 to 28, 30, 42.
Conservancy of forests, prior to Madras Forest Act of 1882, 100; subsequent operations, 101; recent working plans, 102.
Co-operative credit society, 223.
Copper, 12, 18.
Copper plate inscriptions, 24.
Copper pots, 112.
Coppice with standard system of fuel felling, 101, 102.
Cornwallis, Lord, 45.
Coromandel, 35.
Corundum, 16.
Cotton, 78, 127; printing and dyeing, 111; ginning and pressing factories at Jammalamadugu, Proddatūr and Pulivendla, 113.
Cotton, Sir Arthur, 83.
Couvade (hatching) custom, 70.
Cows, 105.
Cox, Mr., 154.
Crime, 169.
Crimes, sensational, 171.
Criminal justice, 168.
Criminal tribes, 160.
Crystalline rocks, 8, 9.
Cuddapah, Meteorological Observatory at, 6; Bugga Vanka near, 12, 138; town on rocks of Kurnool formation, 13; battle of, 44; saffron works and factory at, 75, 113; husking mills and weaving factory at, 113; a principal trade centre, 114; a railway station, 121: outbreak of plague in, 139, Municipal hospital in, 141, 176; high school in, 143; London Mission elementary school in, 145; Deputy Collector at, 159; district m unsif's court at, 166; a Municipality, 174; descriptive note of, 178.
Cuddapah basin, 9.
Cuddapah district, boundaries, latitude and longitude and area of, 2; its transfer to the British, 46
Cuddapah melons, 75, 236.
Cuddapahs or Cuddapah formations, 8 to 11.
Cuddapah slabs, 112, 114 and 121; use of, 60.
Cuddapah taluk, 2, 3; turmeric cultivation in, 75; description of, 177.
Cultivation, wet, 73; dry, 75; modern changes in, 79
Cycads, 99.

D

Dabbala Yerukulas, 69.
Dabbudapalle, 190.
Daggupād, 164.
Dāmalcheruvu, 41, 42.
Dānavālapād, 29.
Daniel, Mr. J. R., 129.
Danthi, 77.
Dasabandham wells, 158.
Dāsaripalle, 203.
Dāsaripalle fuel working circle, 102.
Dāsaris, 71.
Dasavarman, 30.
Date trees, tapped for toddy, 163.
Davies, Mr. R. W., his scheme report for the resettlement of the sub-division, 156, 158.
Deccan, 25, 37, 38, 41; Sugar and Abkāri Company, 163.
Decennial lease of renting, 153.
Deer, 23.
Deities, village, 64.
Delhi, 35.
Demarcation of forests, 107.
Density and growth of population, 52.
Deposits, geological, 8.
Deputy Tahsildars, 159.
Desamukhi, 148.
Desay Mārka Reddi, 230.
Description, physical, 1.
Despondi, 148.
Dēvachōda Mahārāja, 39.
Dēvadāri, 93.
Dēvagiri Ankālamma, 233.
Dēvagudipalle, 32.
Dēvāngas, 68, 108, 110.
Dēvarāya Odaiyār, 36.
Dēvuniboova, 62.
Dēvunimūla, 61.
Dhadiyam, 115.
Dhavalēyarasa, King of the Bānas, 28.
Dhoor taluk, 153.
Diamond mines, 81.
Diamonds, 15.
Diorite, 10, 12.
Diospyros chloroxylon, 93, 99.
Diospyros ebenum, 99.
District, redistribution of the, 1; shape and boundaries, 2; history of the eastern division of the, 30.
District Court, 167.
District Munsifs, 166.
Divisional charges, 159.
Divisions, natural, 2; western, 3; southern and eastern, 4.
Dodonnœa viscosa, 94.
Dogs, wild, 22.
Dolls, 106.
Donga Dāsaris, 169.
Donga Woddars, 169.
Dorasāni Venkatamma, 203.
Doyle, Rev. Fr. Patrick, 56.
Dravida, 26, 27.
Dress, 61.
Drinking vessels, 112.
Dry cultivation, 75.
Dry lands, resettlement of, 157.
D'Souza, Rev. Joachim, 55.
Duck, 23.
Duddine Tippa, 246.
Dūdēkulas, 58, 109.
Duggireddi Venkatreddi, 186.
Duke of Wellington, 46.
Dupleix, M., 43.
Duvvūr, 167; battle of, 44; district munsif's court at, 167; descriptive note of, 198.
Dynasties, earliest known, 26.

E

Earth Salt, method of its manufacture, its interference with monopoly salt, 161; its manufactures suppressed, 162.
Eastern division, 4, ghats, 25.
East India Company, 46.
Economic condition of agriculturists, 87.
Education, 54; according to religions, 143; by the missions, 144.
Educational Institutions, 144.
Edum, 116.
Ekili rājas, 213, 220.
Eleodendron Glaucum, 99.
Ellamma, 64.
Epidote, 16.
Erythroxylon monogynum, 93.
Eugenia alternifolia, 99.
Eugenia Jambolana, 93.
Euphorbia, 20.
Euphorbia antiquorum, 20.

Euphorbia neriifolia, 20.
Euphorbia tirucalle, 20.
European piece goods, 115.
Exports, 114.

F

Factories, 113.
Famines, 127 to 138.
Fath Miah, 42.
Fauna, 21.
Felis Jubata, 22.
Felspar, 9, 10.
Females, deficiency of, 53.
Fennelly, Rt. Rev. Bishop Stephen, 56.
Ficus religiosa, fig tree, 21.
Ficus tsiela, 21.
Fleury, the ship, 97.
Floods, 137, 138.
Flora, 20.
Florican, 23.
Fly shuttle slay, 109.
Food, human, 61 ; of cattle, 79.
Foreign liquors, 163.
Forest produce, minor, 105.
Forests, their situation, area, administration and character, 92 ; planting and sowing, demarcation, 107 ; forest offences, fire protection, 106.
Fort of—Vanipenta, 200 ; Korrapād, 201; Mudireddipalle, Tippireddipalle, Chākaralapād, 203 ; Pārnapalle, 212 ; Midipentla, 213 ; Nūlivēdu, 221 ; Gadikōta, 224 ; Kottakōta, 232 ; Sidhout, 233.
French, the, 43.
Fuel reserves, 101.
Fuel working circles, 102 ; working operations, 103.

G

Gaddam Bāligādu, 172.
Gādelu, 60.
Gadi, 60.
Gadikōta, 224.
Gaggula Tippa, 202.
Gajapati, 36.
Gājubendu, 16.
Gājula Balijas, 212.
Galena, sulphide of lead, 17.
Gālivādu, 221.
Gamble, 98.
Game, 22.
Ganapati of Warangal, Kākatīya king, 34.
Gandagōpāla, 32.
Gandhapurāllu, 212.
Gandikōta, gorge, 3 ; hills, 6 ; sīma, 34 to 36 ; fort, 41 ; descriptive note of, 191.
Gandlūr, 194.
Gangamma, 64.
Gangana, river, 223.
Gangapērūr, 236, 240.
Ganja, 164.
Ganjikunta, 203.
Garden crops, 75.
Gardenia Gummifera, 99.
Gardenias, 99.
Gardenia turgida, 99.
Garuda, 184.
Gathala fuel reserve, 101.
Geese, barheaded, 23.
Gelonium lanceolatum, 99.
Geology, 8 ; industrial products of, 15.
Geriselu, 60.
German silver, materials of, 112.
Ghadia, 117.
Giddalūr, 122.
Ginjee, 43.
Gneiss, 8, 9, 10, 20.
Gneissic series, 8.
Goa, 162.
Goats, 21.
Godavari district, distillery in, 163.
Godavari river, battle on the banks of, 34.
Golconda, 16, 24, 37, 193.
Golla, 64, 67.
Gooty Munsifi, 164.
Gōpālaswāmi Temple, 244.
Gōpāl Reddi, 206.
Gōpavaram, 85.
Gorru, 76.
Gōvinda rāja, 40.
Gōvindaswāmi, 233.
Gōvinda III, 27.
Grain measures, 116.
Granite veins, 9.
Granitoid gneiss, 9.

Gravel, 8.
Grazing and goat browsing, 105.
Green gram, 79.
Green stone, 10.
Gregory, Mr. G., 152.
Gribble, Mr., 128, 130.
Ground-nut, 79, 114.
Gudetti Rāmi Reddi, 170.
Gudhi, 117.
Gumpramānudinne people, 112.
Gunjāna river, 80, 83, 241.
Guntaka, 75.
Guntur famine, 128.
Guriginjakōna, 194.
Guriginjakunta, 223.
Gurramkonda, 41, 42, 45, 48; its cession to the Mahrattas 44; poligārs of, 50.
Guvvalacheruvu, hills, 8, 12; ghat, 41.
Gypsies, 70.

H

Haidar Ali, 40, 43, 44, 45, 148, 199.
Hanbury, Mr., 153.
Handlooms, 108, 109.
Hands, Rev. John, 56.
Hanuman, 71.
Hardwickia binata, 99, 100.
Hariali, 78.
Harihara Bukkarāyalu, 191.
Harihara, founder of the Vijayanagar Empire, 35.
Harihara II, 36.
Harpanahalle, 137.
Harvesting, 79.
Haworth, Mr., 123.
Health, general, 139.
Hemicyclia sepiaria, 99.
Hemp drugs, 163, 164.
Hexandra, 93.
Heyne, Dr., 16.
High Schools, 143.
Hindus, 59.
History, political, 24.
Hœmatite, 17.
Holmespet, 197.
Hornblende, 9, 10.
Hornstone, 16.
Hoskins, Wren, 88.
Houses, 60.
Howell, Mr., 171.
Howell, Rev. W., 56.
Hoysalas, 32, 34, 35.
Hubli, 46.
Hughly, 97.
Humidity, 7.
Husking mills, at Muddanūr, 196; at Jammalamadugu, Kamalāpuram, Cuddapah, 113.
Hwen Thsang, 27.
Hyderabad, 43, 46.

I

Īdigas, 68, 164.
Idupulapāya palmyra plantation, 102, 163.
Implement gravels, 14.
Imports, 115.
Inagalūr, 30.
Income tax, 165.
Indebtedness of the ryots, 91.
Indigo, 114.
Indigo vats, refuse as manure, 73.
Indlūr, 33.
Indra, 184.
Indra III, 29.
Indūri Appayya, 231.
Industrial products, 15.
Infirmities, 141.
Ingallūr Nādu, 29, 30.
Inge Bheema Reddi, 238.
Inman, Rev. Canon, 57.
Inoculation, 139.
Inscriptions at, Rāyachōti, 219; Tsundupalle, 220; Pōrumāmilla, 227; Chennūr, 182; Pendlimarri, 185; Chintakommadinne, 186; Duvvūr, 98; Vanipenta, 200; Rāmēswaram, 201; Korrapād, Gaggula Tippa, 202; Pālagiri, 205; Uppalūr, 206; Animela, 207; Vontimitta, 237; Kōtapād, 238; Gangapērūr, 240; Pottapí, 244; in Soumyanāthaswāmi temple, 246; Sidhēswaraswāmi temple, 247.
Inumbrōlu or Inumpudōli, 33.
Inupakolumulu, 203.
Irasas, 116.
Iron ore, 12, 17; oxide, 10.
Irrigation, general and under river channels, 80; under tanks and wells, 81.

Irrigation works, 83.
Iruvai Okati, 63.
Ixora parviflora, 20, 94, 99.

J

Jackals, 75.
Jaggery, 74, 164.
Jails, 171.
James and Mary, the ship, 97.
Jammalamadugu, Mission hospital at, 57; husking mills and ginning factory at, 113; Mission medical institution at, 142; Campbell Memorial school, caste girls' school and Boarding school at, 144; Deputy Collector of, 159; Sub-Registrar's office at, 168; descriptive note of, 188.
Jammalamadugu taluk, 2, 3, 187.
Jāmu, 117.
Jāndras, 220.
Jangamrāzupalle, lead workings of, 17; valley, 5.
Jasper, 16.
Jātra, 64.
Jesuits, suppression of, 55.
Jinkala Musalmāns, 220.
Jōti, 236.
Judge, District, 166.
Jungle fowl, 23; sheep, 23.
Justice, administration of, 166; civil, 166; criminal, 168.
Juvvi tree, 21.

K

Kachchi or Kanchi (Conjeeveram), 29, 32.
Kadiri taluk. added to Anantapur district, 1.
Kāka Mahārāja, 191.
Kākatīyas of Orangal, 34.
Kākustavijayamu (Telugu poem), 39, 244.
Kālahasti, 28.
Kalakada, 42.
Kalasapād, 5; anicut near, 86, tank, 87; Mission dispensary at, 142; elementary school at, 145; descriptive note of, 231.
Kalikiri, 121, 122; railway station, 218.
Kalinga, 31.
Kalivi, 94.
Kaluvanāyanivāru, 221.
Kaluvāya, 240.
Kamalāpuram, 2, 160; fuel plantation, 100; railway station, 121; railway accident near, 123; private dispensary at, 142; descriptive note of, 204.
Kamalāpuram taluk, 2, 3, 204.
Kamal-ud-din, 45.
Kāmanūr, 200.
Kamar-ud-din, 222.
Kamil assessment, 38, 147; survey, 222.
Kammas, 66, 68.
Kampa I, 35.
Kanamalōpalle, 9; fuel reserve and working circle, 102.
Kandukūr, 32.
Kankar, 19.
Kanna, 16.
Kanna sāles, 242.
Kannekalacheruvu, the story of the origin of the name, 246, 247.
Kannekamma temple, 197, 200.
Kantalam, private dispensary at. 142.
Kantlam, 116.
Kānuga trees, 21, 74.
Kapila, 83.
Kāpus, 66.
Karēpāku, 94.
Karikala Chōla, 26, 28.
Karla, 16.
Karnam Veerappa, 238.
Kārtikam, 74.
Kathāri Mangayya, 185.
Katteragandla, 36.
Kāvaligar, 216.
Kāvali rusums, 223.
Kāzi, 58.
Kērala or Chēra, 26.
Kerosene oil, 115.
Kēsapuram, 224.
Khazipet-Sunkēsula, 186.
Kilpāka or Kilpauk, 31.
Kistna, 5, 26.
Kistvaens or cell tombs, 25, 205.
Kodide Kāpus, 66.
Kōdūr (Jammalamadugu taluk), 190.

Kōdūr (Pullampet taluk), 33; redsanders plantation, 98, 100; fuel reserve, 101; fuel working circle, 102; railway station, 121; mission dispensary at, 142; mission primary school at, 145; descriptive note of, 244.
Koilkuntla lime stone, 13.
Kolar, 28, 122.
Kōlāttam, 62.
Kōmatis, 68, 114, 197.
Kommi, 94.
Kondāpuram, hills, 12; husking mills, 19; railway station, 121, 194.
Kondavāndlu, 230.
Kondavīdu, Reddis of, 36.
Kondūr, 33; anicut near, 39; descriptive note of, 239.
Kondūr rājas, 241.
Kondūr Tippa, 241.
Kōnēti Nāyudu, 212.
Korachas, 169.
Kornād cloths, 110.
Korra, 77, 155.
Korrapād, 201.
Korund or Corundum, 16.
Kōtalapalle, 194.
Kōtapād, 238.
Kōtapalle Bakki Reddi, 238.
Kōthandarāmaswāmi temple, 237.
Kotlūr, 183.
Kottakōta, 6, 226, 232.
Krishna Dēva, 182.
Krishna Naiker of Vijayanagar, 35.
Krishnarāya, the greatest of the Vijayanagar emperors, 36, 192, 200, 201, 222.
Krishnā Reddi, 232.
Krishna III, King of the Rāshtrakūtas, 29, 30, 201, 205.
Krupapalle, leper asylum at, 58, 141, 142, 245.
Kukudu, 94.
Kulōttunga I, Chōla king, 30.
Kulōttunga III, 31, 32, 182.
Kumāra Ananta Rāja, 207, 244.
Kumāra Narasimha Nāyudu, 203.
Kumāra Nāyudu, 213.
Kumāra Sunki Reddi, 202.
Kumphani Government, 40.
Kunchams, 116.
Kunchugattu Yerukulas, 69.
Kunchulu, 69.
Kundēr river, 2, 44.
Kundēr series, 13.
Kundēr valley, 9.
Kunkumam, 65.
Kurivi, 94.
Kurnool-Cuddapah canal, 83, 120; turmeric cultivation under it, 75.
Kurnools or Kurnool formations, 8, 9.
Kurubas, 71, 110, 111.
Kuruguntapalle, 238.

L

Lakkireddipalle, 43, 44, 159; deputy tahsildar of, 168; descriptive note of, 220.
Lakshminarasimhaswāmi temple, 185.
Lambādis, 69, 70.
Land revenue administration, under the Vijayanagar Empire, 146; Visapadi system, 147; Muhammadan system, 147; in the 18th century, 148.
Languages, 54.
Langur, 23.
Lankāmalais, 5, 92, 99; fuel working circle, 102, 103; timber fellings, 103.
Latchmi, goddess of riches, 16.
Lāvu vadlu, 74.
Lead, 12.
Leaf-manure, 73.
Leases, decennial, 153; triennial, 150.
Lēbāka, 31, 34, 39.
Lebbeck, 99.
Leopards, 22.
Leper asylum, 58, 141, 142, 245.
Lime, 19.
Limestones, 8, 9, 12, 18.
Lineal measures, 116.
Linga Balijas, 63
Lingāla Vanka, 215.
Lingāyats, 63, 219.
Liquid measures, 116.
Liquor, 163.
Lithic inscriptions, 24, monuments, 26.
Litigation, 167.

Local boards, 174; their receipts and expenditure, 175.
Local self-government, 174.
London Mission, 56.
Loris, 23.
Lower Secondary schools, 144.
Lutheran Mission, 57.

M

Maba buxifolia, 93, 99.
MacCartie, Mr., 133, 187.
Macdonald, Mr., murder of, 171, 181.
Macfarlane, Rev. G. H., 57.
Madanapalle, and Vāyalpād taluks added to Chittoor district, 2.
Madanapalle, district munsif's court, 165.
Maddicheruvu, iron furnace at, 17.
Maddimadugu fuel working circle, 102.
Mādemma, 189.
Mādhavaram, 4; its silk weaving, 110, 112, 115; descriptive note of, 237.
Mādigas, 67, 68.
Madras and Southern Mahratta railway, 121.
Madurāntakam, 31.
Madurāntakan-Pottapi-Chōla, 31.
Madurāntaka-Uttama-Chōla, 31.
Mahābhārata, 32.
Mahāvishnu, 184.
Mahazid Khan, 41.
Mahrattas, 38, 41, 44.
Maidukūr project, 85; descriptive note of, 203.
Mailavaram, 69.
Mākam Chenchiah, 173.
Malaria, 139, 140.
Mālas, 67, 68; Weavers, 108.
Malēpād, 27.
Malinēnipatnam, 222.
Mallemkondas, 239.
Mallēswaraswāmi temple, 223
Māmandūr, 31.
Māmillapalle fuel working circle, 102.
Māndavya river, 217.
Mangapatnam, railway disaster near, 124.
Mango trees, 20.
Mantapampalle, 6.
Mantolu Sahib (Munro), Colonel, 40.
Manumasiddhi, 32; his settlement of a land dispute of the Brahmans of Perungandura, 33, 247.
Manuring, method of, 73.
Mārellamadaka, 217.
Margosa trees, 20.
Markets, weekly, 175.
Marraya Konigii, 94.
Masthān Sahib, 59, 66.
Matla Ananta, 39, 244.
Matla (Matli) princes, 38, 243, 247.
Matli, 224.
Mattu, 117.
Mayalūr, private dispensary at, 142.
Measures, grain, liquid and lineal, 115; of time, 117.
Mēdaravāndlu, 245.
Medical institutions, public, 141; private, 142.
Meer Jumla, 193.
Meera Khan, 186.
Meer Sahib, Governor of Gurramkonda, 40, 44, 213, 222.
Megasthenes, Greek geographer, 26.
Melons of Cuddapah, 75, 236; of Sidhout, 115.
Mēlpādi, 29.
Memecylon angustifolium, 99.
Mērpāka-Nādu, 31.
Merugulacheruvu, 221.
Metal, industries in, 112; work in Vontimitta, 199.
Metamorphic series, 8.
Metla guntaka, 77.
Mhote, 83.
Mica, 9.
Midde, 60.
Mills, husking, 79.
Mimusops hexandra and elengi, 99.
Mimusops Indica, 93.
Mines, diamond, 81.
Miskin Vali, 212.
Missions, Roman Catholic, 55; London, 56; S.P.G., 57; Lutheran, 57.
Modas or Salt mounds, 161.
Modern changes in cultivation, 79.
Moharram, 58.
Moir, Mr. T. E., his scheme reports, 156; his remarks on the cultivation of groundnut, 80.

Molasses, 163.
Monkey, 23.
Monsoon, N.E., 125; S.W., 126.
Morāri Rao, 42.
Mōtakatla, 222.
Mōtāti Kāpus, 66.
Mouse deer or tragalus memimna, 23.
Muddanūr, 27; husking mills, 79, 196; descriptive note of, 196.
Mudireddipalle, 203.
Mudivēmu, 26.
Muhammad Ali Khan, 42
Muhammadans, their invasion, 34; their invasion rolled back by the Hindus, 35; their fight with the Vijayanagar empire, 37; their system of land revenue administration, 147.
Muhammadans, 42, 45, 48; as weavers, 108; as boot and shoe-makers, 111; brass, copper and bell-metal workers and stone carvers, 112; as shopkeepers, 114; as tree tappers, 164; as masons and builders, 220; as tanners, 222; as shoe and sandal manufactureres, 227; as bangle makers, 212: their worship of the Hindu god Narasimhaswāmi, 196.
Muhūrtam, 117.
Mukkanti-Kāduvetti, 33.
Mukkantīswara temple, 189.
Mukkonda, 202.
Mukundāpuram, 240.
Mūlastānēswaraswāmi temple, 243.
Mulikinādu, 34, 36.
Munelli, 37, 232.
Mungāri pairu, 77.
Municipal government, 175.
Munro, Sir Thomas, 3, 38, 40, 45, 48, 128, 137, 148, 149; Governor of Madras, 153, 156; his work as principal Collector, 46; his reduction of the Poligars, 47; his method of dealing with them, 49; his ryotwari settlement approved by the Madras Government, 50; and by the Directors, 51; his rates of assessment, 150; story of his grant of inam for the Narasimhaswāmi temple, 240.
Munsifs, District and Village, 166.
Muntha, 116.
Mūnūta nālugu, 63.
Mūredu, 116.
Musalnāyadu, 239.
Musalnāyani Cheruvu, 239.
Mushti, 93.
Muzaffar Jung, 43, 221.
Mysore, plateau, 4, 26, 44; breed of cattle, 21; treaty of, 45; Industrial and Arts exhibition, 110.

N

Nābhikōt, 180.
Nagarājupet, London Mission School at, 145.
Nāgreddipalle railway station 245.
Nallamalai group, 12.
Nallamalai hills, 2, 3, 5, 9, 92, 99, 105, 112; fuel and timber working circle, 102; timber fellings, 103.
Nallavadlu, 74.
Nalla Vāgu, 201.
Nandalūr, 4, 31, 101, 102; fuel working circle, 102; railway station, 121; railway dispensary, 142; Lower secondary school, 144; district munsif's court, 166, descriptive note of, 245.
Nandimandalam, 187.
Nandyal, 121, 122.
Nandyālampet, district munsif's court, 167; descriptive note of, 203.
Nandyal shales, 13.
Nārada, 184.
Nārapanāyani Pina Avubala Nāyudu, 200.
Narasimha Dēva Rāya, 205, 206, 222.
Narasimha of Ahōb lam, 69.
Narasimha Reddi, 172.
Narasimhaswāmi temple, 59, 189, 240.
Narasimha III, 32.
Nawabs, of Gandikōta and Cuddapah, 38; of Cuddapah, 39 to 44, 180; of Arcot, 41; of Kandanūr (Kurnool), 41, 43; of Savanore 43
Nazir Jung, 43.
Neelāpuram, 203.
Neiknamabad, 179.

Neiknam Khan, 179.
Nēkunāmpet, 194.
Nemaliadugu, 94.
Nērēdu, 93.
Nerjee limestones, 13, 18.
Nerusupalle, 29.
Newbold, Captain, 16.
Nidujuvvi, 208.
Nim tree, 100.
Nissanka Pratāpa Rāja, 219.
Nizam, 40 to 42.
Nūlivēdu, 221.

O

Obālām,valley, 5; descriptive note of, 239.
Ōbālapathi, 63.
Ōbannapet, 194.
Occupations, 54, 108, 113.
Oddes, 68.
Odeya, a title of the rulers of the Vijayanagar provinces, 36.
Odina Wodier, 99.
Onūtulakōna, 185.
Opium, 163.
Opuntia dillenii, 20.
Oranges of Vēlpula, 115.
Ordeal, trial by, 33.
Orthoclase, 10.
Oudh Regulations, 150.

P

Paddy, 165; its cultivation and method of sowing, 73; its seasons and varieties, 74.
Padigala Kondā Reddi or Kondayya, 195.
Padlu, 116.
Padma Sāles, 110, 242; their caste dispute with the Jāndras, 220.
Pākanādu, 31, 34.
Pākanāti Kāpus, 66.
Pākarāshtra, 30.
Pakka Seer, 116.
Pāla, 93.
Pālagiri, 30, 205.
Pāletti Gangamma, 224.
Pālkonda hills, 2, 3, 92, 99, 102, 103, 114; bullmen fuel working circle, 102; timber fellings, 103.
Pallavas, 26, 27, 32.
Palmyras, 102; tapped for toddy, 163.
Pālnāti Ankālamma, 233.
Pālugurāllapalle, 233.
Palugurāllu, 212.
Pāmalēru, 246.
Pamidi, 191.
Panchalingālakōna waterfall, 215, 240.
Pānch seer, 115.
Pāndavagullu, 25.
Pandums, 116.
Pāndya and Pāndyas, 26, 32, 34.
Pāniam series, 13.
Pāpaghni river, 2, 3, 28, 102, 120, 217; group, 12.
Paraiyans, 67.
Paramatakōna, 225.
Parāntaka I, Chōla king, 28.
Pārnapād, 202.
Pārnapalle, 8, 138, 211.
Partridges, 23.
Pāta Cuddapah, 178.
Patchai bendu, 16.
Pathan chiefs, 43.
Pātravāndlu, 203.
Pattapurāyi, 239.
Patte Khan, 206.
Pattūr fuel working circle, 102.
Pattu Sāles, 242.
Pea fowl, 23.
Pedda althi, 115.
Peddakanti kāpus, 66.
Peddakūdāla, 216.
Pedda madaka, 78.
Peddamma, 68.
Peddamudiyam, 27, 112, 189.
Pedda Orampād, 246.
Peddapasupula, 113.
Peddināyaka, his land survey of Pottapi nādu, 34.
Penagalūr, 33, 247.
Pendlimarri, tank, 87; descriptive note of, 185.
Pennapērūr, 236, 240.
Pennēr river, 2, 3, 4, 5, 6, 27, 101, 115, 137, 138, 241; blown sands of, 15; lithic monuments in its neighbourhood, 26.
Pentas, 105.

Penukonda, 35 ; transfer of the head quarters of the Vijayanagar empire to, 37.
Perumāllarāja, 39.
Perungandura, 33 ; brahmans, their land dispute settled by Manumasiddhi, 247.
Phaseolus Mungo 79.
Phœnix, the ship, 97.
Physical description, 1.
Picottah, 83.
Pidugupalle tank, 87.
Pig, 23.
Pīlēr, 41, 42.
Pinchanadi, 3, 217.
Pistacite, 9, 10.
Plague, 33 ; its outbreak at Cuddapah, 139.
Plantains, 75.
Plantation, the Pullampet and Reddipalle fuel, 100.
Pleistocene, 9.
Plovers, 23.
Pogada, 93.
Pōlēramma, 64.
Police, 170.
Poligārs, 38, 47.
Political history, 24.
Pōlūr, 29.
Pondalūr, 39.
Pondicherry, 43.
Pongamia glabra, 21.
Population, density and growth, 52 ; emigration, birth and death rate, sexes, 53 ; parent tongue, education, occupations, 54 ; religious and social life, 63, 71 ; castes, 66.
Porter, Rev. Edward, 57.
Pōrumāmilla, 34, 35, 121 ; tank and its construction, 81 ; fuel working circle, 102 ; descriptive note of, 227.
Potladurti, 36.
Pottapi, 30, 32, 33, 34, 35, 39, 243.
Pottapi sīma, 39.
Pottipād, 28.
Pratāparudra, 34, 35, 36, 247.
Prehistoric remains, 25.
Preventive force, Salt and Abkāri, 164.
Prices of food grains, 157.
Pringle, Mr. A. T., 95.
Prithvīswara, 312.
Proddatūr, Cotton pressing and ginning factories of, 109, 113, 114 ; a principal trade centre, 114 ; the wealthiest town in the district, 121 ; dispensary at, 142 ; schools in, 144 ; district munsif's court at, 166 ; Sub-Registrar's office at, 168 ; descriptive note of, 197.
Proddatūr taluk, 2, 196.
Pteraspermun suberifolium, 94, 99.
Pterocarpus santalinus, 94.
Public health, 139.
Puckle, Mr., 131.
Pulijūdam, 62.
Pulivendla, 34, 35, 36, 48, 114 ; weekly fair at, 111, 175 ; ginning factory at, 113 ; dispensary at, 142 ; Sub-Registrar's office at, 168 ; descriptive note of, 210.
Pulivendla taluk, 2, 3 ; cultivation of ground-nut in, 80 ; descriptive note of, 208.
Pulivēsham, 58.
Pullampet, 30, 38 ; fuel plantation and working circle, 100, 102 ; weaving industry in, 109 ; embroidery work in, 110 ; Sub-Registrar's office at, 168 ; descriptive note of, 242.
Pullampet taluk, 2, 4 ; turmeric cultivation in, 75 ; descriptive note of, 240.
Pullangi river, 241, 246.
Pulugunāti sīma, 39.
Punganūr, 28, 41, 122.
Pushpagiri, 63, 183.
Putalēshwar, warm springs of, 12.
Putti, 116.

Q

Quadrumana, 23.
Quails, 23.
Quartz, 10.
Quartzites, 8, 9, 20.

R

Rāchapalle, 224.
Rācheruvu, 231.
Rāgi, 62, 74, 114.

Raichur, 167.
Railways, projected lines, 121 ; accidents, 123.
Rainfall, 6.
Rainfall and seasons, 125.
Rajahmundry, 164.
Rājampet, fuel working circle, 102 ; a trade centre, 114 ; dispensary at, 142 ; Sub-Collectorate, 159 ; weekly market at, 175 ; descriptive note of, 241.
Rājarājadēva III, 31.
Rājarāja I, 29, 31.
Rājēndra Chōla III, 32, 33, 34.
Rākshasas, 184.
Rama, his victory over Rāvana, 3.
Rāmarāja, the great Hēmraj of Muhammadan historians, 36, 37, 193.
Ramayya Pantulu, Mr. J., 180.
Rāmēswaram, 200.
Rangarazus or Rangaris, 111.
Ranga, son of Timmala, 37.
Rāshtrakūtas, 27, 28.
Ravikas, 61, 110.
Rāyachōti, rough blankets of 110, 111 ; dispensary at, 142 ; Government training school at, 144 ; Deputy Collector of, 159 ; district munsif's court at, 167 ; Sub-Registrar's office at, 168 ; descriptive note of, 218.
Rāyachōti taluk, 2, 4, 217.
Rāyakāpus, 239.
Rāyalcheruvu, 194.
Rāyavaram, 217.
Rāzus, 187.
Reddipalle fuel plantation, 100.
Reddis of kondavīdu, 36.
Red ferruginous soils, 5, 6 ; their classification, 154.
Redistribution of districts, 1.
Redsanders plantation, at kōdūr, 98, 100, 244 ; in the Pullampet valley, 102.
Redsanders tree, 97 ; its uses, 94.
Redwood posts, 95.
Rēgadipalle, 194.
Regar or black cotton soils, 5 ; their classification, 153, 154.
Registration, 167.
Relief works, famine, 130.
Religions, high percentage of Muhammadans, the Christians, 54 ; Roman Catholics, 55 ; the London Mission, 54, 56 ; the S.P.G. Mission, 54, 57 ; the Lutheran Mission, 57 ; religious practices and superstitions, 64.
Religious life, 63—66.
Rēnādu, 27, 34.
Rēnāndu, 27.
Rēnigunta, 4, 167.
Resettlement, 156 ; of dry lands, 157 ; of wet lands, 158 ; of dasabandham well lands, 158 ; financial results of, 159.
Revenue history, 153, 146 ; under Vijayanagar empire, 146 ; under the Muhammadans, 147 ; in the 18th century, 148.
Revenue settlement, village settlement of, 1800-01, ryotwari settlement of 1801–02, 149 ; triennial leases, 150 , Munro's views thereon, 151 ; ryotwari system, 151.
Rice, 115.
River Channels, 80.
Rivers, 2.
Roads in 1854, 118 ; extensions during famine, 119 ; present administration, 119 ; avenues, 120.
Robinson, Mr., 123.
Roches Moutonnes, 8.
Rock areas, description of, 8.
Roman Catholic Mission, 55.
Romany, 70.
Rugs, 110.
Rumphius, 95.
Russel, Mr. J. W., 153.
Rusums, 45.
Ryots, their indebtedness, 91.
Ryotwari settlement of 1801-02, 149.

S

Sadāsiva, emperor, 36, 37, 39, 186.
Saffron, works, 75 ; factory at Cuddapah, 113.
Sagilēr, river, 2, 3, 34, 226 ; project, 86, 135.
Saiyid Khaja Ghouse Mahiuddin darga, 227.

Sākali, 33 to 35.
Sākali Kōdūr, 33.
Saktibanda, 65.
Sāles, 68, 108, 110.
Salt, 115; former sources of supply, monopoly salt, 161; present sources of supply, 162.
Salt mounds, 161.
Samalkot, 163.
Sambhar, 22.
Sancherla fuel working circle, 102.
Sandals, manufacture of, 111.
Sandal sowing, 105.
Sandibondi, 61.
Sandgrouse, 23.
Sandstone, 8, 11, 20.
Sānipāya, 222.
Sankarānthi, 59.
Sankavaram, 230.
Sannavadlu, 74.
Sanskrit Mahābhārata, 32.
Sapindus emarginatus, 94, 99.
Sārapappu, 114, 222.
Sāris, 110, 111.
Sashagrundipuram, 191.
Sāshtāngamulu, 67.
Scarcities subsequent to the great famine, 134.
Schools, 143.
Seasons, 125; for paddy cultivation, 74; series of bad, 129.
Selection system of timber felling, 103.
Seringapatam, 40, 44; treaty of, 45.
Sēshāchalams, 2, 3, 4, 42, 99; timber working plan for, 103; workers in wood near, 111.
Setti Balijas, 238.
Settigunta, home of doll makers, 106; wood carvers of, 111; descriptive note of, 245.
Settivāripalle, 202.
Settlement department, early operations of, 154.
Settlement, the village — of 1800–01, and ryotwari of 1801–02, 149; triennial leases, 150; Munro's views thereon, 151; decennial leases, 153.
Shales, 9, 11, 13.
Sheep, 21, 105.
Sheep and goats, penning them for manure, 76.
Sheep fair of Simhadripuram, 216.
Sheikhs, 58.
Shoes, manufacture of, 111.
Shorea tumbaggaia and talura, 99.
Siddhavattam sīma, 35, 39.
Siddhavattēswaraswāmi temple, 235.
Siddhēswaraswāmi temple, 235.
Sidhout or Siddhavattam, 30, 38; fort, 44; fuel working circle, 102; melons, 115; dispensary at, 142; headquarters of the district, 152, 181; Sub-Registrar's office at, 168; descriptive note of, 235.
Sidhout taluk, 2, 4, 234.
Silk weaving, 110.
Silpīs, 112.
Simhādripuram, weekly fair at, 194; private hospital at, 142; descriptive note of, 216.
Simhavishnu line of kings, 27.
Sirvēl, 122.
Slates, 8, 11, 19.
Small-pox, 140.
Snipe, 23.
Social life, 66.
Soils, 5.
Sōmapalle, 29.
Somasīla, 2, 240.
Somayāji, 34.
Sōremati, battle of, 29.
Soumyanāthaswāmi temple, 246.
Southern division, 4.
Sowing, 73.
S.P.G. Mission, 57.
Spices, 115.
Spur fowl, 23.
Srīharikōta, 69.
Srī Vēnkatēswara temple, 179.
Stamps, 164.
State granary of Gandikōta, 3.
Steatite, 212.
St. Leger, Colonel, 50.
Stonework, 112.
Storms, 137.
Stratified rocks, 8.
Stream bunding, 106.
Strychnos nux-vomica, 93, 99.
Strychnos potatorum, 93.
Stuart, Major, 154.
Subbamma, T., 172.

Sub-division, the resettlement of, 158.
Sub-registrars, 168.
Suddapalle 83.
Sugālis, 70, 169.
Sugar, 115.
Sugarcane, 74.
Sunkēsula, 83.
Superstitions, 64.
Surabhu valley, 29, 81, 209.
Survey of the Cuddapah district by the king of Golconda, 38; of Pottapinādu by Peddināyaka, 34.

T

Table of weights, 115.
Tada, 94.
Tādpatri cotton ginning and pressing factories, 109, 114.
Tādpatri plain, 5.
Tahsildars and deputy tahsildars, 159.
Talikōta, battle of, 37, 40, 179.
Tāllaproddatūr, 194.
Tamarind topes, 20.
Tangatūr, 4, 31, 39; district munsif's court at, 167; head quarters of the Matla princes, 247; descriptive note of, 247.
Tangēdu, 20.
Tanjai or Tanjore, 29.
Tank irrigation, 80.
Tanks at, Pōrumāmilla and Badvēl, 5, 227; at Pōrumāmilla constructed by Bāskara, 35; at Badvēl constructed by Anantarāmarāju, 39; at Lēbāka, 39; of Vīraballi, 223; of Kalasapād, 231; of Vontimitta, 237; of Settigunta, 245; of Ōrampād, 246; of Penagalūr, 247; of Kamalāpuram, 205.
Teal, 23.
Tellabendu, 16.
Telugu Chodas, 30.
Temperature, 7.
Temples at, Ahōbilam in the Nallamalais, 19; Pālagiri, restored by Bhīma Mahāraja, 30; Athirala, 34; Pondalūr, 39; Sidhout, 39; of Vīrabhadraswami at Rayachōti, 63.
Temple, Sir Richard, 131, 132.
Terminalia chebula, tomentosa and pallida, 99.
Thāndava Pātagāndlu, 172.
Thimma Nāyudu, 193.
Thiti Mallugādu, 172.
Thomba, 219.
Thornhill, Mr. G., 130, 162.
Thrighavari Dēva Mahārāja, 231.
Thumakonda fuel reserve, 101.
Thumus, 116.
Tigers, 22.
Tikkana Somayāji, 32.
Tikka or Gandagōpāla, 32, 33.
Timber and timber operations, 103.
Timber transit rules, 106.
Timmala, 36, 37, 193.
Tippireddipalle, 203.
Tipu Sultan, 40, 44, 45, 148, 212.
Tirumala Madhya Ahōbilam, 183.
Tirumalarāja Matla, 39.
Tirupati, 2, 4, 8, 101, 112, 114, 115; lower, 40.
Tiruvēngalanātha Rāja, 40.
Toddy, 163.
Togatas, 68, 108, 110.
Tōkavadlu, 74.
Tondiarpet, 164.
Tondur, 215.
Tots, 8.
Trade, 108, 113.
Tragalus Memimna or Mouse deer, 23.
Transplanting, 73.
Trap dykes, 10.
Traps, 9, 12.
Travellers' bungalows and choultries, 120.
Trial by ordeal, 33.
Tribes 69, criminal, 169.
Trichinopoly, 42.
Triennial leases, 150.
Trilōchana Pallava, 26.
Tsallādamulu, 61.
Tsoudu, 60.
Tsundupalle, 220.
Tummala vanka, 234.
Tummalūr, 185.
Tungabhadra, 83.
Turmeric, 75, 114, 115

U

Udayagiri, 35, 36.
Ullinda, 93.

Unions, 174.
Uppalūr, 4; poligār of, 50; silk weaving industry at, 110; descriptive note of, 206.
Upparapalle, 239; fuel plantation, 100.
Upparas, 68, 161, 162.
Urampad, 124.
Urutūr, 56.
Uti, 93.
Utukūr tank, breach of, 138.

V

Vaccination, 141.
Vadyānam, 61.
Vāgatikōna fuel reserve, 100, 101.
Vāghi tree, 100.
Vaidumbas, 29.
Vaisākham, 73.
Vallūr, 32, 34, 182.
Vangimalla, 223.
Vanipenta, 106, 112; lead workings near, 17; brass workers of, 106, 112; descriptive note of, 199.
Vannūramma, the only female poligār, 203.
Varikunta, 37.
Vāyalpād and Madanapalle taluks added to Chittoor district, 2.
Velanādu Kapus, 66.
Vēledu, 116.
Veligallu, 22, 221.
Veligonda hills, 2, 4, 9, 92, 99; timber fellings, 103.
Vellālas, 33.
Vēlpulakōna, 239.
Vēlpula, oranges of, 115.
Vēmpalle, 2, 3, 28; dispensary at, 142; district munsif's court at, 167; descriptive note of, 209.
Vēmula, 48, 213.
Venkatādri, 203.
Venkatapathi, 37, 231.
Venkatarāmarāja, 39, 40.
Venkatēsa, 71.
Vēnkatēswaraswāmi temple, 189
Vēnugōpālaswāmi temple, 239.
Vighadia, 117.
Vijayāditya, 26.
Vijaya Gandagōpāla, 34.
Vijayālaya, 28.
Vijayanagar empire, 16, 24, 41; founded by Harihara and Bukka, 35; rolls back the Muhammadan invasion, 35; its history, 35; its policy of appointing relatives of the reigning emperors as viceroys of provinces, 35; its administrative units, 36; the Muhammadan confederation against it, 37; its power broken at the battle of Talikōta, 37; its capital transferred to Penukonda, 37; again to Chandragiri, 37; its final overthrow by the king of Golconda, 37.
Vikrama Chōla, 31.
Village deities, 64.
Village Munsifs, 166.
Villages, 59.
Village settlement of 1800–01, 149.
Vīraballi, 223.
Virabhadraswāmi temple, 63, 185, 219.
Vīra Somēswara, 32.
Visapadi system, 147.
Vishnuvardhana, 189.
Vitex altissima, 94.
Vitex pubescens, 99.
Volcanic rocks, 8.
Vontimitta, 6, 12, 102; valley, 4, 9; fuel working circle, 102; descriptive note of, 237.
Vows, 65.
Vrishabhāsurudu, 210.
Vūra Kunta, 21.

W

Warangal, 34.
Warm springs, 12.
Weavers, castes of, 108; condition of, 109.
Weaving, cotton, 109; silk, blankets and rugs, 110; cotton printing and dyeing, 111.
Webera corymbosa, 94.
Weekly markets, 175.
Weights and measures, 115.
Weights, table of, 115.
Wellesley, Colonel, 46.
Wells, irrigation under, 81; treatment of lands under, 154.

Western division, 3.
Wet lands, cultivation of, 73; re-settlement of, 158.
Wheat, 115.
Whitehead, Mr. T. A., 97.
Wild date, 99.
Wild dog, 22.
Willshaw, Captain, 97.
Winds, 7.
Wittmann, Rev. J. N., 57.
Wolves, 22.
Wood, work in, 111.
Wreath of golden flowers, triumphant, legend of, 3, 217.

Y

Yāli, 198.
Yānādis, 69.
Yarn, 109, 115.
Yappirāla, 239.
Yelamakāpus, 66.
Yellamarasayya, 36.
Yellammadēvata temple, 182.
Yellappa Nāyanigādu, 186.
Yēnugula Pāpā Nāyudu, 191.
Yerraballa, 215.
Yerra bendu, 16.
Yerragudipād, 122, 198.
Yerraguntla 5; husking mills at, 79; railway station, 121, 197; where Cuddapah slabs are entrained, 113; unfashioned prehistoric tombstones found near, 25; descriptive note of, 208.
Yerraguntlakōta, hill range, 8; head-quarters of the Matla princes, 93; fuel reserve, 101; iron furnace at, 17.
Yerrakonda, 191.
Yerramanenipalem, 222.
Yerukula Nānchāramma, 70.
Yerukulas, 69, 111.
Yēruva division, 34.
Yētūr, weekly fair at, 194; descriptive note of, 195.

Z

Zadigam, 76.